Organizing Access to Capital

Organizing Access to Capital

Advocacy and the Democratization of Financial Institutions

EDITED BY

Gregory D. Squires

TEMPLE UNIVERSITY PRESS

PHILADELPHIA

Temple University Press, Philadelphia 19122
Copyright © 2003 by Temple University
All rights reserved
Published 2003
Printed in the United States of America

Library of Congress Cataloging-in-Publication Data

Organizing access to capital : advocacy and the democratization of
financial institutions / edited by Gregory D. Squires.
    p. cm.
  Includes bibliographical references and index.
   ISBN 1-59213-025-9 (cloth : alk. paper) — ISBN 1-59213-026-7
(pbk. : alk. paper)
    1. Bank loans—United States. 2. Financial institutions—United
States. 3. Community development—United States—Finance.
4. Economic assistance, Domestic—United States. I. Squires,
Gregory D.

HG1642.U5 O74 2003
332.1'2–dc21   2002035273

2 4 6 8 9 7 5 3 1

Contents

In Memory of Gale Cincotta

Organizing and advocacy efforts have transformed neighborhoods throughout the United States by turning the financial services industry from an engine of redlining into an agent of reinvestment. One person stands out as the pioneer who brought these problems to the public's attention and devised effective remedies. Gale Cincotta, the mother of the Community Reinvestment Act, is truly one of the few heroes of our age. Sadly, Gale died on August 15, 2001, while we were writing this book and, more importantly, engaging in furthering neighborhood reinvestment. As chairperson of National People's Action and director of the National Training and Information Center, Gale took an idea that came out of the neighborhoods and turned it into a movement. This book is dedicated to her, to the vital work she did, and to the incalculable influence she had on everybody engaged in reinvestment around the country.

Gale probably would not have cared much about this book one way or another. She was driven far more by the exercise of power to achieve desired results. She excelled at simple statements: "We want it, they got it, let's go get it." "We have found the enemy and it isn't us." "We work miracles because it's part of the program." These comments, coupled with her ability to run rings around the bankers and others she faced down over negotiating tables and at the front doors of their homes and offices through the years, were part of her combination of toughness and sensibility.

Some of the contributors to this volume were close personal friends and colleagues of Gale. We were all transformed and inspired by her work. Gale led the effort that created a federal ban on redlining, produced the evidence that showed the world what was going on in the financial services world, and trained the cadre of organizers around the country to make these tools work. I hope that in some small way this book will honor her memory, build on her legacy, and improve the lives of families in all communities.

Acknowledgments

Many individuals and organizations have made this book possible. As editor, I want to thank all of the contributors for their work, and not just that which went into this book. The Department of Sociology at George Washington University has provided a supportive environment that has enabled me to continue my work on organizing and advocacy. We would all like to thank the Charles Stewart Mott Foundation for its generous support of this project.

Acknowledgments

Many individuals and organizations have made this book possible. As editor, I want to thank all of the contributors for their work, and not just that which went into this book. The Department of Sociology at George Washington University has provided a supportive environment that has enabled me to continue my work on organizing and advocacy. We would all like to thank the Charles Stewart Mott Foundation for its generous support of this project.

Gregory D. Squires

I   Introduction:
The Rough Road to Reinvestment

These are the two faces of community development: noisy
protest and quiet accomplishment.... One can act one way
at age 20 and another at age 40. It is called growing up.

—Lawrence B. Lindsey (Lindsey 2000)

If there is no struggle, there is no progress.
Those who profess to favor freedom and yet deprecate
  agitation
Are men who want crops without plowing the ground.
They want rain without thunder and lightning.
They want the ocean without the awful roar of its waters.
Power concedes nothing without a demand.
It never did, and it never will.

—Frederick Douglass, August 4, 1857, West India Emancipation,
Speech delivered at Canandaigua, New York
(Blassingame 1985, 204)

After decades of overt redlining and racially discriminatory lending practices,
financial institutions are once again returning to the nation's cities. Between
1993 and 2000 the share of single-family home-purchase mortgage loans going
to low- and moderate-income borrowers increased from 19 percent to 29 percent. The share of loans going to black households increased from 3.8 percent
to 6.6 percent, while the Hispanic share increased from 4 percent to 6.9 percent (National Community Reinvestment Coalition 2001a, 9). As Paul S. Grogan and Tony Proscio have observed, "Not only have community-based organizations found it vastly easier to line up financing and equity investments
for their projects, but millions of individual borrowers and home buyers have
found credit where for decades there had been only rejections" (Grogan and
Proscio 2000, 120). One result is that homeownership rates are at all-time
record high levels. In the first quarter of 2001 the national homeownership

rate rose to 67.4 percent. African American homeownership climbed to 47.6 percent and the Hispanic homeownership rate reached 46.3 percent (Joint Center for Housing Studies 2001, 14). In central cities the homeownership rate reached a record high of 51.2 percent in 2000 (U.S. Department of Housing and Urban Development 2000a, 38–39). All of these figures were the highest in the nation's history. Though much remains to be done, clearly there has been progress in recent years.

Noting the greater availability of credit in urban and minority markets, some prominent observers attribute such change to the maturing of 1960s-style protesters who grew up and now pursue "progress over protest." Lost in what is in fact a premature declaration of victory is the vital role that advocacy and organizing efforts have played and continue to play in ongoing struggles to increase access to capital in distressed neighborhoods. This book tells the story of how neighborhood groups brought their communities together to change the way financial institutions do business in the nation's cities.

Politics, Protest, and Progress

Community development is big business today. Billions of dollars are spent by a range of investors, development organizations, and consumers. In observing that community development has emerged as an industry, Lawrence B. Lindsey, former economic policy advisor to President George Bush, patronizingly concedes that "The protest banner can still be held reverently in our box of mementos, along with the love beads [and] peace signs." But fortunately, from his perspective, effective proponents of urban communities act differently today; now they are "business people." The evolution is very simple, according to Lindsey: "It is called growing up." In their widely acclaimed book *Comeback Cities* (2000), Paul S. Grogan and Tony Proscio ridicule those with a "preference for confrontation over visible results." As Lindsey would no doubt agree, they applaud the sixties and seventies activists who, they claim, "exhausted by the antagonisms and fruitless turmoil, were more than ready to turn their newfound community-organizing talents to some practical redevelopment *projects.*" Interestingly, they attribute much of the recent success in urban revitalization to the Community Reinvestment Act (CRA), a federal law that emerged from the Alinsky-style radicalism they dismiss. To this day its effectiveness is grounded in large part in the power neighborhood groups have acquired through a range of advocacy and organizing efforts that Grogan and Proscio also scorn.

Community development is clearly changing. Many lenders see investment opportunities in neighborhoods they would not have considered just a few years ago. Financial institutions and community development groups are sitting down as partners and "doing deals." In many cases it is the protest organizations that, as a result of their advocacy, have been able to bring the lenders to the negotiating table. Financial intermediaries like the Local Initiative Support Corporation (LISC) and quasi-governmental organizations like the Neighborhood Reinvestment Corporation and Fannie Mae are providing capital. Community development finance institutions have been created to contribute to these efforts. Government agencies have used the proverbial stick as well as the carrot in passing new laws, like the CRA, and in filing lawsuits to prod reinvestment. No doubt some lenders have simply responded to signals of the marketplace and found profitable loans and investments in areas they had not previously considered. There are many facets to community reinvestment today.

But those who juxtapose organizing and advocacy efforts with accomplishments and results distort both history and current social reality. Community reinvestment is also an emerging social movement. Like other social movements that sought to alter systems of unequal power and privilege (the two most vivid examples of which are the labor movement and civil rights movement), struggle and conflict are intrinsic to community reinvestment efforts. Advocacy and accomplishment are pieces of the same mosaic. And this does not apply just to historical developments. As the heated debates over the recent Financial Services Modernization Act and implementing regulations indicate, conflicting interests persist. If advocacy and organizing are passé, so will be further progress in community reinvestment.

Race, Redlining, and Reinvestment

For at least fifty years it has been very difficult to disentangle the realities of race from the dynamics of urban disinvestment. Racial discrimination has been at the heart of uneven metropolitan development, as the Kerner Commission noted in 1968 and the current debate over urban sprawl reveals today (National Advisory Commission on Civil Disorders 1968; Dreier et al. 2001; Orfield 1997, 2002; Rusk 1999; powell 1998). Housing policy, and particularly housing finance practices, as well as business and community development have all been shaped by the contours of racial inequality, which these policies and practices in turn have reinforced.

The influence of race on mortgage lending in particular and housing policies and patterns in general is now well known (Jackson 1985; Massey and Denton 1993; Yinger 1995; Squires and O'Connor 2001; Ross and Yinger 2002). More than fifty years ago, University of Chicago sociologist and federal housing policy advisor Homer Hoyt ranked fifteen racial and ethnic groups in terms of their impact on property values in a report he prepared for the Federal Housing Administration (FHA). Those having the most detrimental impact were Negroes and Mexicans (Hoyt 1933). In light of this expert advice, the FHA concluded in its 1938 underwriting manual, "If a neighborhood is to retain stability, it is necessary that properties shall continue to be occupied by the same social and racial classes. A change in social or racial occupancy generally contributes to instability and a decline in values" (U.S. Federal Housing Administration 1938, par. 937).

The FHA was also a leading advocate of racially restrictive covenants that virtually guaranteed that properties would be occupied by the same classes over time. These covenants were enforceable in court until the U.S. Supreme Court ruled them unenforceable in the 1948 case *Shelley v. Kramer.*

The FHA has been a major source of home financing for more than seventy years. From 1930 through the 1950s it financed 60 percent of all home purchases. Virtually all FHA insured mortgages were for properties in suburban communities (Lief and Goering 1987, 229). During the 1960s, the FHA altered its policies and began to insure central-city homes in substantial numbers. Liberal loan terms and lower costs attracted low-income buyers. With the costs paid up front and insured by the federal government, they were attractive to many lenders as well. Frequently working with local realtors, lenders would solicit home purchases from families who could not, in fact, afford the acquisition. Exploiting racial fears in many cases, blockbusting resulted in the swift racial transition of urban communities. Thousands of families shortly defaulted on the loans, which led to the deterioration of once vibrant neighborhoods. The linchpin of such destruction was the availability of federally insured loans, which guaranteed the profits of lenders and realtors but cost many families their homes and life savings. The operation of the dual housing finance system—conventional loans for white suburbanites and FHA loans for nonwhite inner-city residents—reinforced the division of American society into the predominantly white, affluent suburbs and largely poor nonwhite central cities foreseen by the Kerner Commission in 1968 (Bradford 1979; Bradford and Cincotta 1992).

Private housing and housing finance industries shared the federal government's racial biases. In 1932 a leading real estate theoretician, Frederick Babcock, observed that "there is one difference in people, namely race, which can result in very rapid decline. Usually such declines can be partially avoided by segregation and this device has always been in common usage in the South where white and negro [*sic*] populations have been separated" (Bradford 1979). The American Institute of Real Estate Appraisers used the following example to illustrate neighborhood analysis into the 1970s: "The neighborhood is entirely Caucasian. It appears that there is no adverse effect by minority groups" (Greene 1980, 9). Until 1950 the National Association of Realtors stated in its code of ethics that "A Realtor should never be instrumental in introducing into a neighborhood a character of property or occupancy, members of any race or nationality, or any individual whose presence will clearly be detrimental to property values in the neighborhood" (Judd 1984, 284). And in 1988 a sales manager for the American Family Mutual Insurance Company advised one of his agents, in a tape-recorded statement, "I think you write too many blacks. . . . You gotta sell good, solid premium paying white people . . .

they own their homes, the white works. . . . Very honestly, black people will buy anything that looks good right now . . . but when it comes to pay for it next time . . . you're not going to get your money out of them" (*NAACP v. American Family Insurance Company* 1992). The explicit attention paid to race has been a key factor in the creation of the dual housing market and hypersegregation of urban neighborhoods throughout the United States (Jackson 1985; Massey and Denton 1993; Massey 2001).

While the overt discrimination of prior decades has been ameliorated, racial inequality and discrimination persist in housing finance markets. African American mortgage loan applications are still denied twice as often as those from whites, even among those with similar incomes. While there is much debate over the causes of these patterns, available empirical evidence reveals that discrimination is still a central feature of the housing finance market. The most comprehensive study to date, conducted by the Federal Reserve Bank in Boston, found that among similarly qualified applicants, African Americans were 80 percent more likely to be denied than whites (Munnell et al. 1996). Paired testing by fair housing organizations, other academic research, and investigations by regulatory agencies find substantial evidence of discrimination in the marketing of loans, terms and conditions of available credit, impact of underwriting guidelines, and other facets of the mortgage lending industry (Goering and Wienk 1996; Turner and Skidmore 1999; Turner et al. 2002a). Within the past ten years the U.S. Department of Justice has settled at least thirteen cases resulting in over $33 million in monetary relief from lenders it concluded were refusing to market in black neighborhoods, rejecting black applicants who were as qualified as whites who were approved, charging higher interest rates and other fees to nonwhite borrowers, using underwriting rules that adversely affected black communities (for example, refusing to finance or varying the terms of loans for older and lower-valued properties), providing different levels of counseling based on the race of the applicant, and otherwise treating racial minorities less favorably (Lee 1999).

If access to credit has improved in recent years, predatory lending may be filling at least part of that void. Many lenders use high-pressure sales tactics to market loan products where the interest rates and fees far exceed the risk and where borrowers are often worse off financially after consummating the loan. Such loans are often based on the value of the home rather than the income of the borrower. Consequently, borrowers often find themselves unable to keep up with the loan payments. Predatory lenders may refinance these loans at even more stringent terms, and eventually many borrowers lose the equity in their homes, or lose their homes altogether (U.S. Department of Housing and Urban Development 2000b; Immergluck and Wiles 1999). To date the Federal Trade Commission has sued fifteen lenders for unlawful predatory practices and is investigating more (Oppel 2001, 1). Predatory lending today is exerting the same adverse impact on urban communities as the FHA scandals did in the 1960s and 1970s.

There are no precise quantitative estimates of the number of predatory lenders or their share of the market. But there has been a substantial growth in subprime lending, which is the segment in which predatory lenders are located. Between 1993 and 1998 subprime lenders increased their share of home-purchase loans in metropolitan areas from 1 percent to 5 percent. In low-income minority neighborhoods their share grew from 2 percent to 15 percent. Growth has been even greater in the refinance market, where the market share in low-income minority areas went from approximately 5 percent to 46 percent, compared to less than 5 percent to 30 percent in upper-income white areas (Joint Center for Housing Studies 2000). Not all subprime lenders are predatory, of course. Many serve an important role in providing access to credit to higher-risk borrowers who could not otherwise obtain a loan or buy or maintain a home. But the sudden expansion of this part of the market is indicative of the increase in predatory lending. And both Fannie Mae and Freddie Mac have estimated that between 30 percent and 50 percent of borrowers receiving subprime loans would, in fact, qualify for less costly prime loans (Ross and Yinger 2002, 9).

Race has also long influenced small-business lending. Small businesses constitute a critical part of the U.S. economy, particularly in major metropolitan areas. The roughly 24 million small businesses nationwide employ 52 percent of the private workforce, contribute 51 percent of private sector output, create the majority of new jobs, and produce 55 percent of innovations. These businesses, and the U.S. economy generally, depend on access to credit, particularly from commercial banks, in order to survive and thrive (Office of Advocacy, U.S. Small Business Administration 1999).

Yet small businesses, particularly small minority-owned businesses in urban communities, often experience difficulty in securing small-business loans. Recent evidence indicates that minority-owned firms receive fewer and smaller loans than white-owned firms with identical traits (Cavalluzzo, Cavalluzzo, and Wolken 1999; Blanchflower, Levine, and Zimmerman 1998; Ando 1988; Bates 1989, 1997). In a 1993 survey the National Bureau of Economic Research found that black business owners were three times as likely as whites to be turned down for small-business loans. Among firms that were comparable in terms of credit rating, age, size, geographic location, and experience of owners, black-owned firms were twice as likely to be rejected—and among those firms that were approved, black ownership paid an average of 1 percent more in interest (Blanchflower, Levine, and Zimmerman 1998).

The historical and contemporary reality of racial discrimination, urban disinvestment, and redlining has generated strong reactions on several fronts. Progress is perhaps best symbolized by enactment of key federal laws, including the Fair Housing Act in 1968, the Home Mortgage Disclosure Act in 1975, and the Community Reinvestment Act in 1977. These statutes and their implementing regulations have been revised significantly over time, and more changes are currently under consideration. Each stage of these developments has been and continues to be enshrouded in political conflict and controversy.

From Redlining to Reinvestment

Community reinvestment and fair lending advocates have used a variety of tools to pursue their objectives of increasing access to credit in underserved markets. These include public education, litigation, demonstrations, partnerships, and direct delivery of services, among others. Critical leverage has been provided by federal law, particularly the Fair Housing Act, Home Mortgage Disclosure Act (HMDA), and Community Reinvestment Act (CRA). Each of these statutes was born in struggle, and controversy continues over their implementation.

The Fair Housing Act

The Fair Housing Act was a product, at least in part, of the civil disobedience that many cities experienced in the 1960s. A combination of political conflicts and compromises resulted in a law that was comprehensive in its coverage but weak in its enforcement. Had it not been for the assassination of Martin Luther King Jr. on April 4, 1968, the bill might never even have made it out of committee to the House floor (this discussion of the Fair Housing Act is drawn from Massey and Denton 1993, 186–216).

The bill did become law in 1968. It prohibited discrimination on the basis of race, color, religion, sex, and national origin in the sale or rental of housing, the terms and conditions under which housing would be made available, the advertising of housing, and the financing of housing. Implementing regulations and court decisions prohibited blockbusting and racial steering, denial of credit due to the racial composition of a neighborhood, property insurance discrimination, and other practices that resulted from unlawful intentional discrimination or had an illegal adverse disparate impact on nonwhites that could not be justified as necessary for a legitimate business purpose.

But the FHA gave the U.S. Department of Housing and Urban Development (HUD), the primary enforcement agency, only the power to engage in "conference, conciliation, and persuasion." HUD could also refer cases to the U.S. Department of Justice for prosecution. The Fair Housing Amendments Act of 1988 added handicap and familial status (for example, families with children) as protected groups and provided HUD with more enforcement authority. It created a process for the agency to take cases to an administrative law judge who could order full compensation for damages plus civil fines up to $10,000 for a first violation and $50,000 for a third offense.

The Justice Department relied on the FHA in settling the lending cases noted above. Private nonprofit fair housing centers have used the Act to secure relief for victims of discrimination in a variety of areas, including housing finance.

Home Mortgage Disclosure Act

In response to a growing number of complaints and accusations about redlining and the failure of bank regulatory agencies to respond, Congress enacted the Home Mortgage Disclosure Act (HMDA) in 1975. This was soon followed by enactment of the Community Reinvestment Act (CRA) described below.

The initial pressure was mounted in Chicago by community groups, inspired by the organizing tactics of Saul Alinsky, that protested the blockbusting and disinvestment of older urban neighborhoods. Two Chicago groups, the Organization for a Better Austin and the Northwest Community Organization, asked local banks to permit community input in the review of loan applications. They were rebuffed, so more aggressive tactics were employed. For example, organizers assembled area residents to open and close $1 checking accounts on Saturday afternoons, flooded bank floors with pennies, and arranged boycotts, effectively prohibiting the banks from conducting normal business on those days. Subsequent meetings produced agreements between the banks and the community groups. Research by the Center for Community Change and the National Urban League provided additional evidence of redlining and disinvestment. In 1972 Chicago organizers Gale Cincotta and Shel Trapp hosted a national conference on redlining in Chicago. That meeting resulted in the formation of the National Training and Information Center (NTIC), which would conduct additional research and coordinate further organizing, and National People's Action (NPA), which would serve as a neighborhood advocacy group. The Chicago City Council and later the Illinois legislature enacted anti-redlining legislation. The Chicago organizers then worked with Wisconsin senator William Proxmire, who sponsored HMDA in 1975 and the CRA two years later.

In 1976 several civil rights organizations sued the major federal financial regulatory agencies for failure to enforce nondiscrimination rules. The litigation was settled when three agencies (Federal Deposit Insurance Corporation, Federal Home Loan Bank Board, and Office of the Comptroller of the Currency) agreed to maintain loan log registers recording information on loan applications, approvals, and denials. But these agencies, which have long been, at best, reluctant to act on fair lending issues, did little with the newly collected data. In the late 1980s Bill Dedman published a series of stories in the *Atlanta Journal-Constitution* revealing widespread racial disparities in mortgage loan denial rates. Nationwide, blacks were rejected twice as often as whites, even among applicants with similar incomes. These reports stimulated substantial organizing activity, more enforcement efforts on the part of bank regulators, and expansion of the information made available under HMDA (Schwartz 1998; Bradford and Cincotta 1992; Pogge 1992; Dedman 1988, 1989).

HMDA made information available to the general public on the mortgage lending activity of most lenders by census tract in metropolitan areas throughout the United States. The basic objectives were to assist in determining the extent to which financial institutions were serving their communities, to help public officials distribute public investments in a manner that would leverage private investment in distressed communities, and to identify possible discriminatory lending patterns.

Initially HMDA only provided census-tract-level data on mortgage lending activity. But the requirements of the law and its implementing regulations have been expanded several times and now provide information on the characteristics of borrowers, loan products, and the disposition of mortgage applications. Today banks, savings institutions, credit unions, mortgage banking subsidiaries of bank holding companies and savings institutions, and mortgage lenders not affiliated with depository institutions are required to report annual loan information. Information that is currently disclosed includes the race, gender, and income of applicant (as of 2003, race and gender must be requested by lenders in applications taken by phone); type of loan applied for (for example, conventional or government insured); purpose of the loan (for example, home purchase, home improvement, refinancing); dollar amount of the loan; disposition of application (for example, loan originated, application denied); and census tract, county, and metropolitan area in which the property is located. As of 2004 lenders are required to identify high-priced loans subject to protections of the Home Ownership and Equity Protection Act (HOEPA), which basically requires additional disclosures for loans priced substantially above the cost of prime market-rate loans. In addition, as of 2004 lenders must report the difference between the annual percentage rate and the yield on comparable Treasury Department securities for loans that exceed the yield by three percentage points for first-lien loans and five percentage points for subordinate-lien loans (Federal Financial Institutions Examination Council 2001; Board of Governors of the Federal Reserve System 2002a, 2002b, 2002c, 2002d). The Federal Reserve Board estimates that virtually all prime loans will be exempt from this requirement but that it will apply to more than 95 percent of subprime loans (Center for Community Change 2002).

In 2000 approximately 22 million loan records for calendar year 1999 were reported by more than 7,800 institutions. Initially, lenders with assets of $10 million or more were required to report. In 1996 the Federal Reserve Board (which enforces Regulation C implementing HMDA) determined that the asset-size exemption would be tied to the consumer price index. For calendar 2002 that limit was set at $32 million (Board of Governors of the Federal Reserve System 2001). As of 2003 lenders with at least $25 million in mortgage loans are required to report. Prior to that year lenders were exempt if the dollar volume of their mortgage lending was less than 10 percent of their total lending. That exemption no longer pertains to lenders whose mortgage lending volume reaches $25 million (Board of Governors of the Federal Reserve System 2002d).

HMDA is simply a disclosure requirement. But the data available from HMDA have been used in conjunction with other tools to increase access to credit in underserved communities. The Community Reinvestment Act has been a particularly valuable complement to HMDA.

Community Reinvestment Act

Under the Community Reinvestment Act most federally regulated depository institutions "have a continuing and affirmative obligation to help meet the credit needs of the local communities in which they are chartered." Federal financial regulatory agencies (the four principal regulators are the Federal Reserve Board, the Office of the Comptroller of the Currency, the Federal Deposit Insurance Corporation, and the Office of Thrift Supervision) periodically evaluate lenders under their jurisdiction. Those evaluations and a final rating (outstanding, satisfactory, needs to improve, or substantial noncompliance) are kept on file and also made available to the public upon request. Regulators are required to take lenders' CRA performances into account when evaluating applications from those institutions they supervise whenever the lenders seek permission to open a new branch, merge or purchase another institution, increase their depository insurance, or to make almost any other significant change in their business practices.

A key provision of the CRA is that third parties can challenge such applications. These challenges often delay consideration of the application and therefore can be quite costly for the financial institution. Regulatory agencies rarely deny applications on CRA grounds. Banking regulators reported that for the ten years prior to 1988 only eight of forty thousand applications were denied because of inadequate compliance with the CRA (Schwartz 1998b, 633). But often they take time to review the challenges and they frequently ask the lender and the organization filing the challenge to seek a voluntary solution. This challenge process provides leverage that several groups have used to negotiate reinvestment or CRA agreements. Community organizations, often in conjunction with supportive public officials, sympathetic reporters and academics, and friendly lenders have exploited the opportunities created by the information made available through HMDA and the affirmative requirements established by the CRA. In light of the growing merger and acquisition activity in the financial services industry in recent years, stepped up enforcement of the CRA in the 1990s, and the increasing capacity of community organizations to conduct research (particularly with HMDA data) and address community development issues in general, the CRA has had a substantial influence on the flow of credit (Marsico 1996).

Institutions subject to the CRA are required to make such information available to the public as a map delineating their service or assessment area, the products they offer, the location of their main office and branch banks, recent CRA evaluations, and any comments they have received pertaining to their community reinvestment activities. Initially, evaluations focused on a range of procedural matters, such as how often bank representatives met with community groups and the extent to which chief executive officers were involved in community reinvestment activities. In 1995 a new regulation was enacted that focused more on performance.

Under the new regulation, lenders with $250 million or more in assets are now evaluated in terms of their lending, investment, and service activities. The lending test focuses on the amount of lending in their assessment area and the distribution of loans by neighborhood and borrower income characteristics. The investment test focuses on the extent of their investments where community development is a primary purpose, including grants to community development corporations, affordable-housing developers, and small businesses. The service test examines the distribution of branch banks, the record of opening and closing branches, and services generally provided to low- and moderate-income markets. Smaller banks are examined primarily in terms of their loan-to-deposit ratio, share of loans in their assessment area and to low- and moderate-income areas, and their response to complaints about their community reinvestment record. Wholesale or limited-purpose banks that do not make direct residential or small business loans are evaluated on their community development lending and services. In addition, lenders have the option of developing a strategic plan, in conjunction with community groups, that is tailored to their own institution but will meet the same basic community reinvestment obligations. One further provision of the 1995 regulation was that lenders with assets of $250 million or more or affiliated with a holding company totaling $1 billion or more in assets must report their small business lending by census tract to their regulators. Tract-level data, however, are not made available to the public for individual institutions. Aggregate data for all reporting institutions combined are available at the tract level by metropolitan area. For individual lenders, data are available on the number and dollar amount of their small business lending by tract income level (for example, tracts where the median income is less than 50 percent of the metropolitan area median) (Marsico 1996; Haag 2000).

There is now substantial evidence that the CRA is having the intended impact. According to the National Community Reinvestment Coalition, more than 390 CRA agreements totaling over $1 trillion have been negotiated by community organizations and lenders (National Community Reinvestment Coalition 2001b, 1). These agreements have been implemented in all regions of the country and in at least thirty-four states. They call for increases in home-purchase, home-improvement, and small-business lending in low- and moderate-income areas and to racial minorities throughout metropolitan areas; changes in underwriting standards to increase the flow of credit to previously underserved areas; new branch banks in urban areas; affirmative action to increase minority employment; and many other activities, along with the establishment of joint monitoring committees (with membership including representatives from community organizations and financial institutions) to implement and provide oversight for these initiatives.

As the following chapters reveal, creating and implementing these agreements is frequently not a smooth process. Often they arise from charges of improper behavior, CRA challenges, and other conflicts. Community groups often organize campaigns highly critical of lending institutions, frequently based on their analyses of HMDA data. In some cases demonstrators "visit" the homes of bank presidents. They contact friendly reporters, who write sympathetic stories. Sometimes it is the reporters' stories themselves that initiate the campaigns (Dedman 1988, 1989; Everett, Gallagher, and Blossom 1988). But the culmination is often a productive partnership in which the community secures increasing access to capital and the lenders find new and profitable markets.

Scholarly research has also begun to demonstrate empirically the benefits of the CRA. In a review of CRA-related research, the Brookings Institution found that in the 1990s home-purchase mortgage lending to low-income and minority households and neighborhoods increased faster than home-purchase mortgage lending generally (Haag 2000). The U.S. Department of the Treasury reported similar findings, with the greatest increases coming after the 1995 performance-oriented regulation was implemented. In addition, the Treasury report found greater increases in communities where there had been at least one CRA agreement signed by a lender with a community group (Litan et al. 2001). Schwartz drew similar conclusions in a nationwide study comparing the lending record of financial institutions that signed CRA agreements with those that had not (Schwartz 1998a). Raphael Bostic and Breck Robinson found that the number of conventional home-purchase loans going to low- and moderate-income and minority borrowers and areas increased significantly in urban counties with the introduction of new CRA agreements in recent years, though these effects were most pronounced in the first two years the agreements were in place (Bostic and Robinson 2002). The Federal Reserve Board also found that CRA-related lending was profitable for the vast majority of covered lenders, though not quite as profitable as other home lending for a majority of institutions (Board of Governors of the Federal Reserve System 2000b). And the Joint Center for Housing Studies found that CRA-regulated lenders make a higher share of their loans to lower-income people and communities and to minority markets than do nonregulated institutions, that this effect was most noticeable in the assessment areas of CRA lenders (where their loans are most closely scrutinized), and that the CRA has had a direct impact on these patterns (Joint Center for Housing Studies 2002, 135–36.)

At the same time, the CRA has been a source of great controversy and contention. A primary and longstanding concern is the argument that the CRA leads to credit allocation, and therefore to inefficiencies in financial service markets. Some contend that enforcement pressure by regulators may have forced some lenders to make loans to low-income borrowers who were not able to handle the payments and therefore subsequently lost their investments when they went into default (Benston 1997, 1999). A related concern is that there may be a conflict between the safety-and-soundness standards lenders are required to meet and the objectives spelled out in the CRA (Gunther 1999). Senator Phil Gramm, then chair of the Senate Banking Committee and longtime critic of the CRA, stated that the Federal Reserve Board's profitability study "demonstrates that CRA lending as it is now practiced is credit allocation" and called for a more in-depth study of the issue (Heller 2000). Gramm has argued that under the CRA, "We have had rampant extortion, fraud, and kickbacks," and has claimed that neighborhood groups use the law to shake down banks for loans (Dodge and Power 1998). He likens CRA proponents to the Mafia and describes the rules as "an evil like slavery in the pre–Civil War era" (Wayne 1998). Others acknowledge the increase in lending to previously underserved markets but argue that market pressures and improved technology that provide more information on potential borrowers (for example, credit scoring and automated underwriting)—and not the CRA—account for increasing lending in previously underserved areas (Gunther, Klemme, and Robinson 1999).

But the evidence is more consistent with the conclusions of two members of the Federal Reserve Board. Governor Edward M. Gramlich has observed that the "CRA does seem to have generated a large amount of new loans. . . . There seems to be little doubt that most of these outcomes would not have occurred in the absence of CRA and other fair lending laws" (Gramlich 1998). Governor Laurence H. Meyer concurred, stating, "At no time in our history has credit been more available and more affordable to virtually all income groups, than it is today. The Community Reinvestment Act has contributed to this increase in the availability and affordability of credit" (Meyer 1998).

Campaigns

Increasing access to capital in distressed areas has been a common focus of organizing and advocacy efforts, which draw from a common toolkit. At the same time, each campaign has particular objectives and uses an array of strategies and tactics to achieve them.

In Chapter 2, "Where the Hell Did Billions of Dollars for Reinvestment Come From?" Joe Mariano of the National Training and Information Center (NTIC) concretely demonstrates the positive impact of a range of direct actions. In describing the origins of HMDA and the CRA, NTIC's efforts to reform the FHA's guaranteed loan program, and anti-predatory-lending activities, Mariano reveals the limits of "being nice." He clearly demonstrates the ongoing need for organizing and shows why it is not simply a historical curiosity.

The critical role of citizen involvement is demonstrated in Chapter 3, "Giving Back to the Future: Citizen Involvement and Community Stabilization in Milwaukee." William R. Tisdale and Carla J. Wertheim, president and executive vice president of the Metropolitan Milwaukee Fair Housing Council, show how local citizen involvement at all levels—as board members, investigators, advisors—can lead to a range of successful fair housing and community development initiatives. As the nature of financial institutions and regulation of those institutions evolves, Tisdale and Wertheim reveal how what began as traditional inner-city fair housing struggles can result in comprehensive community development initiatives that benefit entire metropolitan regions.

Attorney John P. Relman shows the critical role the courts can play in furthering fair lending objectives. In Chapter 4, "Taking It to the Courts: Litigation and the Reform of Financial Institutions," Relman reveals how litigation can enable just one courageous individual to secure significant institutional change in the nation's largest financial institutions. Lenders have powerful friends in Congress, regulatory agencies, and other halls of power. Access to the courts, however, can level the playing field. Through law enforcement victims can obtain substantial remedies. And with the negative publicity litigation can bring, financial institutions can find it very difficult to do business unless they do so equitably.

Chapter 5, "From Living Rooms to Board Rooms: Sustainable Homeownership Deals with Banks and Insurers in Boston," reveals the importance of research, favorable reporting by local media, and supportive elected officials, along with organizing initiatives involving ordinary working people who simply want to own their homes. But these cannot be one-shot or short-term activities. Thomas Callahan of the Massachusetts Affordable Housing Alliance illustrates the need for long-term, sustainable efforts. These lessons are drawn from organizing campaigns against, and partnerships with, banks and property insurers in their underwriting and investment activities.

The importance of local coalition building and the role of research in nurturing the effectiveness of local collaborations are examined in Chapter 6, "A Citywide Strategy: The Pittsburgh Community Reinvestment Group." Stanley A. Lowe and John T. Metzger also describe some of the challenges to local organizing posed by internal staff-management problems, the impact of suburban sprawl, a changing financial and regulatory landscape, and other nonlocal forces.

As Allen J. Fishbein observes in Chapter 7, "Filling the Half-Empty Glass: The Role of Community Advocacy in Redefining the Public Responsibilities of Government-Sponsored Housing Enterprises," one of the best-kept secrets in the affordable-housing industry is the role of government-sponsored enterprises, primarily the Federal Home Loan Banks, Fannie Mae and Freddie Mac. Fishbein examines the role of community advocacy in the creation, expansion, and enforcement of affordable-housing goals, which has been critical to increasing, by perhaps billions of dollars, the amount of mortgage financing available for low- and moderate-income communities across the nation.

Maude Hurd and Steven Kest of ACORN show the power that low-income residents can exercise in Chapter 8, "Fighting Predatory Lending from the Ground Up: An Issue of Economic Justice." They reveal the impact of simply having residents tell their own stories of how they were the victims of predatory lending practices. When such stories are publicized in the media, they often lead to institutional changes on the part of financial institutions and their regulators. Simply the threat of holding a public hearing can cause some lenders to come to the bargaining table so as to avoid becoming the poster child for abusive lending practices.

Success often requires linking reinvestment with other social justice issues. In Chapter 9, "Community Reinvestment in a Globalizing World: To Hold Banks Accountable from The Bronx to Buenos Aires, Beijing, and Basel," Matthew Lee of Inner City Press/Community on the Move illustrates the value in uniting CRA challenges and litigation on a global level. This can require working in conjunction with other social justice issues and organizations, including environmental and labor groups, in order to achieve shared objectives.

The vital role of solid, independent research is the focus of Chapter 10, "Research, Advocacy, and Community Reinvestment," by Malcolm Bush and Daniel Immergluck of the Woodstock Institute. Bush and Immergluck also point to the critical role of independent advocacy groups, and the somewhat limited role that community development corporations and others dependent on bank financing can play in these efforts. This chapter illustrates the application of these principles, whether the objective is legislative or regulatory change or the negotiation of a reinvestment agreement with a financial institution.

John Taylor and Josh Silver of the National Community Reinvestment Coalition demonstrate how community reinvestment can be a win-win situation for lenders and communities. In Chapter 11, "The Essential Role of Activism in Community Reinvestment," they indicate the importance of operating at several levels, including negotiating directly with lenders, working with regulators and legislators, and commenting publicly on merger applications. The end result, however, is often a situation in which lenders find new, profitable business and residents gain access to affordable credit.

Community reinvestment involves a range of actors and actions, as Peter Dreier observes in Chapter 12, "Protest, Progress, and the Politics of Reinvestment." Noting the progress and pitfalls of various campaigns, this chapter assesses the value of organizing and advocacy tools for achieving progress in community reinvestment. Drawing on the findings of the previous chapters, Dreier summarizes the lessons that have been learned about the roles and strategies diverse actors (for example, community organizations, regulators, legislators, financial institutions) have used and could use in the future to further reinvestment objectives. He emphasizes the importance of developing innovative political coalitions with other social justice groups and among urban and suburban constituencies that have not often been on the same side of controversial issues.

Organizing is a means to an end. The prize in community reinvestment struggles has been increased access to affordable credit in traditionally under-served neighborhoods. But each campaign also has specific objectives. The Epilogue, "Where Do We Go From Here?" describes a federal legislative proposal, the Community Reinvestment Modernization Act, that contains several specific goals, each of which on its own, or in conjunction with each other, would constitute fruitful directions for future organizing campaigns. Community reinvestment strategies occupy consistently contested terrain. Specific future objectives will change as developments warrant. But at least some overriding principles will persist. These are captured in the various provisions of that proposal. But it is precisely the contested nature of these issues that promises continued struggles ahead.

Reaction to Fair Lending and Community Reinvestment Initiatives

The CRA and fair lending policies in general have generated a range of attacks. Members of Congress routinely introduce legislation that would provide a "safe harbor" (that is, immunity from CRA challenges, for example) for insti-tutions with "satisfactory" or better CRA ratings—which would include 98 percent of all lenders in 1998, up from 87 percent in 1987 (Woodstock Insti-tute 1998). Small bank exemptions are also frequently proposed. Depending on the definition of a small bank, such proposals could exclude up to 85 per-cent of all covered lenders (Bradford and Cincotta 1992, 267). Other proposals would permit comment on bank applications only at the time that the CRA evaluation is conducted. Some have proposed that lenders be able to "self-certify" their compliance with the CRA. Elimination of the disparate-impact standard of the Fair Housing Act has been offered (Silver 1999). While no seri-ous public effort has yet been launched to eliminate the CRA altogether, the direction of most proposals is evident; less is more.

Lenders, sometimes through their trade associations, have begun to orga-nize in opposition to community reinvestment and fair lending initiatives. Fol-lowing the Justice Department's settlement of its lawsuit against Chevy Chase, the Savings and Community Bankers of America—a trade association representing thrifts and banks—created a $100,000 war chest to fight at least some fair lending enforcement actions. These funds will be used to defend selected institutions and may also support research, public relations cam-paigns, or friend-of-the-court briefs as part of an advocacy campaign (Mere-dith 1994). Edward L. Yingling, the chief lobbyist for the American Bankers Association, stated, "We've gone from a decade in which the consumer activists were really able to push their legislative agenda to a point where they not only can't push forward but we can begin pushing back" (Garsson and de Senerpont Domis 1994).

Another threat to community reinvestment is the wave of consolidation and merger activity among financial institutions. The decline in the number of banks, as well as mergers involving mortgage lenders, insurers, and securities firms, raise questions about commitments to community reinvestment. The number of banks in the United States has declined from almost 20,000 in 1970 to 9,100 by the end of 1997. While some of this decline was due to bank failures, most of it is the result of mergers among healthy institutions (Bradford and Cincotta 1992, 261; Meyer 1998). The merger of Citicorp Bank and Travelers Insurance to form Citigroup, resulting in a $750 billion corporation engaged in banking, insurance, and securities, raised concerns to a new level both because of the scope of the entities involved and the diversity of financial services offered under one roof. In fact, some claimed the merger was illegal under banking law at that time (Seiberg 1998).

Developments like the Citicorp-Travelers merger have provided additional fuel to the twenty-year struggle on the part of some financial institutions to revise Depression-era statutes that limited mergers and consolidations among and across financial industries. Arguing that international competitiveness and maximum efficiency (ultimately for the benefit of consumers) require that financial service providers be able to offer banking, insurance, securities, and other services, proponents have called on Congress for at least twenty years to pass "bank reform" legislation removing remaining barriers to consolidation. Opponents have expressed concern for the safety and soundness of at least some of the financial service companies that such legislation would permit. One basic fear has been that subsidiaries of a holding company would engage in something other than "arms-length" transactions when lending to, insuring, or otherwise financing another arm of that corporation, thus weakening the financial status of that subsidiary or even the entire holding company. Such "crony capitalism" or any number of other developments could lead to more institutions being viewed as "too big to fail," which could result in more taxpayer-subsidized bailouts—a scenario similar to the $180 billion bailout of savings and loans in the 1980s. A related consumer concern is that current prohibitions against "tying" (where in order to obtain one financial service a customer must agree to purchase others from the same company), would be weakened (Bush 1999).

A more direct CRA-related concern is the enhanced opportunity for such providers to shift assets out of institutions covered by the law into those entities (for example, independent mortgage companies, insurers) not currently covered. In fact, institutions that traditionally provided the vast majority of mortgage loans—savings and commercial banks that are covered by the CRA— now make less than half of such loans (Bush 1999; Taylor 1999a). That the impact of CRA has started to wane is evidenced by the fact that fewer than 30 percent of home-purchase loans are now subject to intensive CRA review. This reflects the fact that between 1993 and 2000 the number of home-purchase loans made by CRA-regulated institutions in their assessment areas—the loans that are subject to the most intensive review—dropped from 36.1 percent to 29.5 percent (Joint Center for Housing Studies 2002, iii, v).

Proponents of bank reform finally won a victory in 1999 when Congress passed and the president signed the Financial Services Modernization Act. For the first time since the CRA was enacted in 1977, Congress did enact legislation that rolled back its authority. This legislation permits banks, insurers, and securities firms to enter each other's business more freely. Such conglomeration had been proceeding piecemeal through various regulatory exemptions and loopholes under previous law. Now financial institutions will be able more easily to offer a range of services to their customers. Congress could have established CRA or CRA-like requirements for all providers of financial services, or at least to the lending activities of these firms, resulting in a level playing field that would not disadvantage the federally regulated depository institutions that are now the focus of the law. Instead, the law weakens the CRA requirements for those institutions to which it does apply.

Under the new law, small banks—those with assets below $250 million— will be examined once every five years if they have an "outstanding" rating and once every four years if they have a "satisfactory" rating. Under previous rules they were examined every two years. A so-called "sunshine" provision requires lenders and community groups engaged in reinvestment agreements to file with the regulatory agency supervising the lender a report of the terms of their agreements and annual statements on how the funds are used. This will have a chilling effect on the desire of either community groups or lenders to form such partnerships, in part because some lenders do not want their competitors to know all the details of their marketing plans (Taylor 1999b). The extent to which the CRA has been harmed by these changes can be debated. More significant than these particular changes, however, is the fact that for the first time in more than twenty years the CRA has been weakened, and no doubt Congress will consider further CRA "reforms" in the near future.

These developments have already started to take their toll. As noted above, the share of single-family home-purchase loans to low- and moderate-income borrowers grew from 19 percent to 29 percent between 1993 and 2000, but dropped to 24.7 percent in 2001. The share of loans going to blacks increased from 3.8 percent to 6.6 percent but then declined to 4.8 percent in 2001. For Hispanics the increase was from 4 percent to 6.9 percent before falling to 6.2 percent (National Community Reinvestment Coalition 2002, 5–6).

Interestingly, many of the institutions currently engaged in mega-mergers have made unilateral CRA pledges for what appear to be substantial commitments. Citicorp and Travelers announced a $115 billion commitment to low-income and minority communities over the next ten years. NationsBank and Bank America topped this when they announced a $350 billion commitment as part of their merger plans. But it is difficult to know what these large national commitments actually mean. These announcements were made without any prior research or planning by, or discussions with, neighborhood groups. Precisely what counts in these commitments and how these pledges relate to previous lending practices (that is, do they represent an increase in community reinvestment and, if so, how much?) remain unclear. Mechanisms for monitoring and evaluation are also unclear. For example, these commitments sometimes include credit card debt and loans to wealthy nonwhite households. Community groups in the local communities where these dollars may go would not necessarily view these commitments as responding to current needs (O'Brien 1998). And sometimes these "pledges" actually call for a reduction in community reinvestment and fair lending activity.

In 1993 a coalition of inner-city churches in Milwaukee, the Milwaukee Innercity Congregations Allied for Hope (MICAH), and eight local lenders announced a $500 million, five-year loan commitment. But the requisite homework was not done. A closer inspection of the previous lending records of these institutions revealed that this "commitment" would actually amount to a lower level of lending than these institutions had provided in prior years (Norman 1993; Squires 1993). One lender conceded, "The dollars we pledged are the amounts we were asked to by MICAH. Maybe MICAH didn't seize the negotiating advantage they had. They could have squeezed more" (Norman 1993). Not surprisingly, over the next few years the lenders frequently and proudly announced that they were well ahead of meeting their MICAH goals.

The advent of electronic banking poses additional potential problems. Lenders are reducing their reliance on brick-and-mortar branch offices and human tellers and other employees at various levels to provide basic banking services. Increasingly they use telephones, stored-value or "smart" cards, computers, and the Internet to provide depository, bill-paying, lending, and other services. More employers provide paychecks electronically, and government agencies are increasingly distributing various benefits (for example, grants, pensions, welfare payments) electronically as well. Low-income and minority households, which are less likely to be "wired," run even greater risks of being locked out of traditional banking services as this trend develops, as it no doubt will (Stegman 1999).

Related developments include the widespread use of credit scoring and automated underwriting. With credit scoring lenders use credit reports to determine certain cut-off points to determine who is automatically eligible and who requires a second look. Automated underwriting involves the use of credit scores and other information about borrowers and the properties they want to purchase in the development of computer-generated models for assessing eligibility. Lenders maintain that these practices allow them to process many more applications, and to do so in a more scientific, unbiased manner (Fannie Mae n.d.; Fair, Isaac and Co. 1997). Others are not so sure. Many observers have raised concerns about the inaccuracy of credit reports. Since the factors that go into the models are generally confidential, it is not clear whether each variable in fact reflects ability to repay or if nontraditional credit-related variables are excluded that would enhance the credit record of minorities. Even if no discrimination is intended, some models could have a disparate impact on minorities. And questions remain about what happens to those with borderline scores (Fishbein 1996).

Other problems, some longstanding and others relatively new, threaten fair lending and community reinvestment initiatives. Racial steering and other discriminatory practices remain facts of life, as black and Hispanic home seekers encounter discrimination in approximately 20 percent of their encounters with real estate agents (Turner et al. 2002b). Property insurance discrimination has been documented in cities across the nation, with four of the nation's six largest insurance companies (Allstate, State Farm, Nationwide, and Farmers), among others, settling fair housing complaints since 1995, following the pathbreaking settlement with American Family Mutual Insurance Company in Milwaukee that year (Squires 1997; Toledo Fair Housing Center 2001). Arbitrary and discriminatory appraisal practices persist, undercutting property values in minority areas. In a project carried out by the Cleveland Federal Reserve Bank, one property in that city was valued at $36,000 by one appraiser and $83,500 by another (Pittinger 1996; Appraisal Process Task Group 1994). Each of these practices makes it more difficult for minorities and residents of low-income areas to build financial assets, qualify for mortgage loans, and become homeowners.

Perhaps the greatest threat is posed by the growing evidence of predatory lending discussed above. Predatory lending practices may actually be more damaging than the refusal to provide service. Families subject to these practices frequently find themselves with loans they cannot repay and ultimately lose their homes along with the life savings they have invested in them.

The political pendulum continues to swing. Fair housing and community reinvestment advocates are responding to the new financial service marketplace and the challenges it poses. Ongoing debates suggest that it would be premature to retire the protest banner.

A Fragile Movement

The struggle to democratize access to capital goes on. The latest legislative thrust is the Community Reinvestment Modernization Act, introduced by two Midwestern Democratic congressional representatives, Tom Barrett of Milwaukee and Luis Gutierrez of Chicago. This bill would extend CRA or CRA-like provisions to all mortgage lenders, insurers, and security firms. It would establish HMDA-like disclosure requirements for the property insurance industry. And it would revise those sections of the Financial Services Modernization Act that weakened the CRA. But the prospects for this legislation are uncertain. The future of fair lending and community reinvestment, as ever, depends on community-based organizing efforts.

"Community organizing has been the driving force of the reinvestment movement from the beginning," according to two of the movement's pioneers, Calvin Bradford and Gale Cincotta (1992, 235). "At any given point, a legislator, an agency official, or some government agency can play an important part in an issue or policy; but over the long haul, community reinvestment remains a movement determined by people power" (Bradford and Cincotta 1992, 270).

Even Lawrence Lindsay concedes that "today's successes might not have been possible without the protests of the past." And while protest alone will not sustain any social movement (Andrews 2001), Lindsay is simply wrong when he concludes, "But that is a point about the past. Today we must look to the future." That future, according to Lindsay, means announcing to the world, "We are grown up. We're business people" (Lindsay 2000, 54). NTIC's Shel Trapp responded to the same advice 17 years ago in his book *Blessed Be the Fighters,* when he offered the following observation:

> "Confrontation was good for the '60s, but this is the . . . age of partnerships." That really sounds great, but the basis of partnership is equality and respect. My experience in the '60s, '70s, and '80s has been that while we are willing to form partnerships with anyone who is willing to come to the table and seriously discuss the issues, I have not seen too many of our opponents come to the table willingly. . . . Partnerships are great as long as there is mutual respect. Community organizations usually have to fight to get that respect. It reminds me of the story of the farmer who was asked why he hit his mule over the head with a two-by-four. His response was, "That is just to get his attention." In all the partnerships we formed, we first had to get the attention of our opponents. Translated, that means we've had to confront them. (Trapp 1986, 13–14)

No doubt Shel Trapp would echo these sentiments for the new millennium.

The following chapters describe how the progress of the past has been won. Despite real successes, they remain incomplete. Saul Alinsky argued that there are no permanent friends or permanent enemies. And there are few, if any, permanent victories. Progress has been made in fair lending and community reinvestment, but that progress is threatened. Homeownership may be at record levels today, but low-income and minority neighborhoods remain underserved. While lending to racial minorities has increased, as indicated earlier, at their peak in 2000 African Americans received just 6.6 percent of single-family home-purchase loans (dropping to 4.8 percent one year later), and Hispanics received 6.9 percent (before falling to 6.2 percent), but each group accounted for more than 12 percent of the nation's population (U.S. Department of Commerce 2001; Joint Center for Housing Studies 2001; Federal Financial Institutions Examination Council 2002). One result is the persistent gap in homeownership. As noted above, 73.8 percent of white households own their homes, compared to just 47.6 percent of black and 46.3 percent of Hispanic households (Joint Center for Housing Studies 2001, 14). Fair housing has been referred to as "a fragile movement" (Saltman 1990). One price of progress is the proverbial eternal vigilance.

References

Ando, Faith. 1988. Capital Issues and Minority-Owned Business. *Review of Black Political Economy* 16 (4): 77–109.

Andrews, Kenneth T. 2001. Social Movements and Policy Implementation: The Mississippi Civil Rights Movement and the War on Poverty, 1965–1971. *American Sociological Review* 66 (1): 71–95.

Appraisal Process Task Group. 1994. Report of the Appraisal Process Task Group, a subcommittee of the Residential Housing and Mortgage Credit Project of the Federal Reserve Bank of Cleveland (June 1).

Bates, Timothy. 1989. Small Business Viability in the Urban Ghetto. *Journal of Regional Science* 29 (4): 625–43.

———. 1997. Unequal Access: Financial Institution Lending to Black- and White-Owned Small Business Start-ups. *Journal of Urban Affairs* 19 (4): 487–95.

Benston, George J. 1997. Discrimination in Mortgage Lending: Why HMDA and CRA Should Be Repealed. *Journal of Retail Banking Services* 19 (3): 47–57.

———. 1999. *The Community Reinvestment Act: Looking for Discrimination That Isn't There.* Washington, D.C.: Cato Institute.

Blanchflower, David G., Phillip B. Levine, and David J. Zimmerman. 1998. Discrimination in the Small Business Credit Market. National Bureau of Economic Research Working Paper No. 6840.

Blassingame, John W., ed. 1985. *The Frederick Douglass Papers.* New Haven: Yale University Press.

Board of Governors of the Federal Reserve System. 2000a. Press Release (Dec. 14) accessed at <http://www.federalreserve.gov/BoardDocs/Press/BoardActs/2000/20001214/default.htm> on March 8, 2001.

———. 2000b. The Performance and Profitability of CRA-Related Lending. Washington, D.C.: Board of Governors of the Federal Reserve System.

———. 2001. Press Release (Dec. 19) accessed at <http://www.federalreserve.gov/boarddocs/press/boardacts/2001/20011219/default.htm>.

———. 2002a. Press Release (January 23) accessed at <http://www.federalreserve.gov/boarddocs/press/boardacts/2002/20020123/>.

———. 2002b. Press Release (May 2) accessed at <http://www.federalreserve.gov/boarddocs/press/boardacts/2002/20020502/>.

———. 2002c. Press Release (June 24) accessed at <http://www.federalreserve.gov/boarddocs/press/bcreg/2002/20020621/attachment.pdf>.

———. 2002d. Press Release (June 24) accessed at <http://www.federalreserve.gov/boarddocs/press/bcreg/2002/20020621/attachment1.pdf>.

Bostic, Raphael W., and Breck Robinson. 2002. Do CRA Agreements Influence Lending Patterns? Working Paper. University of Southern California, Lusk Center for Real Estate.

Bradford, Calvin. 1979. Financing Home Ownership—The Federal Role in Neighborhood Decline. *Urban Affairs Quarterly* 14 (3): 313–35.

Bradford, Calvin, and Gale Cincotta. 1992. The Legacy, the Promise, and the Unfinished Agenda. In *From Redlining to Reinvestment: Community Responses to Urban Disinvestment.* Ed. Gregory D. Squires. Philadelphia: Temple University Press.

Bush, Malcolm. 1999. The Challenges to Community Reinvestment from Bank Modernization. Memo prepared for the Woodstock Institute (Feb. 5).

Cavalluzzo, Ken S., Linda C. Cavalluzzo, and John D. Wolken. 1999. Competition, Small Business Financing, and Discrimination: Evidence from a New Survey. In *Business Access to Capital and Credit.* Ed. Jackson L. Blanton, Alicia Williams, and Sherrie L. W. Rhine. Washington, D.C.: Federal Reserve System.

Center for Community Change. 2002. Center for Community Change Policy Alert # 259. Washington, D.C.: Center for Community Change (January 28).

Dedman, Bill. 1988. The Color of Money. *Atlanta Journal/Constitution* (May 1–4).

———. 1989. Blacks Turned Down for Home Loans from S&Ls Twice as Often as Whites. *Atlanta Journal/Constitution* (January 22).

Dodge, Robert, and Stephen Power. 1998. Gramm Takes Shot at CRA—Kirk Fights Back. *Dallas Morning News* (Nov. 5).

Dreier, Peter, John Mollenkopf, and Todd Swanstrom. 2001. *Place Matters: Metropolitics for the Twenty-first Century.* Lawrence: University Press of Kansas.

Everett, David, John Gallagher, and Teresa Blossom. 1988. The Race for Money. *Detroit Free Press* (July 24–27).

Fair, Isaac and Co. 1997. Credit Bureau Scores in Mortgage Lending: Strategies for Improving Operations. San Rafael, Calif.: Fair, Isaac and Co.

Fannie Mae. N.d. What Are Credit Scoring and Automated Underwriting? Washington, D.C.: Fannie Mae.

Federal Financial Institutions Examination Council. 2000. Press Release. Washington, D.C.: Federal Financial Institutions Examination Council (August 8), accessed at <http://www.ffiecj.gov/hmcrpr/hm080800.htm> on March 12, 2001.

———. 2002. Press Release. Washington, D.C.: Federal Financial Institutions Examination Council (August 1), accessed at: <http://www.ffiec.gov/hmcrpr/hm080102.htm> on August 7, 2002.

Fishbein, Allen J. 1996. Is Credit Scoring a Winner for Everyone? *Stone Soup* (spring): 14–15.

Garsson, Robert M., and Olaf de Senerpont Domis. 1994. GOP Win Looks Good for Banks. *American Banker* (Nov. 10).

Goering, John, and Ron Wienk, eds. 1996. *Mortgage Lending, Racial Discrimination, and Federal Policy.* Washington, D.C.: Urban Institute Press.

Gramlich, Edward M. 1998. Remarks by Edward M. Gramlich at Widener University, Chester, Pennsylvania (Nov. 6).

Greene, Zina G. 1980. *Lender's Guide to Fair Mortgage Policies.* Washington, D.C.: Potomac Institute.

Grogan, Paul S., and Tony Proscio. 2000. *Comeback Cities: A Blueprint for Urban Neighborhood Revival.* Boulder: Westview Press.

Gunther, Jeffrey. 1999. Between a Rock and a Hard Place: The CRA-Safety and Soundness Pinch. *Economic and Financial Review* (2d qtr.).

Gunther, Jeffrey, Kelly Klemme, and Kenneth Robinson. 1999. Redlining or Red Herring? *Southwest Economy* 3 (May/June): 8–13.

Haag, Susan White. 2000. Community Reinvestment and Cities: A Literature Review of CRA's Impact and Future. Paper prepared for The Brookings Institution, Center on Urban and Metropolitan Policy.

Heller, Michele. 2000. Capitol Hill Partisans Spin Lessons from CRA Profit, Delinquency Report. *American Banker* (July 18).

Hoyt, Homer. 1933. *One Hundred Years of Land Values in Chicago.* Chicago: University of Chicago Press.

Immergluck, Daniel, and Marti Wiles. 1999. *Two Steps Back: The Dual Mortgage Market, Predatory Lending, and the Undoing of Community Development.* Chicago: Woodstock Institute.

Jackson, Kenneth T. 1985. *Crabgrass Frontier: The Suburbanization of the United States.* New York: Oxford University Press.

Joint Center for Housing Studies. 2000. *The State of the Nation's Housing: 2000* (January 24), accessed at <www.gsd.harvard.edu/jcenter> on March 8, 2001.

———. 2001. *The State of the Nation's Housing 2001.* Cambridge: Joint Center for Housing Studies, Harvard University.

———. 2002. *The Twenty-fifth Anniversary of the Community Reinvestment Act: Access to Capital in an Evolving Financial Services System.* Cambridge: Joint Center for Housing Studies.

Judd, Dennis R. 1984. *The Politics of American Cities: Private Power and Public Policy.* Boston: Little, Brown.

Lee, Bill Lann. 1999. An Issue of Public Importance: The Justice Department's Enforcement of the Fair Housing Act. *Cityscape* 4 (3): 35–56.

Lief, Beth J., and Susan Goering. 1987. The Implementation of the Federal Mandate for Fair Housing. In *Divided Neighborhoods: Changing Patterns of Racial Segregation.* Ed. Gary A. Tobin. Newbury Park: Sage Publications.

Lindsay, Lawrence B. 2000. Community Development at a Crossroads. *Neighborworks Journal* (winter): 54–55.

Litan, Robert E., et al. 2001. *The Community Reinvestment Act after Financial Modernization: A Final Report.* Washington, D.C.: U.S. Department of the Treasury.

Marsico, Richard D. 1996. The New Community Reinvestment Act Regulations: An Attempt to Implement Performance-Based Standards. *Clearinghouse Review* (March): 1021–33.

Massey, Douglas S. 2001. Residential Segregation and Neighborhood Conditions in U.S. Metropolitan Areas. In *America Becoming: Racial Trends and Their Consequences,* vol. 1. Ed. Neil J. Smelser, William Julius Wilson, and Faith Mitchell. Washington, D.C.: National Academy Press.

Massey, Douglas S., and Nancy Denton. 1993. *American Apartheid: Segregation and the Making of the Underclass.* Cambridge: Harvard University Press.

Meredith, Robyn. 1994. Thrifts Set War Chest for Fight on Fair Lending. *American Banker* (Oct. 18).

Meyer, Laurence H. 1998. Remarks by Laurence H. Meyer before the 1998 Community Reinvestment Act Conference of the Consumer Bankers Association, Arlington, Virginia (May 12).

Munnell, Alicia H., Geoffrey M. B. Tootell, Lynn E. Brown, and James McEneany. 1996. Mortgage Lending in Boston: Interpreting HMDA Data. *American Economic Review* 86 (1): 25–53.

NAACP v. American Family Mutual Insurance Company (1992). Statement taken from case files, Milwaukee, Wisconsin.

National Advisory Commission on Civil Disorders. 1968. *Report of the National Advisory Commission on Civil Disorders.* New York: Bantam Books.

National Community Reinvestment Coalition. 2001a. Home Loans to Minorities and Working Class Populations Increase, but Policymakers Do Not Address Remaining Credit Gaps: A Review of National Data Trends from 1993–2000. Washington, D.C.: National Community Reinvestment Coalition.

————. 2001b. *CRA Commitments.* Washington, D.C.: National Community Reinvestment Coalition.

————. 2002. Home Loans to Minorities and Low- and Moderate-Income Borrowers Increase in 1990s, but Then Fall in 2001: A Review of National Data Trends from 1993 to 2001. Washington, D.C.: National Community Reinvestment Coalition.

Norman, Jack. 1993. Lending Pledges Are a Step Back, Group Says. *Milwaukee Journal* (August 17).

O'Brien, Timothy L. 1998. For Banks, a Big Nudge to Do More. *New York Times* (July 5).

Office of Advocacy, U.S. Small Business Administration. 1999. Small Business Lending in the United States, 1998 Edition. Washington, D.C.: U.S. Small Business Administration.

Oppel, Richard A. 2001. U.S. Suit Cites Citigroup Unit on Loan Deceit. *New York Times* (March 7).

Orfield, Myron. 1997. *Metropolitics: A Regional Agenda for Community and Stability.* Washington, D.C. and Cambridge: Brookings Institution Press and the Lincoln Institute of Land Policy.

————. 2002. *American Metropolitics: Social Separation and Sprawl.* Washington D.C.: Brookings Institution.

Pittinger, William L. 1996. Managing the Appraisal Component of Fair Lending Compliance. *ABA Bank Compliance* (March/April): 11–15.

Pogge, Jean. 1991. Reinvestment in Chicago Neighborhoods: A Twenty-Year Struggle. In *From Redlining to Reinvestment: Community Responses to Urban Disinvestment.* Ed. Gregory D. Squires. Philadelphia: Temple University Press.

powell, john. 1998. Race and Space: What Really Drives Metropolitan Growth. *Brookings Review* 16 (4): 20–22.

Ross, Stephen, and John Yinger. 2002. *The Color of Credit: What Is Known about Discrimination in Mortgage Lending.* Cambridge: MIT Press.

Rusk, David. 1999. *Inside Game, Outside Game: Winning Strategies for Saving Urban America.* Washington, D.C.: Brookings Institution Press.

Saltman, Juliet. 1990. *A Fragile Movement: The Struggle for Neighborhood Stabilization.* New York: Greenwood Press.

Schwartz, Alex. 1998a. Bank Lending to Minority and Low-Income Households and Neighborhoods: Do Community Reinvestment Agreements Make a Difference? *Journal of Urban Affairs* 20 (3): 269–301.

————. 1998b. From Confrontation to Collaboration? Banks, Community Groups, and the Implementation of Community Reinvestment Agreements. *Housing Policy Debate* 9 (3): 631–62.

Seiberg, Jaret. 1998. City-Travelers Gets the Nod for Financial Powerhouse. *American Banker* (Sept. 24).

Silver, Josh. 1999. E-mail message to membership of National Community Reinvestment Coalition (Jan. 26).

Squires, Gregory D. 1993. MICAH's Lending Agreements. Memorandum to the Fair Lending Coalition.

————, ed. 1997. *Insurance Redlining: Disinvestment, Reinvestment, and the Evolving Role of Financial Institutions.* Washington, D.C.: Urban Institute Press.

Squires, Gregory D., and Sally O'Connor. 2001. *Color and Money: Politics and Prospects for the Community Reinvestment Movement in Urban America.* Albany: SUNY Press.

Stegman, Michael A. 1999. *Savings for the Poor: The Hidden Benefits of Electronic Banking.* Washington, D.C.: Brookings Institution Press.

Taylor, John. 1999a. Testimony before the Committee on Banking of the U.S. House of Representatives, Washington, D.C. (Feb. 11).

———. 1999b. Letter to William Jefferson Clinton (October 29).

———. 2001. NCRC Statement at National League of Cities Press Conference (January 18).

Toledo Fair Housing Center v. Farmers Insurance Group. 2001. Consent Decree. Case No. CI 99-1339. Lucas County (Ohio) Common Pleas Court.

Trapp, Shel. 1986. *Blessed Be the Fighters.* Chicago: National Training and Information Center.

Turner, Margery Austin, Fred Frieberg, Erin Godfrey, Carla Herbig, Diane K. Levy, and Robin R. Smith. 2002a. *All Other Things Being Equal.* Washington, D.C.: Urban Institute.

Turner, Margery Austin, Stephen L. Ross, George C. Galster, and John Yinger. 2002b. Discrimination in Metropolitan Housing Markets: National Results from Phase I HDS 2000. Washington, D.C.: Urban Institute.

Turner, Margery Austin, and Felicity Skidmore, eds. 1999. *Mortgage Lending Discrimination: A Review of Existing Evidence.* Washington, D.C.: Urban Institute.

U.S. Department of Commerce. 2001. United States Department of Commerce News. Washington, D.C.: U.S. Department of Commerce (March 12), accessed at <http://www.census.gov/Press-Release/www/2001/cb01cn61.html> on March 12, 2001.

U.S. Department of Housing and Urban Development. 2000a. *The State of the Cities 2000: Megaforces Shaping the Future of the Nation's Cities.* Washington, D.C.: U.S. Department of Housing and Urban Development.

———. 2000b. Unequal Burden: Income and Racial Disparities in Subprime Lending in America. Washington, D.C.: U.S. Department of Housing and Urban Development.

U.S. Federal Housing Administration. 1938. *Underwriting Manual.* Washington, D.C.: U.S. Government Printing Office.

Wayne, Leslie. 1998. Panel Clears Overhaul Bill on Banking. *New York Times* (September 12).

Woodstock Institute. 1998. Community Reinvestment in an Era of Megamergers and Financial Modernization. Presentation at the Nonprofit Center of Milwaukee (November 12).

Yinger, John. 1995. *Closed Doors, Opportunities Lost: The Continuing Costs of Housing Discrimination.* New York: Russell Sage Foundation.

Joe Mariano

---

2 ## Where the Hell Did Billions of Dollars for Reinvestment Come From?

*They say we are not nice when we protest and demon-
strate at people's homes and offices. But bad housing isn't
nice, redlining isn't nice, high oil prices aren't nice, crime
on our streets isn't nice.*

—Gale Cincotta, national chairperson of
National People's Action and executive director of
National Training and Information Center

Cincotta's words are the most obvious answer to Larry Lindsey and other
detractors of organizing on financial and other issues. This chapter refutes
him at greater length and documents three financial advocacy victories: the
organizing work of the early 1970s that led to creation of the Community
Reinvestment Act; a campaign to reduce the number of foreclosures and
abandoned buildings that result from the 100 percent guaranteed home loan
program run under the auspices of the Federal Housing Administration (FHA)
and its parent agency, the Department of Housing and Urban Development
(HUD); and passage of city and state laws and regulations against predatory
lending in Illinois.

Financial accountability has been a key goal of community organizing and
training through the National Training and Information Center and National
People's Action. Chicago-based NTIC is a nonprofit resource center that provides community organizing, technical assistance, and research on issues,
especially in the areas of housing and reinvestment, to grassroots neighborhood groups across the country. Its affiliate, NPA, is a national coalition of
some 302 grassroots neighborhood groups based in thirty-eight states. Both
groups were formed in 1972 to promote more responsive and sound housing
and banking policies.

Direct Action

What is a "noisy protest"? Whether it's called a "direct action," a "hit," a "house call," an "office visit," or just an "action," it is sometimes the only way for groups to signal that something is wrong and work to right that wrong. Organizing an action is not a casual undertaking. All successful actions are preceded and followed by hard work, and the group or person to be protested is first invited to meet with protestors to see if goals can be reached without the need for an organized protest. Protest goes against a fundamental instinct. Individuals absorb unwritten rules as they grow up, one of which is the commandment to "be nice." Yet if ordinary people are to make significant changes to our system, they have to break this rule. Ordinary people lack the financial resources and clout of big business and big government. As Cincotta put it, "they have their corporate jets and we have our . . . school buses."

Direct actions are controversial. It was a protest at the home of former Texas GOP senator Phil Gramm, led by Cincotta and Shel Trapp, cofounder of NPA, that sparked Larry Lindsey's comment that "There are two faces of community development: noisy protest and quiet accomplishment" (Lindsey 2000). But if people in power won't meet to discuss the issues, how can one enter into a constructive dialogue with them except by taking what one observer called "the stealth schoolbuses" to their homes or offices? "When we go into a fight we have to have something the enemy wants," Trapp says. "What they want is for us to get out of their lives and the only way to do that is to come to the negotiating table. To me that is the reason we do actions" (Trapp 2001).

Uncritical deference to the "cult of the expert" is an obstacle to widespread public support for direct actions. Financial policies are complex, and many people have been raised to believe that "the experts know best." But one lesson of the 1970s, learned for example by the victims of urban renewal policies, was the extent to which public policy and other experts are both fallible and corruptible. (See, for example, the report of the National Commission on Neighborhoods to the President and Congress of United States, March 19, 1979.) Neighborhood residents are the real experts on what their neighborhoods need, and they have a right to participate in decisions that affect them. Knowledge of what it's like to live next to an abandoned building and a street-level understanding of how it came to be abandoned are often more valuable and relevant to housing policy than a Ph.D. in economics. Practical experience shows that direct action works. "I cannot remember when a bad thing happened out of a hit," Trapp says. "Somebody grows, the enemy says something stupid or reacts in a way that gets people angry and gives a chance to organize even harder, or they cave and give you what you want" (Trapp 2001).

In the words of Calvin Bradford, a social scientist who has worked closely with NPA and NTIC since their inception, financial organizing that grows out of local knowledge succeeds for specific historical reasons:

The organizing process was first designed to build leadership and people's confidence in their knowledge and abilities, regardless of expertise and credentials of the opposition. Nowhere was this process of building confidence and individual faith more important than in organizing around the banking system in the United States. All the experts were telling people, "your neighborhood is obsolete." The economists and the real estate industry said they were following the market and avoiding risks—not redlining. These industry experts would say time and again they did not create decline, but simply avoided declining neighborhoods, whose decline was the result of market forces beyond control. The organizers built on the people's own understanding that there was nothing wrong with them or their neighborhoods. What was most critical was that these organizers forged organizations that involved both the existing white residents and the newly arrived minorities into a single organization. (Bradford and Cincotta 1994)

It is an axiom of community organizing that there are two kinds of power: organized money and organized people. Few situations are more polarized than those between lending institutions, or organized money, and community groups, or organized people. The work of both lenders and organizers is superficially similar in that both have to do with relations between people. The only "products" in both businesses are pieces of paper, whether loan applications or picket signs, both accessories after the fact to the work done in each profession. But their goals are opposite: bankers dream of high returns without high risk, while organizers (and leaders) dream of better service to communities. Another defining feature of organizing is the importance of stories to the process. The three war stories below trace the roots of reinvestment as well as the development of direct action methods, as applied to national issues such as redlining, from the 1970s to the present.

Roots of Reinvestment

This is the story of why many believed the nation needed a law to coerce banks into community reinvestment, even before the word redlining was coined. Slumlords and urban renewal issues were already subjects of intense discussion at the Northwest Community Organization (NCO), one of Chicago's most powerful Alinsky-style groups, with civic associations, churches, and other institutions on the membership rolls in the early 1970s (NTIC 1975). In the fall of 1971, two people came into NCO's office in the space of a week; National Security Bank had turned both down for a loan, one for a business loan, the other for a home mortgage.

A committee from one of NCO's civic associations visited the bank to discuss its lending policies. They were told not to worry, that the bank made loans in the community. "Special circumstances" made it impossible to grant loans in these two cases, they said. Pressed, the officials admitted that the only "special circumstance" was the neighborhood in which the two applicants lived.

The delegation demanded immediate processing of these two loans, establishment of a $4 million mortgage pool for the community, and the right to review any application for a loan that was rejected. Impossible, the bankers said.

A larger group of leaders and staff met to determine the next step. It was first suggested that everyone take their money out of the bank. The assets of the bank were $60 million, and the total deposits of everyone in the room amounted to $29,000. This tactic would be of little value. Picketing a bank has been illegal since the Depression, so NCO leaders decided to hit the bank on a Saturday morning and pass out flyers to customers. Little was accomplished after leafleting on two consecutive Saturdays. A change in tactics was needed.

One woman's gut instinct to up the ante turned out to be the spur for the first reinvestment victory. Trapp, executive director of NCO at the time, recalls what happened:

> The lady who dropped her pennies and saved the action, Josephine Koziol, was a quiet old lady. She was never outstanding as a leader—I can't remember her chairing a single meeting. We had been picketing the bank and gotten nowhere. We had a leadership meeting and Josephine Koziol said, let's have a bank-in. Not wishing to appear stupid in front of the people who were paying my salary, I said well, Josephine, maybe you should explain what a bank-in is. I went out and got a case of beer, so we were knocking back beers and came up with what a bank-in would look like. That was the kickoff for the whole fight.
>
> The third Saturday, we were there two hours with 50 or 60 folks. People were walking up to the window with hundreds of pennies and asking the tellers to count them, or asking for withdrawals in pennies. It was just total chaos, but it wasn't getting the bank president out of his office. I was wondering how the hell to get out with dignity when Josephine said, "Oh, shit," and dropped all her pennies on the floor. That re-energized the troops and the second time she did it, it got the bank president out of his office. We won a meeting with the board of directors of the bank that same afternoon. . . .
>
> Someone from another civic association in NCO said, "We heard about National Security. Could we do something like that at Liberty Savings at North and Milwaukee?" Next someone outside NCO's turf called and said, "Do you guys do these bank-in things?" Then I remember getting a call from some other city and this woman says, "My sister tells me you guys can make banks reinvest." The thing just seemed to be like an avalanche, gathering more snow and power as it started from the top of the hill. For Josephine to end up with that place in history as the catalyst was probably the most unlikely turn of events and person that could be. But that's where $80 billion in reinvestment came from. (Trapp 2001)

The next step came when a leader called a large financial institution for a mortgage and was told over the phone, "that is our FHA area." Leaders were troubled by the discrepancy between mortgages guaranteed by the Federal Housing Administration and mortgages from conventional sources. The FHA was already known in the loan business as a "lender of last resort." Implicit in receiving government insurance on a loan is the idea that conventional private lenders choose not to offer the borrower favorable terms. In the early 1970s, problems with FHA and Veteran's Administration loans were so bad that a book about them was titled *Cities Destroyed for Cash* (Boyer 1973). To be told that a bank does not make conventional loans in a community makes the people there suspect that the bank knows something bad about the community that they don't know. Even today, many people have the idea that bankers are very intelligent people who have all kinds of privileged information, so that when they pass judgment on a community, they must be right.

While Trapp was running NCO, Cincotta was president of another grassroots group, the Organization for a Better Austin (OBA). The two had met when Trapp was an organizer at OBA. Panic peddling and abandoned buildings, two issues intimately related to lack of access to credit, were key issues in her area (Bailey 1972). Cincotta and Trapp had already begun to collaborate on urban renewal and other issues through what became known as the West Side Coalition. Driven by the scandals at FHA, what was becoming known as redlining by conventional lenders, and the relationship between these two sectors of the banking business, the coalition worked to plan and host a national housing conference for grassroots community groups.

In March 1972 the first-ever conference of community groups to discuss housing drew two thousand delegates from thirty-six states and seventy-four cities to Chicago. Delegates passed a series of resolutions and agreed to meet again a month later in Baltimore, where their first-ever protest targeted HUD secretary George Romney. A consensus emerged to create a national network of groups that would come together periodically to discuss the state of the nation's housing and would create a resource center to monitor housing and banking issues. Cincotta and Trapp opened the National Training and Information Center office to address these issues and provide training—for example, on how to do bank-ins—and the national network became National People's Action (NTIC 1997a).

Leaders of these new organizations recognized that they needed evidence to back up their experiences of geographical discrimination in lending and demands for reinvestment. Anecdotal evidence would not suffice; they needed more solid and conclusive proof that banks were refusing to make loans in their communities. Their first rallying cry became loan disclosure, and their target was the directors of the Federal Home Loan Bank in Chicago and the Home Loan Bank Board in Washington, which regulated savings and loans. The S&Ls took many neighborhood residents' deposits and were the first place where many applied for loans. Trapp recalls what happened next:

> They were terrified of us because they viewed us as totally irrational people. After we hit their headquarters they brought in a director of the Federal Home Loan Bank who was supposed to be a tough guy sent to Chicago to straighten out the community groups named Robert Bartell. We had him out to a public meeting and he just was arrogant as hell. So we found out where he lived and I scouted his place out. It was in some hoity-toity suburb and a big hedge ran all the way

around his house. I figured, let's get some red crepe paper, to wrap around those hedges. I went to the dime store and got six or seven rolls. My idea was to wrap it around the bushes.

We get there and I look down the side of the house and there in the back yard is the family, having a barbecue. I'm carrying all those rolls of crepe paper, and I wanted to get there before they got inside. So I threw the paper to someone and said, here, redline the house, the rest of you come with me. We're having a confrontation around the barbecue pit and suddenly out of the corner of my eye I see a red flash and this red crepe paper lands in the back yard. Apparently, it's gone over the top of the house. People thought that looked pretty neat, so they threw it back. This guy decided he wanted to deal with us in the board room, not his back yard. That's where our clout came from. This was just so far outside their experience, they didn't know what we'd do next. (Trapp 2001)

The end result of that action—along with others performed almost every week—was an agreement by board officials to survey S&Ls in Chicago to determine their deposits and loans by Zip code. The survey was voluntary, and board employees cut institutions' names off the survey questionnaire and threw them away, making it impossible to identify those with the best and worst records. Each institution presented data on the number of conventional loans, FHA/VA loans, construction loans, and home improvement loans, and the amounts involved, in addition to the totals for savings accounts as of June 30, 1973. Responses came from 127 Chicago-area S&Ls, and the data was sorted by zip code.

The survey produced clear evidence that disinvestment of the city and redlining in older neighborhoods were occurring. First, while deposits for the time period covered increased overall, the dollar value of both home improvement and new construction loans decreased in Chicago's Rogers Park, Austin, Uptown, Lakeview, Kenwood, and South Shore areas. Even poorer neighborhoods had relatively large deposits in their local institutions, but the banks were lending money out in the suburbs at these communities' expense. To gain a charter, a bank, then as now, had to apply to serve a specific geographic area. At the time, the definition of service became part of the controversy. Today, service area is an integral part of the Community Reinvestment Act (CRA). Community pressure intensified after this survey data became public, leading to a meeting with Illinois governor Dan Walker.

Meanwhile, after the second National People's Action conference, in 1973, the Chicago City Council passed an ordinance requiring banks that held municipal deposits to disclose lending data. The Chicago ordinance became one model for the Home Mortgage Disclosure Act (HMDA). The Commission of Savings and Loan Associations for Illinois amended its rules and regulations in January 1974 to include the first official definition of redlining: "the practice of arbitrarily varying the terms of application procedures or refusing to grant a . . . loan within a specific geographic area on the grounds that the specific parcel of real estate proposed as collateral for the loan is located within said geographical area" (NTIC 1975). This was not only the first anti-redlining regulation in the country; it also specifically referred to geographical discrimination. The regulation served as a model in other states.

The following year Congress passed William Proxmire's Senate Bill 1281, the Home Mortgage Disclosure Act. It wasn't everything community groups had asked for. Data on small business loans, for example, remained secret. So did deposits. Bradford recalls:

> The banking lobby opposed the bill, but did not take the power of the community coalitions pushing for the bill very seriously. The community supporters took the bill very seriously. The Senate had scheduled a single hearing with brief statements by several community groups. But the groups brought with them well-documented stories of redlining and did not intend to leave until they had all told their stories. Proxmire agreed to let them all speak until they were done. When they had ended, the hearings had lasted from May 5 through May 8, 1975. They produced two volumes of evidence. (Bradford and Cincotta 1994)

The Act required commercial banks and savings institutions with federally insured deposits and assets of $10 million or more to disclose mortgage lending in urban areas annually. The legislation did not include all requirements proposed by the community groups, such as disclosure by mortgage companies as opposed to depository institutions, data on race or income of applicants, data on the decision to accept or reject applications, business loan data, or deposit data. But it was a substantial form of disclosure, and a victory for community groups. Senator Proxmire noted later that "this disclosure bill would never have become a law but for the research and local organizing activity undertaken by NPA." Community organizations had maintained that if they had the data, they would create reinvestment on their own, if need be. At the same time, the community movement felt the government had an obligation to outlaw redlining. The push for an anti-redlining law evolved rapidly into the bill that established the Community Reinvestment Act. In this process, the scope of the law moved from a prohibition against redlining to a more inclusive focus on the role and obligation of federally insured depository institutions (commercial bank and thrift institutions) to provide their full range of resources to reinvest in what community groups called "historically underserved communities."

Next steps were considered at a national conference, "From Redlining to Reinvestment," in September 1976. Conference participants explored not only reinvestment by banking institutions but leverage of public funds, pension fund investments, and reinvestment through insurance companies (Bradford and Cincotta 1994). Shortly thereafter, Senator Proxmire introduced Senate Bill 406, the "Community Reinvestment Act of 1977," to the 1st Session of the 95th Congress. The first draft, along with a background statement, was sent out to a range of people in December 1976 for comment. In the background paper Proxmire noted that "the regulators have . . . conferred substantial economic benefits on private institutions without extracting any meaningful quid pro quo for the public" (Bradford and Cincotta 1994). In January 1977 NPA drafted its own version of the act (NPA 1977). Later that year the bill passed, with the legislation mandating two years before the act became effective in 1979.

The CRA passed without a clear statement of the reinvestment obligations and standards for which community groups had lobbied. The wording of the Act was short and in many respects vague. It stated that "regulated financial institutions have a continuing and affirmative obligation to help meet the credit needs of the local communities in which they are chartered" (U.S. Congress 1977). Regulators were simply required in their examination capacity to "encourage" lending institutions to serve the needs of their local communities. When reviewing applications for charters, acquisitions, mergers, relocations, and branches, the regulatory agencies were required to "assess the institution's record of meeting the credit needs of its entire community, including low- and moderate-income neighborhoods," and to "take such record into account in its evaluation of an application" (U.S. Congress 1977).

Many groups that had been active in the national reinvestment campaign were already developing challenges to lending institutions using the CRA. The Northwest Bronx Community and Clergy Coalition was developing several challenges in New York City. In Cleveland, the Buckeye-Woodland Community Congress was preparing a massive campaign against Ameritrust Bank, and the Union Miles Community Coalition was preparing its campaign against Security National Bank.

Meanwhile, organizers focused on the federal regulatory agencies that would draft the regulations. In January 1978, the regulatory agencies that would be required to enforce the Community Reinvestment Act (the Comptroller of the Currency for national banks, the Federal Reserve Board for bank holding companies and state banks that belonged to the Federal Reserve System, the Federal Deposit Insurance Corporation for state-chartered banks that were not members of the Federal Reserve System, and the Federal Home Loan Bank Board for savings institutions) announced they would hold hearings to "receive suggestions from the public on how to implement the new law" (Bradford and Cincotta 1994).

The CRA makes no mention of community groups, yet they were soon forced to assume the role of de facto enforcer and regulator for the Act. Initially there was hope that the regulators would actually assume the enforcement obligations given them under the law, and at first there were some bright signs. In April 1979 the FDIC rejected an application by the $1.5 billion Greater New York Savings Bank that was being protested by the Brooklyn-based group Against Investment Discrimination. This was most encouraging because the lender had already signed an agreement with Bank of Brooklyn the previous year, but it was cited by the FDIC for falling short of its goals (Bradford and Cincotta 1994).

This kind of denial was rare, however. Applications in Toledo and St. Louis were approved in spite of community challenges. Challenges filed in Cleveland by the Buckeye-Woodland Community Congress against a merger application and applications for additional branches of Ameritrust dragged on for more than two years. Then, in 1980, the Federal Reserve Board granted all the applications. In the decision, the Fed admitted that Ameritrust had violated the Equal Credit Opportunity Act but refused to penalize the lender. The Fed even granted Ameritrust membership in the Federal Reserve System, allowing it the privileges of borrowing from the Federal Reserve at favored rates (Bradford and Cincotta 1994).

An interesting consequence of the CRA fight came at a conference on insurance redlining. A few years after CRA passed, NPA held a conference on redlining by sellers of home insurance. One audience member stood up and told the insurance executives in the room that he hoped they would listen to NPA. He hoped that they would respond immediately and that they would develop the products and services necessary to serve all communities. If they did not, he predicted, they would suffer a long period of confrontation that the communities would win anyway. He expressed regret that he himself had a chance to do just this but had failed to respond to it, much to his regret, and said he hoped that his experience would be a lesson to others. That man was Robert Bartell, the "arrogant" bank board representative who was the target of the first actions to win disclosure.

From the early 1970s on, NTIC and NPA worked consistently to hold both urban and rural lending institutions accountable to communities and to promote policies that would strengthen community reinvestment. In Cincotta's words, "We never asked for a handout or a government program and the CRA is neither. It doesn't cost taxpayers a cent. All it's supposed to do is to make sure the market works for neighborhoods, the same way it works for the wealthy parts of town and the suburbs."

Reforming the Federal Housing Administration's Guaranteed Loan Program

Disinvestment itself is not an issue that comes to people's minds when organizers knock on their doors. Rather, they point out its effects, of which the most harmful may be abandoned buildings. This problem has been exacerbated for years by interaction between lenders and the Federal Housing Administration (FHA), part of HUD. Formed in 1935 by President Roosevelt to stimulate the economy by increasing home construction, the FHA evolved into a program to promote homeownership among less affluent Americans when Congress extended its reach to urban communities after the wave of riots in 1968. One of its key functions is to guarantee mortgages on single-family homes for people who might not qualify under private banking guidelines. Mismanagement and fraud plagued the agency in the 1970s, creating a legacy it has never managed to shake, as shown by a reform campaign that began in 1997 (Boyer 1973).

The FHA paid lenders for more than seventy thousand failed mortgages in 1997, according to HUD's own numbers (NTIC 1997b). The more than forty thousand properties in HUD's nationwide inventory at any given time have to be maintained: grass mowed, abandoned buildings boarded up and protected from vandals. In some neighborhoods of Buffalo, Chicago, Indianapolis, and other cities, it is difficult to find a block without one or more abandoned HUD buildings, recognizable by the broken windows, ripped-out plumbing, overgrown grass and weeds. Community leaders and staff collect news items and neighborhood stories about the rapes, molestations, murders, and drug activity in and around these buildings. Residents report trouble getting or maintaining homeowner's insurance because of abandoned buildings next door, and report that fires in adjacent FHA buildings sometimes spread to their own properties (WJLA News 1998).

New homebuyers' stories of FHA-related scams are also common. For example, investors may buy a damaged property cheaply at auction, perform cosmetic rehab, such as adding siding and new paint to hide major system and structural defects, and then sell the property as a "gut rehab" (Pitt 1998; Harney 1999). One homeowner in Joliet, Illinois, found a hole in the exterior wall filled with old socks after her toddler tore away some wallpaper. Buyers are often told they don't need an inspection because their FHA loan is guaranteed. Sometimes repairs are promised but never done. Homes are sold to buyers who believe, as one person put it, "when they told me the mortgage was guaranteed by the government, I thought that meant I couldn't lose. I didn't understand that the FHA was backing the lender, not me!"

In 1997 community groups decided to demand that the FHA and its parent agency, HUD, get the system under control. They demanded, first, that the agency prevent these abuses by beefing up prepurchase inspection and appraisal requirements. Improving maintenance and marketing of foreclosed properties was probably the most important demand, since this would contribute to eliminating abandoned buildings. Finally, community groups sought more flexible policies that would allow nonprofit community development agencies to buy foreclosed properties at below-market prices and convert them into affordable housing.

Andrew Cuomo, then HUD secretary, had the authority to implement policies to end or at least reduce FHA abuses. In April 1997 NPA invited Cuomo to its twenty-sixth annual neighborhoods conference in Washington, D.C., so that he could hear groups' complaints firsthand. Previous HUD secretaries had accepted such invitations, but Cuomo declined this as well as several subsequent meeting requests. That fall, NPA groups presented data from an NTIC study, *The Devil's in the Details: An Analysis of FHA Default Concentration and Lender Performance in Twenty U.S. Cities*, to the media and congressional staffers. The report used numbers HUD had been collecting since 1991 but never used to analyze loan delinquencies and foreclosures in urban census tracts. Prior to *Devil's in the Details*, available data covered default rates on FHA loans at the regional level, areas that might be as large as half an entire state. As a result, the study found, the agency's successful lending to more affluent homebuyers in the suburbs masked loan failure rates as high as 40 percent in some lower-income, "inner-city" census tracts.

The news coverage of the study and the community leaders' demands sent a warning that all was not well at FHA. Many community groups used this data, provided free by NTIC to interested groups, in studies showing their cities' problems. The release of the study kicked off more than a year of organizing, media outreach, and advocacy. For example, in February 1998 more than fifteen groups across the country celebrated Groundhog Day by picketing HUD offices. "Even the Groundhog comes out once a year, why won't Cuomo come out and meet with us?" they asked. Meanwhile, congressional Republicans, who had their own political motives, were delighted to pound the politically ambitious Cuomo. New York representative Rick Lazio, chair of the House Banking Committee that oversees the FHA, willingly held hearings on community groups' complaints and threatened legislation to force HUD to clean up its act.

The conflict between NPA and HUD intensified. Another neighborhoods conference rolled around in 1999. As she was leaving the office to fly to Washington, D.C., for the event, Gale Cincotta received a call from Cuomo. He would meet to hear community leaders' concerns—but only if she would agree to endorse unrelated policy changes he wanted to make at FHA. And he would not guarantee action on FHA reforms.

This was too little, too late. A dozen yellow school buses brought five hundred leaders from around the country to Cuomo's McLean, Virginia, mansion a couple of days later. They carried pictures of abandoned buildings and maps showing bad FHA loans concentrated in their neighborhoods. Cuomo was at home. The leadership team demanded that he reform the FHA program, bar crooks from using the program to rip off homebuyers, and take better care of FHA properties. Cuomo refused. The next day NPA's yellow school buses rolled up to the HUD building, where a thousand people filled the plaza and put Andrew Cuomo on trial before a "people's court." As victims of bad FHA loans told their stories to the public and press, the unanimous verdict was that with regard to foreclosures and abandonment, "Cuomo Ain't Done Shit." To personify his crime, people unloaded a large porcelain toilet bowl from one of the buses and left a life-sized Andrew Cuomo dummy propped up the seat.

Embarrassment and political pressure through high-profile actions were only part of the story. Dozens of smaller actions, countless neighborhood hearings, and much behind-the-scenes work took place over the next two years. In response to continuous pressure, several HUD officials actually came out and listened to neighborhood residents. Eventually, in part as a result of

NPA efforts, a new, more sympathetic FHA commissioner was appointed in the person of Bill Apgar, the former head of Harvard University's Joint Center on Housing Studies.

From 1998 through 2000, the single-family guaranteed loan program received intermittent coverage on national network television and in newspapers across the country, and drew increased attention from HUD's Office of Inspector General and Congress's General Accounting Office. Both agencies found serious flaws in the way HUD regulates the lenders that participate in the program. Apgar worked with NPA leaders to create the next-best thing to mandatory inspections, an eighty-part report that must now be filled out as part of the FHA guaranteed loan process and highlights potential problems with homes before they are sold. The agency created a program called Credit Watch to examine foreclosures by lenders and sanction those with high rates of loan failure. By privatizing the process of managing and marketing foreclosed homes for resale, and by setting aside more properties for rehab into affordable housing, HUD improved the process and at the same time created new targets for reform throughout the country. At the twenty-ninth NPA conference in 2000—which Apgar attended—neighborhood leaders gave him a pair of boxing gloves while the theme from *Rocky* played, to thank him for battling it out with the mortgage lenders and other real estate interests who had opposed the reforms.

Predatory Lending

The approach taken by NTIC and NPA in their work on predatory lending has been similar to the methods used to pass the original CRA: a bubble-up campaign to promote more city and state ordinances like those passed in Chicago and Illinois, with the ultimate goal of national legislation passed by Congress. Predatory lending, as defined in the previous chapter, is one of the most unscrupulous financial practices communities face today. These high-cost loans, which are generally targeted at low- and moderate-income neighborhoods, can be just as damaging to communities as lack of credit for home purchases. Many people consider predatory lending reverse redlining, as access to quality credit that won't bankrupt the borrower becomes ever scarcer.

Predatory lending targets less affluent homeowners, carries high interest rates, and comes packed with fees. Mortgage lenders who specialize in this business usually try to justify their exorbitant interest rates and fees on the grounds of borrowers' poor credit ratings. Subprime lending rates can range up to 25 percent for a home equity loan, compared to rates that hover near the prime rate (currently around 7 percent) for more affluent borrowers. A common duplicitous technique is to persuade a borrower to finance relatively useless "single premium credit insurance" when the loan is taken out, or to refinance the loan several times, paying new fees each time. These practices suck the equity out of a homeowner's property (NTIC 1999).

Thanks to their fight with the FHA, NTIC staff and community leaders have become experts on foreclosure-related issues. Given recent reforms at the FHA, they expected to see foreclosures begin to decline, but instead they have seen the opposite (Rumbler and Rodriguez 1999a). Using data provided by a company that specializes in reporting on foreclosures in Chicago and the surrounding area, NTIC performed an analysis that suggested that the dramatic increases in foreclosures was the result of predatory lending. Organizers turned to Neighborhood Housing Services of Chicago (NHS), a citywide community development corporation and counseling provider. NHS staff confirmed an increase in defaults on loans by subprime lenders. Scores of homeowners had been coming to NHS looking for a way to escape predatory loans. Many had been enticed by the lure of quick and easy approval and unrestricted cash to be used for home repairs, repaying unsecured debt, or even taking a vacation. Predatory lenders were actually pushing many of these homeowners out of low-interest loans they had gotten from NHS and into high-interest predatory loans.

NTIC's initial response was to contact individuals in foreclosure, according to court records, and invite them to a meeting; forty homeowners attended. Key leaders emerged from this small group and were supplemented by others who attended subsequent meetings. The newly formed Chicago Loan Shark Taskforce decided to meet officials from the state agency charged with policing the mortgage lenders and brokers, the Office of Banks and Real Estate (OBRE). In the spring of 1999, the victimized homeowners brought family, friends, fellow parishioners, and neighbors to the meeting. The suburban bureaucrat from OBRE pointed out that many of the predatory practices homeowners described were legal. In response to a request that his agency investigate the top five predatory lenders identified by the group, he asked those in attendance to fill out official complaint forms, which would establish a pattern of illegal practices, before OBRE could investigate.

The taskforce turned to state legislators over the following spring and summer. State representative Dan Burke of the city's South Side listened to personal stories, appeared amazed at the number of foreclosures in his own district, told a story about arson, crime, and gang-banging at an abandoned building on his own block, and promised to attend a citywide meeting on the issue. Dozens of homeowners offered testimony at that meeting, and Burke, chair of the legislature's executive committee, held hearings in Chicago. None of the lenders or trade association lobbyists who attended the first hearing chose to speak.

Meanwhile, NTIC published *Preying on Neighborhoods: Subprime Mortgage Lenders and Chicagoland Foreclosures* in September 1999. The study documented a dramatic rise in foreclosures completed by subprime lenders between 1993 and 1998. The thirty foreclosures by subprime lenders in 1993 accounted for less than 2 percent of all foreclosures that year, compared to 1,417 foreclosures, or nearly 36 percent of all foreclosures in the Chicago metro area, in 1998. As part of the study, NTIC surveyed a thirty-six-block area in the Chicago Lawn neighborhood. On average, two properties per block were in foreclosure in 1998. A third of the buildings in foreclosure that were secured by loans originating after 1990 were abandoned. Nearly two-thirds of these abandoned properties had loans from subprime lenders. The study also profiled the loans of several subprime borrowers.

A week after releasing the study, NTIC held a national conference on predatory lending attended by 116 people from fifty-one organizations in nine states. Neighborhood leaders, community developers, advocates, and other stakeholders in financial issues from the city of Chicago participated. Nearly two years of organizing followed, in which neighborhood leaders, NTIC staff, and many others held actions and worked to create legislation at both the city and state levels to rein in predatory lending. The first action took place at a small firm in downtown Chicago, where a "loan shark," complete with costume, attempted to hug the loan officers.

The following winter saw the beginning of a legislative battle that brought together unlikely partners and lasted for more than a year, resulting in the passage of at least three laws restricting predatory lending in the state of Illinois. One bill went down to defeat in the spring of 2000 due to lobbying by the Illinois Bankers Association, a potent force in the state capital. But other legislation authorized the state's executive branch to rewrite regulations governing high-interest lending.

Since Illinois's Legislature adjourns in late spring, organizers spent the summer of 2000 working to move a predatory lending ordinance through Chicago's city council. Under the provisions of the ordinance, institutions wishing to hold municipal deposits would be required to pledge not to engage in predatory practices and to disclose interest rate data to prove they were in compliance. Actions against the Illinois Bankers Association (IBA) and several banks that opposed the regulations, such as BankAmerica, were integral to the campaign. When the ordinance failed to pass in midsummer, grassroots leaders took their school buses down the street to confront the IBA directly. The action isolated the IBA and put bankers and members of Mayor Richard Daley's administration on notice that they could be targeted with protests as well. The major banks naturally wanted to weaken the proposed ordinance; Citigroup officials in particular had lobbied heavily to cut prohibitions against credit insurance. While banks ultimately won this point, a weakened ordinance, the first of its kind, passed late in August. A week later Citigroup announced that it would buy The Associates, another company notorious for predatory lending and one that relied heavily on credit insurance for its outstanding profit. NTIC shifted its focus that fall to include not only legislative but also regulatory changes to Illinois's lending system. The state finally approved those regulations in April 2001. These victories came in part as a result of a broad-based, ad hoc coalition of many organizations that by the end included even the city government. The national fight against predatory lending continues, and can build on these victories and the connections forged between various groups.

Conclusion

Gale Cincotta passed away on August 15, 2001. She left a legacy that has inspired others to continue her pathbreaking work. A *Chicago Tribune* editorial published upon her death read in part:

> Community organizers are constantly at risk of two occupational hazards. They may become so entranced by their own screaming and theatrics that they won't quit even when such tactics become counterproductive. Or they get co-opted by the politicians or the corporate "suits" and cease to be effective. Gale Cincotta ... never succumbed to either temptation, and that is what made her one of the most effective community activists in the nation. . . . That effective combination of tenacity, style and realistic approach made Cincotta and her National Training and Information Center here a Mecca for community organizers nationwide. (*Chicago Tribune* 2001)

Sympathetic observers regard Cincotta's action against Phil Gramm, mentioned at the beginning of this chapter, as a climactic moment in NPA organizing history. But the Gramm hit was only a high-profile action, and for every such action there are many others, just as important in their own right, that never make the evening news. Together these efforts have brought, and will continue to bring, positive change to low-income urban neighborhoods.

In 1977 Congress passed the Community Reinvestment Act because people protested after they were told they could not get loans because of where they lived. In 1999 the Federal Housing Administration started cutting off lenders whose loans were contributing dramatically to abandoned buildings in lower-income neighborhoods. In 2001 Illinois state government regulated predatory lending by restricting the kinds of rates and fees home equity lenders could charge borrowers. Not quiet negotiation but noisy protests engineered these victories. The question for the future is, when do we board the buses?

Acknowledgments

Gordon Mayer, a former NTIC staff member, contributed to this chapter. Assistance was also provided by current staff members Jason Kiely, George Goehl, and Tracy Van Slyke.

References

Bailey, Robert Jr. 1972. *Radicals in Urban Politics: The Alinsky Approach.* Chicago: University of Chicago Press.
Boyer, Bryan. 1973. *Cities Destroyed for Cash.* New York: Follett Publishing.
Bradford, Calvin, and Gale Cincotta. 1994. *No One Will Save Us But Us.* Unpublished manuscript.

Chicago Tribune. 2001. Aug. 17.

Harney, Ken. 1999. FHA About to Hit Lenders Who Have Lax Practices. *Washington Post* (May 14).

Lindsay, Lawrence B. 2000. Community Development at a Crossroads. *Neighborworks Journal* (winter): 54–55.

National Commission on Neighborhoods. 1979. *Report to the President and Congress of the National Commission on Neighborhoods.* Washington, D.C.: U.S. Government Printing Office.

National People's Action (NPA). 1977. *The Community Reinvestment Act of 1977: Amended version proposed by National People's Action.* Chicago: NPA.

———. 1984. *Reclaim America* (video). Chicago: NPA.

National Training and Information Center (NTIC). 1975. *The Grassroots Battle against Redlining: From the Streets to the Halls of Congress* Chicago: NTIC.

———. 1997a. *Twenty-five Year Report.* Chicago: NTIC.

———. 1997b. *The Devil's in the Details: An Analysis of FHA Default Concentration and Lender Performance in Twenty U.S. Cities.* Chicago: NTIC.

———. 1999. Preying on Neighborhoods: Subprime Mortgage Lending and Chicagoland Foreclosures. Chicago: NTIC.

Pitt, Leon. 1998. FHA Blocks Foreclosures on One Hundred Rehabbed Homes. *Chicago Sun-Times* (Sept. 11).

Rumbler, Bill, and Alex Rodriguez. 1999a. Mortgage Foreclosures Here Go through the Roof. *Chicago Sun-Times* (March 28).

———. 1999b. High-interest Loans Soar, and So Do the Complaints. *Chicago Sun-Times* (April 4).

———. 1999c. Foreclosures Scar Roseland. *Chicago Sun-Times* (April 5).

Trapp, Shel. 2001. Interview by Gordon Mayer (June).

U.S. Congress. 1977. Community Reinvestment Act.

WJLA News. 1998. Ten O'Clock News (April 11). Washington, D.C.: WJLA (ABC affiliate).

William R. Tisdale and
Carla J. Wertheim

3   Giving Back to the Future:
     Citizen Involvement and Community
     Stabilization in Milwaukee

Building a Foundation for Citizen Involvement

Citizen activity in community issues may seem, to some, a remnant of a bygone era replaced now by power brokering, influence peddling, and so on. Yet, as the actions of a civil rights organization in Milwaukee demonstrate, citizen participation continues to be a powerful means for effecting community change.

This chapter describes an innovative approach by a fair housing organization to engaging citizens in identifying and dismantling obstacles to community development and stabilization in the metropolitan Milwaukee area. The Metropolitan Milwaukee Fair Housing Council (MMFHC) is a private nonprofit organization, established in 1977 by a group of citizens to eliminate illegal forms of discrimination in the sale, rental, financing, and insuring of housing. Founded on the idea of citizen empowerment, MMFHC uses community volunteers in all aspects of its program, including its board of directors, advisory committees, and the investigation of illegal forms of housing discrimination. An outgrowth of a highly successful community-based organization in Milwaukee, MMFHC's very beginnings are rooted in citizen involvement. In the spring of 1977, the U.S. Department of Housing and Urban Development (HUD) commissioned a national study to determine the level and extent of illegal discrimination against African American home seekers in housing markets across the country. HUD's Housing Market Practices Survey (HMPS) included metropolitan Milwaukee as one of the forty areas selected for study. The Sherman Park Community Association (SPCA), a neighborhood group located in a racially integrated part of the city of Milwaukee, was asked to participate as the local coordinating agency. The SPCA was actively organizing residents around issues of racially integrated neighborhoods at that time and was therefore a logical choice for this role.

HUD conducted this study using the method of "testing." Testing is a controlled method of measuring and documenting variations in the quality, content, and quantity of information and services provided to home seekers by housing providers. A test is actually a simulation of any housing transaction for the purpose of comparing the responses given by housing providers to renters or buyers of real estate, insurance, appraisal, and/or financing to determine whether differential treatment may be occurring.

The test results demonstrated extremely high levels of racial discrimination in the Milwaukee area. African American home seekers were treated differently from whites in 43 percent of the tests in the rental market and in 63 percent of the tests in the sales market. The volunteer testers were immensely concerned about the levels of discrimination revealed in this study and sought ways to address the concurrent problems of housing segregation and discrimination in the Milwaukee area. The executive director of SPCA, who had served as the local project coordinator, resigned his position in order to establish a private organization that would combat the discriminatory practices and entrenched patterns of residential segregation that plagued Milwaukee's housing market. In October 1977 forty citizens incorporated the MMFHC as an organization whose mission was to promote fair housing throughout the Milwaukee metropolitan area by guaranteeing all people equal access to housing opportunities and by creating and maintaining racially and economically integrated housing patterns.

MMFHC was structured so that citizen involvement was the very foundation of the organization. Organizers ensured citizen participation by establishing MMFHC as a membership-based organization electing its board of directors from that membership. The committee structure was designed to facilitate two-way communication between the organization and the community at large.

Since its inception, MMFHC has maintained its original organizational structure and continues to depend heavily on community participation. In addition to decision-making roles, volunteers from the community continue to actively address issues of discrimination through their participation as fair housing testers. Volunteer testers serve as the backbone of fair housing enforcement in the Milwaukee area by investigating practices within the rental, sales, financing, and insuring of housing.

Volunteers are carefully trained to conduct testing according to MMFHC's highly systematized program and may serve as witnesses in court proceedings, administrative actions, or other venues that may remedy claims of unlawful discrimination. While testing is a method commonly employed by private fair housing organizations to investigate allegations of housing discrimination, MMFHC remains the only private enforcement organization that regularly uses unpaid volunteer testers to ensure a high level of community involvement. Rather than opting for stipends or payments, MMFHC has continued to use volunteers in order to maintain citizen participation in remedying community problems.

The founders of MMFHC recognized that issues of housing segregation, discrimination, and community development receive inadequate attention from both policymakers and the general public. Yet these issues have a far-reaching impact on all segments of a metropolitan area, even outside those racially and economically impacted neighborhoods of the inner city. MMFHC's strategy of community involvement therefore focused on reaching residents throughout the four-county metropolitan area, extending even into predominantly white, affluent communities.

This strategy had a twofold effect. On the micro level it empowered residents to take charge of issues that affected them directly. Rather than passively waiting for "someone" to ameliorate patterns of discrimination, citizens were able to actively develop and participate in activities that would bring about community change. Even people who initially did not feel directly affected by housing discrimination came to see that they were in fact affected as members of the community, and were spurred to take action and thus took responsibility for resolving the issues.

On the macro level, citizen participation became a force for social change. Through its base of community support, MMFHC was able to achieve a number of political and social changes. These included the strengthening of the state fair housing law, elimination of systemic practices of racial discrimination in local rent-assistance programs, expansion of housing opportunities for low-income and minority persons in previously all-white suburban communities, and the realization of some community and economic development initiatives. One reason for the success of these efforts was the inclusion of community residents in formulating these local housing strategies. MMFHC organized citizen participation through its board of directors and committees, networks with community-based organizations, and religious congregations. MMFHC's diversified decision-making structure allowed people with the most knowledge and investment in the issue to play leadership roles.

Citizen Involvement in Insurance
Redlining Issues

Equal access to homeowners insurance had been a concern in the greater Milwaukee area since the mid-1960s, when insurance companies began to withdraw services from the inner city. It was believed that the action by insurers was in response to widespread racial disturbances in many cities throughout the country (Squires and Velez 1988). Inner-city residents reported being denied homeowners insurance coverage as well as receiving substandard coverage at higher rates. In addition to restricting coverage, many companies and agents began moving their offices out of inner-city neighborhoods with sizeable minority populations to white neighborhoods on the city's periphery, or to suburban locations. Unequal access to insurance services continued for the next twenty years. Allegations of redlining in Milwaukee's inner city escalated to the point that in 1983 the Community Housing Resources Board (CHRB) initiated a study that concluded that "insurance redlining is evident in Milwaukee County" (Hoeh 1983).

Several academic studies also documented the relationship between race and insurance activity in Milwaukee. A study by Squires and Velez concluded that agents were more eager to sell homeowners insurance to residents in white neighborhoods but placed more obstacles in the path of homeowners who lived in racially integrated or predominantly nonwhite neighborhoods. Squires and Velez also found that after controlling for variables such as age of the housing stock, income, poverty level, and residential turnover, market activity still decreased as minority concentration increased within neighborhoods in the city of Milwaukee. Three years later Squires, Velez, and Taeuber did another study that showed that homeowners insurance was difficult or impossible to obtain in many inner-city neighborhoods of Milwaukee and that companies had systematically pulled their agents from those areas (Squires, Velez, and Taeuber 1991).

The reality of insurance redlining was also evidenced by other events. In 1988 six former insurance agents from American Family Insurance Company who worked in metropolitan Milwaukee filed a civil lawsuit in federal court alleging that firm officials instructed them not to sell policies to African Americans or people who did not speak English. Information obtained through the litigation process revealed that in 1988 a sales manager at American Family told agents, "I think you write too many blacks. . . . You gotta sell good, solid premium paying white people . . . they own their own homes, the white works" (*Milwaukee Journal* 1988b).

The local branch of the National Association for the Advancement of Colored People (NAACP) also became acutely aware of the problem in 1987, when their leaders were approached by three black insurance agents. The NAACP held a town meeting a few months later at which African American homeowners testified about the difficulties they faced in obtaining affordable comprehensive auto and homeowners insurance. As one resident said at the meeting, "insurance is so damned bad in this area that people who have it are afraid to file claims, so what good is it?" (*Milwaukee Journal* 1988a). In 1990 the NAACP, the American Civil Liberties Union (ACLU), and eight African American homeowners filed a lawsuit in federal court, alleging that American Family had violated federal and state fair housing law by discouraging the sale of homeowners insurance to blacks in seven zip codes with predominantly black populations (*Milwaukee Journal* 1990).

Other forms of empirical data showed racial differences in the availability of homeowners insurance in Milwaukee. In May 1994 the National Fair

Housing Alliance (NFHA) released the results of a ten-city study of insurance practices. Testing conducted in Milwaukee by MMFHC indicated that African Americans encountered discriminatory treatment in more than 60 percent of the tests (Tisdale and Wertheim 1994). On the basis of this evidence a complaint was filed with HUD in May 1994 alleging that Allstate, State Farm, and Nationwide Insurance Companies engaged in discriminatory insurance practices.

In 1996 State Farm settled the complaint with HUD, agreeing to modify its underwriting guidelines to eliminate restrictions on the maximum age and value of housing, stop using credit reports as the sole reason for declining applications, and establish new sales and service centers in several cities. State Farm later engaged the services of NFHA to conduct education and testing activities. The HUD complaint against Allstate was settled in 1997 for terms similar to those of State Farm. State Farm also agreed to undertake additional marketing initiatives and to provide $1 million to support community investments in Toledo and pay $100,000 in reimbursement to NFHA and the Toledo Fair Housing Center.

In 1997 a settlement was reached with Nationwide Insurance that modified its underwriting policies (including age and value of housing requirements), established sales and service centers in fifteen cities, provided training of employees, and contributed $13.2 million in reinvestment funds.

Because of continuing redlining practices by property insurers and the resulting effects of disinvestment within urban communities, MMFHC developed a plan to address this issue. In 1994 MMFHC submitted a proposal to HUD and was granted funds to implement a two-year investigation of insurance redlining practices in Milwaukee. The proposed activities were conducted in partnership with NFHA and three private fair housing organizations—Housing Opportunities Made Equal (H.O.M.E.) of Cincinnati, Ohio, Housing Opportunities Made Equal (H.O.M.E.) of Richmond, Virginia, and the Toledo Fair Housing Center. Using the method of testing, this investigation was structured to determine whether residents of minority and racially integrated neighborhoods had the same access to homeowners insurance as did residents of white neighborhoods. Through this methodology, company practices and policies regarding the availability of homeowners insurance products could also be detected. Additionally, MMFHC and its partners were prepared to take appropriate enforcement action if warranted by the investigation results.

In 1995 MMFHC once again turned to the community for assistance in identifying and eliminating illegal housing discrimination. By this time there was a heightened community awareness of redlining practices, due to the settlement agreement of the NAACP lawsuit against American Family Insurance. Local media coverage of the $14.5 million settlement and discussion of the illegal practices that led to the filing of the complaint was extensive, and many homeowners were evaluating their current policies. Growing recognition of illegal practices helped MMFHC approach volunteers and local supporters for assistance as testers, for the use of residents' homes for testing purposes, and for participation in an interview survey of homeowners, which would compile data about the practices of various insurance companies in the Milwaukee area.

MMFHC recruited thirty-three new testers for participation in a specialized training program on homeowners insurance testing. Posing as homeowners seeking insurance for their homes, these volunteer testers called local insurance agents to obtain information regarding the procurement of homeowners insurance.

In order to form a basis of comparing treatment provided to homeowners in predominantly white versus nonwhite neighborhoods, insurance testing requires the use of similar homes located in neighborhoods of differing racial composition. These "test homes" need to be matched on features considered by companies/agents when ascertaining coverage and the price of insurance products. These features include the structure, size, and age of the housing. MMFHC used residents in both white and nonwhite neighborhoods to develop a pool of matched homes. Working with its membership and networks within the community, MMFHC secured the agreement of homeowners to have their properties used as test homes, even though they themselves were not testers on this project.

Although this kind of testing was ruled to be a legal and viable means of investigating practices of housing discrimination (*United States v. Wisconsin*, 1975), the courage and commitment of these individuals must be emphasized. They knew that they might be exposing themselves to protracted litigation against large insurance companies, criticism from other local residents, scrutiny by the media, and possible retaliation by their own insurance company for their involvement—yet they volunteered willingly. MMFHC also relied on community participation in conducting interviews of homeowners in the city. Networking with community-based organizations and neighborhood associations, MMFHC identified forty-five homeowners in both African American and white neighborhoods to participate in a survey to collect data on the procurement of insurance. These interviews provided anecdotal examples of the process and experience of homeowners and current and former policyholders regarding their homeowners insurance.

At the conclusion of the two-year investigation, the MMFHC board filed administrative complaints with HUD against Liberty Mutual, Aetna, Travelers, and Prudential Insurance Companies. MMFHC announced the filing of these administrative complaints in September 1997, in simultaneous press conferences with three other fair housing organizations that participated in the investigation. Unable to resolve these complaints through HUD, MMFHC subsequently filed and settled lawsuits against Liberty Mutual and Travelers Insurance (which had purchased Aetna). The lawsuit against Prudential Insurance Company is still pending at the time of this writing.

Community Approach to Resolution

MMFHC had long recognized the need for a coordinated and collaborative approach to institutional impediments to stable, racially and economically integrated neighborhoods. The long-term impact of disinvestment, mortgage lending, and homeowners insurance redlining were major contributing factors to the demise of Milwaukee's inner-city neighborhoods. In efforts to combat these obstacles, the organization decided to establish a program to provide direct funding to existing advocacy and community-based organizations (CBOs) that provide services to residents of the city of Milwaukee.

Using funds provided through the settlement of the lawsuit against Liberty Mutual, MMFHC established its Housing Opportunities Made Equal Program (H.O.M.E.) in the spring of 1999. MMFHC's H.O.M.E. is the first and to date the only grant-making entity operated by a private fair housing organization. It was established to provide direct monetary support to community-based programs and organizations that help maintain, stabilize, and improve the quality of life in Milwaukee neighborhoods.

In order to ensure efficient allocation of limited resources, H.O.M.E.'s strategic plan included a comprehensive community needs assessment designed to answer three questions: 1) what types of programs and services are offered by CBOs and advocacy agencies to Milwaukee-area residents; 2) what programs and services are desired by Milwaukee-area residents served by CBOs and advocacy agencies; and 3) what steps are necessary to ensure maximum collaboration between housing service providers operating programs in the same or contiguous geographic areas?

MMFHC visited twenty-two CBOs and advocacy agencies to assess gaps in housing service delivery. These contacts served not only to acquaint MMFHC staff with the community's executive directors and program coordinators, but also to provide these service providers with a detailed description of services offered by MMFHC. In order to develop the most comprehensive accounting of Milwaukee-area housing services providers possible, the lists of Milwaukee County and City of Milwaukee Community Development Block Grant (CDBG) recipients, as well as United Way of Greater Milwaukee annual recipients, was compiled on thirty additional agencies for future collaboration.

These assessments focused on both the services available to client populations and the management and staffing capacity of Milwaukee-area organizations to provide services that promote homeownership and stabilize neighborhoods. The organizations were also evaluated as to effectiveness of service delivery and verification of outcomes (that is, client perceptions of the level and value of services actually provided). Not surprisingly, initial assessments showed recurring gaps in community housing services and identified the need for 1) assistance to homeowners on fixed incomes, who could not qualify for participation in government home-repair programs due to delinquent taxes; 2) more collaboration between housing services agencies operating programs in the same geographic areas; 3) better home-buying counseling services—specifically post-purchase counseling and home-maintenance training and repair programs; and 4) a coordinated home-buying counseling referral system. In response to housing service gaps identified, H.O.M.E. staff encouraged collaboration and partnerships between CBOs to strengthen the level of services provided to housing consumers, especially those organizations and agencies offering similar assistance to contiguous service areas.

H.O.M.E. funds are not available to individuals, for-profit corporations, or government agencies designated solely for private nonprofit organizations serving residents of the city of Milwaukee. This geographic designation was important, as MMFHC wanted these resources to be used for remedial compensation—that is, for investment in neighborhoods that had suffered most from neglect and disinvestment. H.O.M.E. grants are awarded to local nonprofit organizations through a competitive grant application process.

H.O.M.E. serves as an alternative funding source for CBO program activities that are not eligible for funding from traditional sources (CDBGs, private foundations, religious institutions, and so on). Generally, CBOs have limited funding options for essential program support activities such as staff training, administrative and managerial support assistance, strategic planning, and so on. These are the very programs and services that, if adequately funded, allow CBOs and other housing service providers the flexibility to tailor and expand program activities to specific community need.

H.O.M.E. funding criteria allow members of the community to use H.O.M.E. funds directly or to combine with other leveraged funds to carry out a variety of activities that would otherwise go unfunded. Among these are efforts to revitalize neighborhoods, address issues relating to repair and maintenance of housing stock, housing affordability, and neighborhood stability.

H.O.M.E. funds organizations that do work in the following areas:

- *Community/Neighborhood Improvement:* This category includes programs to develop and implement plans to address identified needs, which are currently unfunded and designed to sustain, promote, and/or enhance neighborhoods.
- *Outreach and Education:* This category includes programs designed to educate or inform community residents about available programs and services.
- *Housing Search Assistance:* Includes programs designed to expand housing choices and/or improve the quality of life for Milwaukee-area residents.
- *Program Enhancement:* Includes programs designed to improve organizational operations and/or broaden the scope of existing programs.

As with all of its initiatives, MMFHC sought community input in determining its grant-making criteria. The organization established a grant allocation committee to review proposals and recommend funding levels for successful projects. This committee was composed of five experienced MMFHC volunteers, whose experience combines longstanding community involvement with active participation in MMFHC programs. Their perspectives on community reinvestment issues meld pressing community needs with fair housing goals.

MMFHC also initiated extensive outreach to the community on the availability of H.O.M.E. funding through CBO newsletters, newspaper articles, media advertisements, and direct mailings to CBOs and advocacy organizations. In early 2000 MMFHC conducted an informational meeting for eligible organizations to announce H.O.M.E.'s grant-making process and the first grant-making cycle.

MMFHC received nineteen proposals from CBOs and advocacy agencies requesting funding for twenty-one projects. After screening the preliminary applications, H.O.M.E. requested and received fourteen full proposals requesting a total of $465,532 during the first funding cycle.

Community Groups Funded to Carry Out Reinvestment Initiatives

Since the inception of H.O.M.E., MMFHC has processed two cycles of grant allocations to fund innovative housing programs and has funded a total of ten organizations in the amount of $141,000. Below is a list of some of the initiatives funded by H.O.M.E.

- A fair lending advocacy organization was awarded an $8,000 grant to produce and distribute a *Mortgage Product Comparison Workbook*. The workbook covers a variety of topics, including an explanation on the Truth in Lending and Equal Credit Opportunity Acts. This information is designed to assist homebuyers in securing the mortgage loan most appropriate to their needs. The workbook is available to home seekers participating in presentations, home-buying seminars, and HUD-designated home buyer counseling agencies, as well as upon request.
- *University of Wisconsin–Extension (UW-Extension)* received $30,000 to develop a *Post-Purchase Counseling Curriculum and Training Program.* This program, in conjunction with the efforts of UW-Extension's Home-ownership Counselor Training Consortium, prepares counselors to provide effective services to low- and low-moderate-income households, helping them maintain their home after purchase.
- *The Milwaukee Realtist Association* received a $12,000 grant to provide pre-purchase homeownership training and counseling to Milwaukee-area home seekers. These services assist first-time homeowners in navigating the home-purchase process—from home selection through closing.
- A homebuyer counseling agency received a $35,000 grant to expand its first-time homebuyer support programs and services by adding a post-purchase technical specialist. The specialist conducts workshops covering escrow analysis and paying property taxes, financial management, benefits

of maintaining property, routine maintenance, insurance, and safety. This program is marketed to homebuyer counseling program graduates and offered as a citywide referral resource to lenders, community groups, religious congregations, neighborhood associations, and community development corporations—as well as through print and broadcast media.

- A disability advocacy agency was awarded a $10,000 grant to provide a foreclosure prevention and emergency maintenance services fund for households assisted through its peer counseling program. The *Homeownership Initiative for Persons with Disabilities Program* provides persons with disabilities with mortgage payment assistance.
- A local community development corporation (CDC) received $12,000 to cover the implementation cost, not covered by any other funding sources, associated with the city of Milwaukee's Target Investment Neighborhood (TIN) commitment, to stabilize and increase homeowner occupancy. This CDC works with residents to enhance the sense of community and increase property values by improving the physical appearance of both business and residential districts.
- The local Legal Aid's *Advocacy for Low Income Neighborhood Equity (A-Line) Project* was awarded $50,000 to provide civil legal representation to combat predatory lending practices relating to home equity and refinance loans. Legal Aid's program combats predatory lending via loan foreclosure mitigation and/or prevention advocacy (particularly home equity and refinancing loan foreclosure), and class action and impact litigation directed at predatory lending practices to obtain restitution, penalties, and other monetary remedies for low-income homeowners. Legal Aid's project also incorporates a revolving home-improvement loan fund to assist in alleviating obstacles, which may cause many low-income, inner-city homeowners to consider predatory lending enticements.

Lessons Learned in the Milwaukee Experience

This study of the Metropolitan Milwaukee Fair Housing Council's involvement of community residents in fair housing enforcement actions as well as community development initiatives demonstrates the far-reaching benefits of organized citizen participation. This model has proved to be mutually beneficial to both the organization and the individuals involved. Specifically, MMFHC's experience demonstrates a number of significant results. First, community reinvestment can be an outgrowth of fair housing enforcement activities. Traditionally, fair housing enforcement has not been used to address reinvestment issues. Although both fair housing and reinvestment advocates seek to remedy racial and economic disparities, they frequently use different methods and approaches to achieve those goals. The establishment of MMFHC's grant-making program is an innovative approach to community reinvestment based on the principle that neighborhoods can be rebuilt by returning resources stripped from them by the actions of the housing industry.

MMFHC's work also illustrates that fair housing initiatives can be integrated into existing community development initiatives. Community development activities generally do not include fair housing components, such as expansion of housing choice to nontraditional populations, affirmative marketing strategies, or inclusion of all persons protected under fair housing laws. MMFHC mandates that such fair housing measures are incorporated into the provision of community services, thus ensuring that the goals of equal housing opportunity are part of each of its funded community development projects.

Above all MMFHC's experience confirms that citizen involvement is a necessary component for comprehensive resolution. The inclusion of volunteers in selecting which projects to fund, as well as their participation in carrying out those funded projects, ensures appropriate and successful solutions to community problems. This model demonstrates that, once made aware of problems in their communities, people are willing to work to solve them. These volunteers experience a sense of empowerment as they work to dismantle institutional forms of disinvestment and rebuild their communities.

The MMFHC's endeavor also shows that collaboration between private fair housing organizations, CBOs, and economic development agencies is an important component of comprehensive community reinvestment. Uncoordinated efforts within the community, although well intended, have often resulted in duplication of effort and poor use of limited resources. The MMFHC assists organizations in identifying community needs and funds organizations to establish partnerships to address those needs.

Finally, MMFHC's approach to redressing neighborhood destabilization and disinvestment demonstrates that effective change can be accomplished through creative use of partnerships between community residents, community-based organizations, advocacy groups, and a fair housing volunteer base. Stabilizing communities is a multifaceted endeavor that requires innovative methodologies. The MMFHC model demonstrates that citizens can become mobilized to resolve community problems if provided with education and information, an opportunity to participate, and assurance that their efforts will result in real change.

References

Hoeh, David. 1983. *Access to Residential Property Insurance in Milwaukee County.*
   Milwaukee: Milwaukee Community Housing Resources Board.
Milwaukee Journal. 1988a. March 3.
Milwaukee Journal. 1988b. Six Insurance Agents Allege Sales Bias (Apr. 8).

Milwaukee Journal. 1990. Ruling Toughens Task for NAACP in Lawsuit (Dec. 12).

Squires, Gregory D., and William Velez. 1988. Insurance Redlining and the Process of Discrimination. *Review of Black Political Economy* (winter): 66.

Squires, Gregory D., William Velez, and Karl E. Taeuber. 1991. Insurance Redlining, Agency Location, and the Process of Urban Disinvestment. *Urban Affairs Quarterly* 26 (4).

Tisdale, William R., and Carla J. Wertheim. 1994. Testimony presented before the U.S. House of Representatives Subcommittee on Consumer Credit and Insurance of the Committee on Banking, Finance, and Urban Affairs. January 4.

United States v. State of Wisconsin, 395 F. Supp. 732 (W.D. Wis. 1975).

John P. Relman

4 Taking It to the Courts:
Litigation and the Reform of Financial Institutions

For many years, lawsuits against lending institutions alleging discrimination on the basis of race or national origin were relatively rare. Most civil rights lawyers did not know how to bring such a claim, and loan applicants turned down for loans had no way of knowing whether they had been victims of illegal discrimination. All of that changed in the early 1990s. Following the pioneering efforts of the Clinton administration's lending discrimination enforcement program, and with the help of new disclosure laws and increasingly sophisticated software programs that make it easier to track where banks make loans, private civil rights lawyers are now in a better position than ever before to challenge the lending practices of large financial institutions as they affect underserved and minority communities.

This chapter focuses on three lending discrimination cases brought by private civil rights lawyers and organizations[1] over the past decade, lawsuits that—in very different ways—are typical of cases that have served as catalysts for reform within the industry. The first, *Boyer and the Fair Housing Council of Greater Washington v. First Virginia Bank, Maryland*, demonstrates the power of an individual plaintiff to force discovery of a bank's loan files to search for differential treatment of loan applicants, and in the process both prove discrimination and win substantial damages. The second case, *Lathern, et al. v. NationsBank*, a class action, takes the *Boyer* model and uses it to force relief for a much broader range of plaintiffs. *Lathern* is also a case study of how federal disclosure laws can be used by both civil rights organizations and civil rights lawyers to identify lending institutions that may be engaged in discriminatory practices. Thanks to media coverage of this case, public attention was focused on the bank's practices, forcing both public debate and scrutiny of little-known underwriting rules and customs that worked to the disadvantage of minority applicants. The media storm won the attention of NationsBank's CEO and unquestionably forced internal rethinking of the bank's practices.

The third case, *Hargraves, et al. v. Capital City Mortgage Corp.*, dramatically highlights the predatory lending practices of a company that represents among the worst of a group of lenders who are increasingly targeting their poisonous products at minority and elderly communities. *Hargraves* shows how a carefully crafted lawsuit can both expand the coverage of existing civil rights laws and, by focusing attention on the bad conduct of lenders, galvanize public support for legislation designed to reform an entire industry. *Hargraves*, along with several other high-profile predatory lending cases, has fundamentally changed the way politicians and policymakers think about subprime lending. All of this has been accomplished through the sheer power of the personal stories these lawsuits tell.

The thread that connects these three cases—and the message they require us to take away—is the power of the courts and litigators to effect significant change in institutions that can be highly resistant to criticism and fearful of innovations designed to benefit the less fortunate. The purpose of this chapter is to explain what makes private litigation uniquely effective in spurring reform of lending institutions, and why the use of this tool for social and financial reform is unlikely to abate anytime soon.

One caveat is in order. The focus of this chapter is *private* litigation. Beginning in the early 1990s, the Justice Department embarked on a remarkably successful series of lending-discrimination enforcement actions that forced wide-ranging changes within the industry. Those efforts have been documented elsewhere and are not reviewed here.[2] In part this is because of scope and space restraints, and in part because private and government enforcement efforts in the lending field are not truly comparable. The Justice Department, with the cooperation of federal banking regulatory agencies, has the power and resources to conduct a comprehensive review of a bank's files before deciding whether to initiate an enforcement action. Private civil rights lawyers and advocates do not have this luxury. This makes for different strategic decisions and different advocacy tactics.

This is not to minimize what the government has accomplished. To the contrary, as noted above, the Justice Department's efforts are largely responsible for the private enforcement actions discussed below. But if reform of the lending industry is to continue, the government cannot do it alone, particularly given the susceptibility of these programs to the changing political winds and the proclivities of the administration in office. Responsibility for continuing reform rests equally with private civil rights lawyers and the government. It is the unique aspects of private litigation, and the elements that have made for success in this arena, that are intended as the focus of this discussion.

The *Boyer* Litigation and the
Power of an Individual Plaintiff

Professor Boyer and His Allegations

In 1992 Professor Spencer Boyer applied for a $50,000 home equity loan at the local branch office of First Virginia Bank–Maryland. Professor Boyer was the most senior law professor at Howard University Law School in Washington, D.C., when he applied. He had lived at his home in Silver Spring, Maryland, for more than twenty-two years, had assets of more than $1.2 million, equity in his home of more than $350,000, and the highest possible current credit rating, indicating that he was fully up to date on all of his charge accounts, credit cards, and mortgage payments. Yet after visiting First Virginia Bank and speaking to the branch manager, William J. Grippo, about securing a home equity loan, he became convinced that he would not get the loan. Although he had never filed a discrimination complaint before, there was, as Professor Boyer put it, something about the way Mr. Grippo spoke to him and looked at him that "as an African American man, just told me it wasn't going to happen. Nothing overt was said about race, it was just something you understand intuitively as a black man living in America."[3]

As expected, two weeks later Professor Boyer received a rejection letter from Mr. Grippo stating that the Bank had denied his loan because of "delinquent credit obligations." No further explanation was given. Professor Boyer quickly applied for a loan in the same amount with another lender, and was immediately accepted. Convinced that his race had played a role in First Virginia's decision, Professor Boyer filed a discrimination complaint with the local human rights commission. In the Bank's response to the complaint, it asserted that Professor Boyer had not been the victim of race discrimination, but rather had not met First Virginia's underwriting guidelines because he had eleven thirty-day late payments on revolving credit cards over the past ten years. In other words, although Professor Boyer had always paid his credit card bills, on eleven occasions over a ten-year period he had paid his credit card bill between one and twenty-nine days after it was due. Unbeknownst to him, this information had been recorded on his credit report. When asked during the litigation why he had occasionally paid late, Professor Boyer responded as any unsuspecting customer would have—that he didn't know. For all he or anyone else could determine he had been on vacation, or there was a mix-up with his wife about who was to pay the bills for a given month. The point was, he did not know that it mattered. He never failed to pay the late fee and the interest, whatever it was.

The lines for Professor Boyer's discrimination claim were now clearly drawn. If it were the case that all applicants, black and white, who had eleven or more thirty-day late payments on their credit cards, and qualifications similar to those of Professor Boyer, were turned down for home equity loans in the approximate amount of $50,000, the Bank could not be guilty of unlawful discrimination. While it might not be a profitable business practice to turn away loan applicants with Professor Boyer's qualifications, nothing in federal law makes it illegal for a lender to make bad business decisions, provided those bad decisions are made on an "equal opportunity" basis to both black and white applicants. If, on the other hand, similarly situated white applicants with eleven or more thirty-day late payments had no difficulty obtaining a $50,000 home equity loan, First Virginia Bank could be held liable by a jury for race discrimination. This would be purely circumstantial evidence of discriminatory intent on the part of the bank, but in the absence of direct evidence of discrimination (a memorandum, for example, explaining the Bank's use of race in the underwriting process)—which is exceedingly rare—it is this type of evidence that is used to prove discrimination cases.

The problem for Professor Boyer at this point, however, was more practical than legal. How could one file a lawsuit alleging discrimination without knowing the answer to these critical questions? Yet finding an answer required reviewing the Bank's loan files, and clearly that could not be accomplished without filing suit. The problem was further compounded by the lack of precedent. Few had tried a lawsuit on these facts, and there was no litigation template to follow. Of the few private lawyers who had attempted a similar case, none had won a court ruling giving a plaintiff the right to invade the privacy of bank files in order to determine whether there had been discriminatory treatment.

Convinced that his financial qualifications were simply too good to justify the denial and that corroborating evidence would be uncovered once the discovery process began, Professor Boyer elected to go ahead and file the lawsuit. In December 1992, joined by the Fair Housing Council of Greater Washington, Professor Boyer filed suit against First Virginia Bank–Maryland, and Mr. Grippo, alleging that he had been denied the right to purchase a home equity loan because of his race.[4]

The Loan File Review

Aware that the loan files held the key to proving the case, the Bank fought ferociously to prevent Professor Boyer from seeing the files. After extensive briefing and a hotly contested hearing, the court sided with Professor Boyer, ruling that the only true measure of whether the denial had been based on race depended upon a full and fair comparative loan file review. That meant sifting through hundreds of confidential loan files of accepted and rejected loan applicants to determine which applicants were similarly situated, and how those applicants had been treated. The race of the applicant could generally be found in the file—in many instances because the application contained a copy of the applicant's drivers license (with photo), and in other instances because the bank was required under certain federal disclosure laws to identify the race of the borrower on the application and report that information to federal bank regulatory agencies.[5]

In the end, Professor Boyer's legal team reviewed more than 1,700 home equity loan applications processed by First Virginia Bank–Maryland at or around the time that Professor Boyer applied for his loan. The results were stunning. They showed that the Bank routinely approved loans for white applicants with credit histories comparable to, or worse than, Professor Boyer's. White applicants with as many as fifty late payments, and in one case seventy-six late payments, were approved for loans in greater amounts than that sought by Professor Boyer. In most instances white applicants with troubled credit histories were approved without providing any explanation for credit blemishes, but in situations where cursory explanations were provided by white applicants they were provided at the Bank's prompting. The Bank did not approve any applications from applicants it knew to be African American with more than eleven late payments, and the files revealed that few African Americans were afforded the opportunity to provide a written explanation for blemishes on their credit reports.

The loan file review also revealed what fair lending advocates have come to call the "thick file, thin file" syndrome. This is a pattern identified in underwriting audits in which the files of white applicants are routinely found to be "thicker" than those of black applicants. The cause is paper correspondence between the underwriter and the applicant, or between officers at the bank, for the purpose of overcoming problems identified in the applications of what are usually white applicants. In other words, the size of the white loan files reflects greater flexibility on the part of the Bank in the application of its underwriting guidelines to white applicants. "Thin" files are more typical of African American applications, like Professor Boyer's, in which little or no effort is made to seek a solution to a perceived problem—such as a credit blemish.

A bank like First Virginia need not violate its own guidelines in order to help these white applicants. Most bank underwriting guidelines allow loan officers wide discretion in approving problem loans where there is evidence of "compensating factors," such as large cash reserves, a history of timely mortgage payments (as opposed to credit card payments), steady employment or income, and equity in the collateral. First Virginia Bank–Maryland's underwriting guidelines were no exception to industry practice. They allowed loan officers wide discretion in weighing all factors before deciding whether to accept or reject a loan. Bank employees had the power to use bank guidelines to justify the approval of white loans and the rejection of black loans whenever they chose.

As expected, this evidence proved to be the turning point in the case. The court denied the Bank's efforts to dismiss the case and ordered the matter set for trial. In the spring of 1994, shortly before the trial was to begin, the Bank agreed to settle the case for $210,000, more than four times the amount of the loan that Professor Boyer had originally sought.

The Significance of the Boyer Litigation

The outcome of Professor Boyer's lawsuit proved groundbreaking in several important respects. First, the case demonstrated the power of one individual to force a comprehensive comparative review of all loans of a particular type issued by a major bank over a predetermined period of time. The bank's files were turned inside out, underwriters were deposed, executives were required to explain under oath how their underwriting guidelines operated, and loan decisions were scrutinized under the pressure of an impending public trial. If lending institutions up until this point had doubted that either federal regulators or the private plaintiffs' bar would have the ability or means to subject their operations to close examination, the *Boyer* case erased their doubts. The *Boyer* litigation made clear that any individual plaintiff could potentially force an exhaustive review simply by filing suit. In short, the case proved that private litigation could level the playing field in an area where many had traditionally thought the bank held all the cards.

Second, the litigation served as a case study of how discrimination typically happens—not with open refusals to sell loans, but through more subtle means. The case educated regulators, advocates, and industry executives about where to look for discrimination and about the importance of focusing on the gray areas where exceptions are made for whites with blemished credit but not for African Americans. For lending compliance officers who paid attention to the case (and there were many), the lesson to take from *Boyer* was the importance of setting up second-look programs and internal comparative file reviews to find patterns of disparate treatment and correct them *before* a lawsuit is filed. And for fair lending advocates, the litigation provided a case study in how to prove discrimination without spending tens of thousands of dollars on complicated statistical analyses and experts.

Third, and perhaps most important, the case served as a warning shot fired across the bow of the industry. Here, after all, was one courageous individual who had forced a time-consuming inspection of bank files, cost the bank $210,000 in damages and hundreds of thousands more in litigation costs—and he was only *one* customer. Apparent to any executive who took notice was the fact that the costs of neglecting potential discrimination problems within a bank and failing to take preventive steps could never be as high as the costs resulting from multiple lawsuits filed by scores of rejected loan applicants. In this sense, as a tool for reform, the *Boyer* litigation forced changes within the industry that far outstripped the dollars at risk for one bank defendant. All of this was made possible by the attention the case received in both the mainstream press and industry trade journals. This in turn was the result of strong facts, an appealing and deserving plaintiff, and the careful planning and execution that went into the litigation itself.

From a strategic standpoint, however, the *Boyer* case left two critical questions unanswered for private-sector advocates determined to reform the industry. First, Professor Boyer had the courage to file suit without knowing what the comparative loan file review would show because his financial qualifications were so strong. But what about individuals who did not have Professor Boyer's credentials? If the premise of Professor Boyer's suit were correct, many African Americans are the victims of the "thick file, thin file" syndrome. Yet how is one to know which banks to target for litigation (and an ensuing loan file review) before the review is actually carried out? And second, if the bank were engaged in discrimination, how can private civil rights lawyers ensure that all of the victims—not just those lucky enough to have found experienced lawyers ready and willing to file suit—will receive their just rewards?

It is to these concerns that the second case study, involving NationsBank, turns.[6]

NationsBank and the Use of HMDA Data

The Washington Lawyers' Committee Report

In 1994 the Washington Lawyers' Committee for Civil Rights and Urban Affairs set out to answer the questions left unanswered by *Boyer.* The focus of the Committee's efforts was the data produced and reported to federal regulators under the Home Mortgage Disclosure Act (HMDA).[7] As Professor Squires notes in the introductory chapter, HMDA requires lenders of a certain size to report where home-mortgage loans originate and to whom the money is lent. The law also requires lenders to report information about loans that are denied. The data reported to the government captures information about the reasons for rejection, and about the income level, race, sex, and national origin of the applicant. The Committee set out to determine whether this data could be used to learn more about possible discrimination by Washington, D.C.–area lenders in two key areas of the lending process: failure to market or solicit home-mortgage loans in minority neighborhoods because of race, and disparate treatment of minorities in the underwriting of loans.

Up until this time, most studies that had attempted to use publicly available loan data to examine bank lending practices failed to control for important factors that could explain racial disparities in underwriting and marketing practices. For this reason they were of limited use in identifying which lenders might be engaged in discriminatory practices. The Committee's proposed study was different. Relying on statistical methods used by the Justice Department in its pattern-and-practice lending cases, the Committee controlled for the income of applicants and the numbers of loans processed, and took into account the lender's reasons for rejection. This latter control was significant, because it allowed for a comparison of rejection rates for African American and white loan applicants among the pool of applicants most likely to be subjected to discriminatory practices. This is the group of individuals rejected for blemished credit and high debt-to-income ratios—an area where banks like First Virginia have traditionally been willing to bend the rules and make exceptions for applicants they choose to favor.

Released to the public in December 1994, the study ranked Washington, D.C.–area lenders based on their rejection rates and on where they originated their loans.[8] A closer look at lenders with significantly higher rejection rates for African American loan applicants showed that the disparity between rejection rates for African Americans and whites increased significantly when controls were applied that allowed one to focus on the pool of applicants rejected for reasons of credit history or debt-to-income ratios. In short, the data suggested that among banks already rejecting African Americans at significantly higher rates than the industry norm, African Americans were significantly more likely to be rejected for alleged problems with credit history or debt-to-income ratios. This, of course, did not prove that a particular bank was discriminating on the basis of race. For any given transaction it could well be that credit problems or debt-to-income ratios were so pronounced as to require denial of the loan. But the findings raised troubling questions. Why would African American applicants making between $80,000 and $120,000 per year, for example, be eight, ten, or in some cases twelve times more likely to be rejected for credit blemishes at certain banks than white applicants in the same income category?

The bank with the highest rejection-rate disparity was NationsBank, one of the country's largest and best-known lenders. The study found that, overall, high-income black applicants were five times more likely to be rejected than high-income whites. But when the data was further controlled for reasons for rejection, black applicants at NationsBank Mortgage Company were twelve times more likely to be rejected because of credit histories or debt-to-income ratios. Another of the country's largest lenders, Citibank, placed second on this list, rejecting African Americans for reasons of credit or debt-to-income ratios at a rate nearly five times greater than that for whites.

The Results of the Study and the NationsBank Litigation

When the study was published and reported in the *Washington Post*, the response was overwhelming. Area banks listed at the top of the rejection rate disparity list scurried to hire legal counsel and compliance consultants to review their files. Although the study made clear that no bank was being accused of unlawful practices, the authors pointedly noted that "racial disparities in underwriting and marketing raise serious fair lending concerns that require further investigation."[9] Given the Committee's history of success in championing civil rights causes in the courts, it was clear to all that banks at the top of this list would be subjected to increased legal scrutiny.

In September 1995 the study became more than an academic exercise. Eleven plaintiffs, representing a class of rejected African American loan applicants in the Washington, D.C., metropolitan area, filed a class action against NationsBank and NationsBank Mortgage Corporation alleging that the Bank had engaged in a pattern and practice of lending discrimination against African American applicants.[10] The plaintiff class was represented by the Washington Lawyers' Committee and a private firm. The complaint recounted the details of numerous loan transactions and rejections reminiscent of Professor Boyer's case, and cited much of the statistical evidence contained in the Committee's study. Shortly after the NationsBank suit was filed, private counsel in Chicago filed a similar class action against Citibank, which, as noted above, had been identified in the Committee's study as the lending institution with the second-highest rejection rate disparities.

As with the *Boyer* case, the NationsBank suit received extensive press coverage. Unlike First Virginia Bank, however, NationsBank was not shy about asserting its position to the media. Having contributed millions of dollars to community groups to improve its image and keep a steady stream of its own bank mergers and acquisitions moving smoothly with federal regulators, a stunned and angry NationsBank organized a media campaign designed to discredit the lawsuit and intimidate the plaintiffs and their counsel.

NationsBank's chief defense was that its high rejection-rate disparity was due to its aggressive efforts to solicit loan applications in underserved and minority neighborhoods. The Bank claimed that because it trawled farther and wider for minority loans, it was natural that more unqualified loan applicants would be caught in its net. The problem with this defense was that Nations-Bank had relied for years on the assistance of community groups, which it funded lavishly, to screen loan applicants in underserved neighborhoods and ensure that only the best-qualified applications were sent to NationsBank's headquarters in Charlotte, North Carolina, for review. The rejection-rate disparity was derived only from the loans that made it to Charlotte; it did not include those screened out by the Bank's agents and employees in Washington's minority neighborhoods and never made it into the application process. Given the careful screening, NationsBank's HMDA data should have reflected one of the region's lowest rejection-rate disparities, not the highest.

This debate, which was carried out in the newspapers and industry trade journals, focused attention as never before on the significance and purpose to which HMDA data could and should be put by federal regulators, banks, and community activists. The merits of the case aside, this debate served an important and useful public policy purpose. But the fact that it arose in the context of specific allegations of discrimination focused NationsBank's attention (and no doubt that of its industry competitors) as never before on the need for internal loan file reviews and assessments, because the stakes were now higher. Were NationsBank to be found in violation of federal fair housing law, the expansion of its empire—which until that time had seemed as inevitable as the manifest destiny that had carried early settlers to the Pacific coast— would be thrown into question.

The NationsBank litigation lasted nearly three years. Every step of the process was fiercely contested. In the end, a settlement was reached. Although the terms were confidential, the settlement fairly remedied and resolved the concerns of the plaintiffs and the class they sought to represent. Notwithstanding the confidential terms, the filing of this private class action, the first of its kind to be brought against a major lending institution, had lasting significance.

First, the case served notice on the lending industry that no lending institution, not even the country's largest or the ones with the best public relations departments, could count on being spared the enormous expense and scrutiny that class action litigation brings. Defense counsel across the country reported a significant rise in the number of major banks seeking assistance with voluntary compliance programs and internal reviews.

Second, and equally important, the publication of the Committee report and the filing of the NationsBank litigation effectively answered the questions left hanging at the conclusion of the *Boyer* case. It was, in fact, possible to harness the power of nonprofit civil rights organizations to identify lenders who were likely to have discriminatory underwriting and marketing practices, and it also was possible to bring cases that would redress injuries for more than one applicant at a time, even against the largest banks.

Finally, the NationsBank litigation demonstrated yet again that only the threat of litigation, followed by the litigation itself, could fracture the aura of invincibility that surrounds these enormously powerful institutions. As with *Boyer*, it was the litigation, and the risk of a judicial finding of discrimination—with all that would entail for the bank's standing and dreams of expansion—that forced the bank to review and rethink its guidelines, operations, and programs to ensure they were in full compliance with the Fair Housing Act. It was no longer enough for top bank officials to make promises and delegate responsibility; the internal review and the reforms could not wait for another day—they had to happen now.

NationsBank and Citibank were prime lenders accused of refusing to make loans in African American neighborhoods to African American applicants. But the suits against these banks did not begin to address the growing chaos and discrimination that began to emerge in the 1990s in the subprime lending market. It is this problem that the third case study addresses. The story of the Capital City Mortgage Corporation demonstrates how litigation can be used not just to document and educate the industry and the general public about a pernicious and destructive lending practice, but how litigation can be used creatively to reform the lending industry by actually expanding the scope and coverage of civil rights laws.

Capital City Mortgage and Predatory Lending

The Rise of Subprime and Predatory Lending

While the Justice Department and fair housing advocates were focused on underwriting and marketing discrimination by prime lenders in the early

1990s, a new phenomenon was emerging in the lending industry. Subprime lenders, offering home-mortgage and refinance loans at rates significantly above the competitive rates offered by prime lenders, began to take root in cities across the country, lending to applicants with blemished credit or no credit history at all, who could not obtain "A" paper loans from prime lenders like NationsBank or Citibank. Many subprime lenders began in the early 1990s as small-volume companies but quickly expanded as demand for capital in the inner cities grew rapidly and access to capital from prime lenders remained tight. The explosive rise in subprime lending in the 1990s surpassed all expectations. From 1994 to 1999 subprime loan originations increased from $35 billion to more than $160 billion.[11] During the same time period, the subprime market share increased from less than 5 percent of all mortgage originations to almost 13 percent.[12]

By definition, subprime lending takes advantage of the fact that certain borrowers with blemished credit do not have access to capital at the most competitive rates, and charges more for the same loans to compensate for the added risk. As Squires observed in the introductory chapter, some advocates have argued that responsible subprime lending provides an important service because it makes capital available in underserved financial markets. But in the early 1990s—and in many jurisdictions still today—there are no rules or regulations that place limits on what subprime lenders can charge or the practices they can engage in. The result has been a chaotic, "wild west" mentality among subprime lenders that has given rise to "predatory" lending. Predatory lending is marked by abusive and fraudulent practices designed to strip equity from borrowers and return high rates of profit by charging unsuspecting customers excessive fees and penalties.

The Capital City Litigation

Capital City Mortgage Corporation is one such lender. A family-owned business formerly run by a white, polo-playing chief executive by the name of Tom Nash, Capital City's practices first came to light in the mid-1990s when the *Washington Post* reported the company had foreclosed on a Baptist Church in northeast Washington, forcing Sunday School children out onto the street. The *Post* conducted an investigation that revealed a pattern of foreclosures by Capital City on properties that had been used as collateral for relatively small loans made by the company to unsuspecting borrowers that began at 24 percent interest rates and escalated to 31 percent in the event of a single late payment. Careful review of the foreclosures and loan records indicated that virtually all of Capital City's loans were made in heavily African American census tracts in the Washington, D.C., metropolitan area.

In 1998 the Washington Lawyers' Committee for Civil Rights and Urban Affairs filed suit on behalf of five victims of Capital City's predatory lending practices: the Greater Little Ark Baptist Church and four individuals who, in several instances, had watched helplessly as their property was seized by Capital City after they were misled into signing loan contracts with usurious interest rates, deceptive terms, and crippling penalties.[13] What happened to the Greater Little Ark Baptist Church is typical of Capital City's practices.

Little Ark received an unsolicited call from a broker who worked for Capital City. The broker told Reverend Hargraves, Little Ark's pastor, that he had heard the church was in need of a loan. Little Ark was, in fact, hoping to obtain a loan for approximately $60,000 to pay back taxes owed on certain of the church's operations. After meeting with the broker, Rev. Hargraves agreed to pledge the church property to secure a $160,000 loan. The amount was far more than the church needed, but Rev. Hargraves agreed to the loan based on the broker's advice that it would be difficult to obtain a smaller loan. The loan still left Little Ark "equity rich," because the property was worth $400,000 and had only a small amount due on the original mortgage.

The broker also told Rev. Hargraves that while the interest rate for the loan was high—18 percent—the church would be able to refinance the property at a lower interest rate shortly after the closing. Prior to the closing, Capital City had Rev. Hargraves sign the loan documents, with many of the loan terms left blank. Capital City did not explain the documents or ask anything about the church's financial condition, ability to pay, income, or debts. At settlement, Rev. Hargraves learned for the first time that the loan had a $26,000 origination fee (16 percent of the loan), $12,800 of which had gone to the loan broker; that for the first four years the loan had an interest rate of 25 percent; and that in the fifth and final year the interest rate would jump to 30 percent, with monthly payments of $4,000. At the time, the church's monthly income was less than $4,000. Shortly after settlement, the loan broker disappeared. The pastor called repeatedly to obtain a coupon payment book and find out where the loan proceeds were, but the broker's phone had been disconnected.

Over the course of the next two years, Capital City demanded from the church arbitrary payments that escalated beyond anything resembling the terms of the note. At the end of two years, the church was forced into bankruptcy, Capital City foreclosed on the church property, and a subsidiary of Capital City obtained the property at auction for $235,000. Little Ark Baptist Church was evicted, and Capital City resold the church to another African American congregation for $450,000.

The pattern was virtually the same with each of the other plaintiffs. In one case Capital City charged an initial interest rate of 24 percent, tacked on fraudulent penalties, attorneys' fees and late fees, and drove the borrower into bankruptcy. In another, Capital City tricked a mother and daughter into signing three separate but identical loan notes in the belief that they were signing copies of the same loan. Instead of being liable for one monthly payment of $794, they were liable for three payments totaling $2,383, an amount that exceeded their monthly income. Capital City knew this at the time of closing and entered into the loan in order to force a foreclosure and obtain title to the property.

On one level, the Washington Lawyers' Committee brought the case in order to stop these fraudulent practices and win redress for its victims. Not surprisingly, therefore, the complaint was replete with allegations of fraud and violations of the Racketeer Influenced and Corrupt Organizations Act (RICO). At another level, however, the case was about something potentially more significant and groundbreaking.

One of the plaintiffs was the Fair Housing Council of Greater Washington,[14] whose mission it is to eradicate housing discrimination in the Washington metropolitan area and, in the process, champion broad enforcement of the Fair Housing Act. Careful scrutiny of Capital City's loans and foreclosures by the Council and experts revealed a clear pattern of making and marketing these predatory loans primarily in African American neighborhoods. The loan data demonstrated that 94 percent of Capital City's loans in the District of Columbia, and 74 percent of its loans in Prince George's County, were on properties located in majority African American census tracts. Ninety-seven percent of the properties Capital City foreclosed on in the District of Columbia were in majority African American census tracts. This contrasted sharply with the practices of other subprime lenders in the Washington metropolitan area. On average, subprime lenders as a whole made fully as many loans in white areas as they did in African American neighborhoods.

In simple terms, the Council alleged that Capital City was deliberately and intentionally targeting and marketing its poisonous and predatory loans in African American neighborhoods because of the race of the potential applicants and the racial makeup of the neighborhood. The complaint alleged that this racially motivated marketing effort was accomplished with the assistance of a cadre of "runners and brokers" who worked within African American neighborhoods, searching for vulnerable potential borrowers to lure into fraudulent loan transactions. This practice, the Council alleged, violated the Fair Housing Act, which makes it illegal to offer or market home-mortgage or refinance loans on the basis of race.

Capital City's response to this allegation was predictable. It contended that it provided access to capital in precisely those neighborhoods that had been historically discriminated against by prime lenders. In this sense, Capital City argued, it was acting in a manner consistent with the purposes of the Fair Housing Act, not contrary to the statute. In the company's view, "reverse redlining," as the Council's allegation was known, could not violate fair housing laws because the practice made housing available to those who would not otherwise be able to obtain a loan.

Not so, the Council responded. The pattern of foreclosures and the evidence that Capital City knew the plaintiffs could not have afforded the loans even before they were made proved that the company was in the business of taking housing away—of stripping equity, not building it.

Never before had this issue been joined in a court of law. No court, to date, had been asked to decide whether predatory lending could also be a violation of fair housing laws. The stakes were considerable. If the court found that reverse redlining was covered under the Fair Housing Act, advocates would have a potent new weapon with which to attack predatory lenders. Unlike RICO or common law fraud claims, the Fair Housing Act provides for compensatory damages for humiliation, embarrassment, and emotional distress; unlimited punitive damages; and a potentially limitless statute of limitations (known as the "continuing violations theory") that allows plaintiffs to reach back as far into the past as a continuous pattern of discriminatory conduct extends. For purposes of this case, the claim would be heard by a jury composed of District of Columbia residents, who would have a very powerful stick with which to punish the company should it determine that Capital City's practices had undermined and destabilized Washington's minority communities and intentionally stripped equity from African American neighborhoods. Indeed, the stick would be strong enough to put Capital City itself into bankruptcy.

The decision would have ramifications far beyond the banks of the Potomac. If successful, the case would open the door for reform-minded juries to bring to justice predatory lenders in cities across the country. And if ever there were to be a test case, this was it—not simply because of the sympathetic nature of the plaintiffs' claims and the heinous nature of the company's alleged practices, but also because of the demographics of Washington itself. Washington is a highly segregated community. More than 90 percent of African Americans in the District of Columbia reside in majority African American census tracts. This meant, as a practical matter, that it would be relatively easy to demonstrate the racial aspect of Capital City's marketing practices. In a less polarized community, it would be far more difficult to identify whether loans were made and marketed in African American or white neighborhoods.

During the course of discovery in the case, additional documents and evidence were uncovered that supported the plaintiffs' claims. The history of the Nash family business—operated in the heart of Washington's poorest African American neighborhoods for more than two generations for the benefit of the Nash family fortune and polo farm in the Maryland suburbs—told what the plaintiffs believed to be a chilling story of exploitation and outright fraud aimed at African American neighborhoods and churches. At the close of discovery, Capital City moved to dismiss the Fair Housing Act claim. With the assistance of the Justice Department, which filed a friend-of-the-court brief supporting the plaintiffs' position, the plaintiffs and the Fair Housing Council made their argument explaining why the Fair Housing Act covered reverse redlining. The participation of the Justice Department in this motion was significant, for it represented the first time that the government had taken a public position on the issue.

In September 2000 the U.S. District Court for the District of Columbia handed the plaintiffs a ringing victory, holding for the first time in a court of law that predatory lenders could be held liable under the Fair Housing Act if their loan schemes were marketed to minority communities on the basis of race.[15]

Yet even before the court handed down its decision on the fair housing claim, the Capital City case was receiving continuing and extensive coverage in the *Washington Post* and around the country because of the egregiousness of the company's predatory practices. Capital City quickly became a pariah within the industry, and other subprime lenders moved to distance themselves from the company, anxious to head off efforts to legislate reforms for the subprime industry as a whole. This, however, proved to be a losing fight. As the volume of subprime lending (and with it, predatory lending) rose dramatically, the call by advocates for legislative reforms grew as well. State after state began to debate new legislation. In many cases, Capital City's practices were cited as examples of the type of lending abuse that the proposed legislation was designed to avoid.

The Significance of the Capital City Litigation

The significance of the Capital City litigation as a catalyst for reform has been profound. It has made important new law and in the process empowered minority communities. It has spurred important new legislation and contributed to a climate in which private companies in the secondary market, like Fannie Mae and Freddie Mac, have now issued new guidelines for purchasing subprime loans that are designed to ensure that primary lenders that sell loans on the secondary market do not underwrite predatory loans. These developments in the secondary market are important, for they have helped impose a powerful measure of private-sector regulation and control on the chaos of the subprime industry. And, not least, the case has educated the public about the evils of predatory lending and the importance of outlawing the abuses of the subprime market before minority communities are damaged further.

All of these achievements have been possible because advocates chose as a vehicle for reform a test case that so captured the destructive nature of predatory lending that everyone—including the court—could understand the importance of bringing it to an end. In short, the Capital City litigation demonstrates well the power of a court case to make law, to tell a story, to win publicity, and ultimately to shape public opinion and frame public debate.

Choosing the Courts: Lessons for Reform

Reforming financial institutions from the outside is never an easy task. The difficulty lies in the massive imbalance in resources. Lending institutions sit at the center of political and financial power in any society, and the United

States is no exception. Politicians and business leaders are unlikely to support a public advocate's proposed reforms as long as the battle is waged in the halls of Congress or lobbyists' offices—places where banks are comfortable because of the advantage they enjoy in terms of money and influence.

Litigation changes the battlefield and in many instances can go a long way toward leveling it. The American court system has always afforded private individuals, whether represented or not, the opportunity to vindicate their rights. Resources are not always fairly allocated in this process either, but as the cases discussed in this chapter demonstrate, careful selection of a case can harness the power of the judiciary in a manner that may well help reform even the largest lenders.

There are several reasons for this, each of which is reflected in the case studies. The first rests with the intrinsic power of a judge or jury to find a bank in violation of the law, and to order it to provide relief to victims and change its ways. The second has to do with the consequences of being found in violation of the law. Once a reputation is sullied, even the largest financial institutions face greater resistance in Congress and more scrutiny from bank regulators when they attempt to expand their business. And the third has to do with the unique confluence of the courts and the press. Increasingly, court cases are forums for the education of the public because they are places where gripping and vital stories are told—where rights, interests, human needs, emotions, money, and power all clash—stories that have intrinsic appeal to the media.

Lending institutions fear all of this because it forces them to fight on a field with players and decision makers they cannot control. Once the court ordered First Virginia's files opened in the *Boyer* litigation, the battle was no longer in the bank's hands. The threat of an adverse court ruling, and all that would mean to NationsBank's plans for expansion, forced that enormous institution to take seriously the charges brought by the plaintiffs. The court's willingness to hold Capital City potentially liable for punitive damages under the Fair Housing Act meant that this company—for the first time—had to face the risk that it might not survive an adverse jury ruling, to say nothing of the attendant media scrutiny that made Capital City the target of public opprobrium. The predicament in which each of these institutions found itself has caused others in the industry to take a hard look at their own practices and, in many cases, change their ways. In the case of Capital City, legislators around the country were encouraged to enact legislation designed to curb a whole new area of lending abuse.

This is not to say that litigation is always the path to reform. Not every situation lends itself to a court case, and not every cause is personified by sympathetic plaintiffs. But as the case studies discussed in this chapter make clear, where openings and opportunities are carefully chosen, private litigation has been and will continue to be a necessary and vital catalyst for the reform of financial institutions.

Notes

1. The author served as co-counsel in each of these cases.

2. See, for example, Richard Ritter, "Redlining: The Justice Department Cases," *Mortgage Banking* (Sept. 1995); Richard Ritter, "The Decatur Federal Case: A Summary Report," in *Mortgage Lending, Racial Discrimination, and Federal Policy*, ed. John Goering and Ron Wienk (Washington, D.C.: Urban Institute Press, 1996).

3. These comments are given in quotation marks but they are in fact a paraphrasing of comments made by Professor Boyer in interviews about the transaction. They are not intended to represent a verbatim statement or recorded testimony.

4. The case was filed in federal district court for the Southern Division of the District of Maryland as *Spencer H. Boyer and The Fair Housing Council of Greater Washington v. First Virginia Bank–Maryland and William J. Grippo*, C.A. No. HAR 92-3632 (D. Md. 1992).

5. Disclosure of this information is required under the Home Mortgage Disclosure Act (HMDA), 12 U.S.C. Section 2801 *et seq.*

6. NationsBank has since merged with Bank of America and now goes by that name.

7. U.S.C. Section 2801 *et seq.*

8. "Ranking the Lenders: Investigating for Patterns of Racial Discrimination in the Making of Home Loans," Washington Lawyers' Committee for Civil Rights and Urban Affairs (December 13, 1994).

9. Ibid., at 3.

10. *Lathern, et al. v. NationsBank Mortgage Corp.*, C.A. No. 95-CV-1805 (D.D.C. 1995) and *Stackhaus, et al. v. NationsBank Mortgage Corp.*, C.A. No. 96-CV-1077 (D.D.C. 1996).

11. "Curbing Predatory Home Mortgage Lending: A Joint Report," U.S. Department of Housing and Urban Development; U.S. Department of Treasury (June 2000) at 2.

12. Ibid.

13. *Hargraves, et al. v. Capital City Mortgage Corp.*, C.A. No. 98-1021 (D.D.C. 1998).

14. The Council is now known as the "Equal Rights Center."

15. *Hargraves, et al. v. Capital City Mortgage Corp.*, 140 F.Supp. 2d 7 (D.D.C. 2000).

5   # From Living Rooms to
     Board Rooms:
     ## Sustainable Homeownership Deals
     with Banks and Insurers in Boston

I Want to Buy a House

As Diana Strother went to answer her doorbell one evening in 1988, little did she know that she was about to become involved in one of the largest and ultimately most successful community battles that Boston has seen in the past twenty-five years. Leaving dinner cooking on the stove, she strode down the hallway of her third-floor apartment in one of Boston's famed triple-deckers. She was tired from her day at Massachusetts General Hospital, where she worked. A single mother of two children, Diana was already juggling a lot. The organizer from the Massachusetts Affordable Housing Alliance (MAHA) said he wanted to talk with her for thirty minutes about a new group that was forming to tackle affordable homeownership issues.

Diana knew that she wanted to own her own home. She had been paying someone else's mortgage for too long and was tired of landlords who only collected the rent and didn't fix what was broken. Diana remembered joining a picket line with her mother years before to protest the lousy landlord who owned their building on Columbia Road. Listening to the MAHA organizer, Diana was intrigued. She didn't know if she had the time, but the organization sounded promising—and it would be composed of people like herself, who were getting priced out of homeownership in Boston. Maybe she would go to a meeting and check them out, she thought.

After seeing the organizer out, she returned to the more pressing matter of fixing her son and daughter's dinner. But when MAHA called again, this time with an invitation to its next meeting, she decided to attend. She wanted des-

perately to buy a home of her own one day, and with Boston's rapidly esca-
lating real estate prices, she felt that chance slipping away. At the meeting,
it dawned on her that things might be different. There were a lot of women
like herself, women of color who were angry. Angry at the city, angry at banks,
angry at the system. "The women in the room were so articulate. I was frustrated too but I couldn't put it into words like these women were. For a while
I just blended into the background and watched."

Diana felt that this group had potential, but its agenda was very ambitious.
Slowly, Diana began speaking up. She offered the group a potential starting
point. Just a few blocks from her triple-decker, the city was building affordable condos, but Diana didn't know how to get one. Was there a list? Did
you have to know the mayor? One day she made some inquiries of a construction worker, and he informed her that she needed an income of around
$40,000 in order to be eligible to buy a unit, and there was already a long
waiting list.

"Most of the people I knew in our community didn't make $40,000. They
made $15,000 or $20,000 or $25,000. We couldn't afford those condos. And
even if we could, we would be on a waiting list forever. We had to do something. I had to do something. So when MAHA asked me to get more involved,
I knew I had nothing to lose."

In large part because of Diana's experience, the group, which had named
itself the Homebuyers Union (HBU), decided to invite city officials to the
next meeting and ask them to set up a city hotline and clearinghouse where
information about affordable homeownership opportunities could be widely
broadcast. Diana found herself agreeing to take a leadership role in the meeting, although she had never done anything like that before. The meeting was
a success; the city agreed to set up a hotline, which later evolved into a city-
sponsored Home Center that today provides information to twenty thousand
people each year.

The Day Boston Stopped

January 11, 1989. The *Boston Globe* ran a front-page story about a draft study
by the Federal Reserve Bank of Boston showing racial bias in Boston mortgage lending (Marantz 1989a). Diana and others in the Homebuyers Union felt
that their world had changed, but it wasn't clear to anyone how (Campen
1992). For a few days phone lines across the city burned up. Community
groups talked across issue, race, and neighborhood lines. Elected officials,
from the chair of the state legislature's banks and banking committee to
Mayor Raymond Flynn, thought about what it meant for the city.

State Representative Thomas Finneran, then chair of the Joint Committee
on Banks and Banking, said to the *Boston Globe,* "You wonder if the banks
who would have been embarrassed by [the Fed study] squashed it. I'm from

Dorchester and Mattapan and it's fairly well known I'm no great fan of banks. I hate to think a fair number of people out there in Roxbury or Mattapan or Dorchester are being denied because of the color of their skin or the location of property they want to purchase. I would hit the ceiling about that" (Marantz 1989a).

And bankers, at least some of them, slowly grasped that this story had the potential to change things for them as well. In June 1989 the president of Bank of New England remarked, "Everybody involved needs to abandon old ideas about how this will be solved. Certainly banks will have to stop saying 'we've never done it this way before' or 'our current policies prevent us from doing that' or 'it's not my problem, let's give it to the government'" (Marantz 1989b).

Up until January 11, 1989, the Community Reinvestment Act was a little-known and little-used law in Boston. One group, the Massachusetts Urban Reinvestment Advisory Group (MURAG), had reached agreements with banks in the first few years after the 1977 passage of the law. By 1989 MURAG and its leader were under investigation by government agencies and had stopped seeking to win commitments from banks for low-income communities. ACORN's Boston chapter had won a good low-cost checking account agreement from Shawmut Bank in 1987, but that was the sum total of all the Community Reinvestment Act (CRA) work done in Boston's neighborhoods in several years.

Out of many meetings and conversations during the next few months emerged a community coalition. After many hours of deliberation about who would be part of this coalition, a labor union, two neighborhood groups, two CDCs, and MAHA's Homebuyers Union became the Community Investment Coalition (CIC). Local 26 Hotel Restaurant Workers Union brought to the table an aggressive, confrontational style that was bound to be noticed by the banks. Greater Roxbury Neighborhood Authority lacked grassroots punch but featured a core group of experienced nonprofit professionals who were passionate about their neighborhood. Dudley Street Neighborhood Initiative was beginning the organizing drive that led the group to gain control, through eminent domain, of substantial parcels of land in the lowest-income census tracts in Boston. Urban Edge and Nuestra Comunidad were respected CDCs with a reputation for getting things done. And MAHA's Homebuyers Union was a group with potential, but less than one year old. It was a formidable coalition, to be sure, but it did not strike fear into the hearts of bankers as it was still an unknown quantity. Diana said of this new alliance, "it was impressive that we were able to put aside some differences we had with each other and begin to focus on the banks." She knew the Homebuyers Union could not take on the banks alone but she was unsure about the chances of the new coalition. How effective could these groups really be? she wondered. She was about to find out.

She was also about to find out a lot about herself. One of the cochairs of the Homebuyers Union, Terry Parson, was packing up and moving to Florida.

Terry was frustrated. "I kind of lost faith in the banks. . . . I've stopped look-ing and my family and I have decided to relocate" (Devine 1989). Terry's departure left a leadership void in the Homebuyers Union that Diana would be asked to fill.

CIC members spent many months putting together a community rein-vestment plan. The plan called for increased lending for affordable-housing developments, new branches, ATMs, and investments in minority-owned businesses (Community Investment Coalition 1989). At the center of the plan was an affordable mortgage program that HBU members thought would make it easier for some in their ranks to buy a home.

CIC released the plan in August and scheduled a community meeting for Sep-tember, when the plan could be formally presented to the bankers—if they showed up. The meeting was held at the William Trotter elementary school in Roxbury, a location most of the city's bankers couldn't find with a map; but some of them came nevertheless. Most sent mid-level executives rather than the CEOs who had been invited. Most of them sat in the back of the room.

The meeting went smoothly enough until Diana spoke. She had already emphasized to the coalition that the banks had to be held accountable. A simple five-word question—"Will you agree to negotiate?"—changed the tone. The bankers agreed to talk about the CIC's plan, but they would not use the word "negotiate." Diana and other members of the Homebuyers Union were insulted by the bankers' attitude. New though she was to the world of com-munity activism, Diana was not willing to settle for the crumbs the bankers were willing to throw at the community. She wanted a deal—a real deal—in writing, negotiated like any other business deal.

With the banks unwilling to negotiate, the CIC kept the pressure on. Com-munity groups planned protests and prepared to file CRA challenges. The *Boston Globe* and *Boston Herald* continued to cover the controversy. A few small banks agreed to negotiate, but the four big Boston banks (Bank of Boston, Shawmut, Bank of New England, and BayBank) were not yet at the table. One of them, however, had misgivings about the "no-negotiation" strategy. The president of Bank of New England was one of the few top executives who actu-ally knew some members of the community. He had a good relationship with Mossik Hacobian of Urban Edge, a CDC in Roxbury and a member of CIC. He talked with Mossik and decided to come to the CIC's first "negotiation" session. It was quite a scene. Twelve community residents, with Diana and fellow Roxbury resident Adrianne Anderson representing MAHA, sat around a table with half a dozen bankers. Not much was accomplished, but the Bank of New England executive got to see that people were serious and prepared, a message he took back to the other bankers.

In preparing for the next meeting, community groups made their first con-cession. The first meeting had been at 7:00 P.M. in a community room at the Dimock-Bragden apartments owned by Urban Edge. Bankers weren't used to these nighttime community meetings. They suggested 7:00 A.M. downtown instead. No way, said the community groups, it's too early and too far from the community. But they did agree to a 7:00 A.M. meeting at Urban Edge in Roxbury. Urban Edge served a catered breakfast to bank presidents and community leaders while the CEOs' limos idled out front. The battle was joined. The negotiations began in earnest and real progress began to be made.

MAHA and its allies kept up the organizing pressure nonetheless. MAHA and the CIC filed challenges to applications by BayBank and State Street Bank to open branches in locations outside Boston's minority neighborhoods. In response to these challenges, BayBank announced an unprecedented commitment to open five new branches and twenty-five ATMs in low-income neighborhoods in Boston. Days later MAHA members led a protest on the Copley Square BayBank branch and a march to the bank president's Back Bay condominium. Protestors delivered a letter to the banker reminding him that branches alone were not enough; affordable mortgages and other loans and investments were a necessary part of being involved in any community.

By December 1989 there was an agreement in principle for loans to affordable-housing developers and minority businesses, and for new branches and ATMs. Missing from the agreement, however, was the issue that had brought banks to the table in the first place: affordable mortgages. The banks offered a Fannie Mae/GE product with one new feature: it allowed low-income buyers to spend even more of their income on mortgage payments than had been previously allowed. While most of the activists supported this feature, it was not enough in itself. The product applied only to single-family homes—not the two- and three-family homes that dominated the heavily minority neighborhoods of Roxbury, Dorchester, and Mattapan.

MAHA members stood firm on the demand for an affordable-mortgage commitment and enlisted the support of the Flynn administration in this cause. Hours before his annual state-of-the-city address, Flynn succeeded in getting Shawmut Bank's president to cut a deal. Flynn used his annual address to announce that Boston banks had agreed to a $30 million one-shot mortgage deal that was 1 percent below the market rate. The Massachusetts Bankers Association (MBA) made its own announcement at the annual Martin Luther King Jr. breakfast, hosted by Reverend Charles Stith of the Organization for a New Equality; but the MBA did not mention the mortgage plan. CIC later made its own announcement, at the Dudley Square library in Roxbury, and laid out all the details of the deal.

The euphoria surrounding the deal was short-lived. The CRA had helped CIC win a huge victory, but implementation would mean another battle. Bank representatives told MAHA members that the 1 percent below-market-rate loans they had agreed to were *adjustable* rate loans. But MAHA and other coalition members had fought for fixed-rate loans. Low-income families simply could not take the risk of an adjustable-rate mortgage loan.

HBU members flooded the banks with postcards. They went to the media. They went to the mayor. The city of Boston came up with $1 million to help further reduce interest rates, but only if the banks offered the loans at below-market rates. Joe Flatley and Clark Zeigler of the Massachusetts Housing Partnership proposed a soft-second loan structure and a $1 million state subsidy. The "soft second" structure included a first mortgage at 75 percent loan-to-value and a second mortgage worth 20 percent of the purchase price. This would allow banks to drop private mortgage insurance and charge interest only on the second mortgage for ten years, with public subsidy payments picking up as much as 75 percent of the buyers' payments on the second loan.

The banks made a counteroffer: they would switch to fixed rates but at only 0.5 percent below market. MAHA members were frustrated but took solace in the assertion by BayBank's president that 0.5 percent was a sustainable rate. This was music to their ears because it meant that this program would be around for a long time to come.

Finally, eighteen months after the original *Globe* article about the Fed study, a mortgage program was announced. Diana Strother hosted a press conference with executives of Shawmut, BayBank, and Bank of Boston. It would take another four months before the program was officially operational, but Diana breathed a sigh of relief. She had won. They had won.

I Was Depressed

A few months later, Florence Hagins was applying for a mortgage. She had seen the house of her dreams—a beautiful two-family home atop Jones Hill in Dorchester. But she was denied the mortgage because the mortgage insurer thought she was a high-risk borrower. "I was depressed," she said, "because the minute I saw this house, I fell in love with it. I never dreamed I would be denied."

A few weeks earlier, Florence had attended an informational session about a mortgage program with a funny name but a great interest rate. She wanted to apply for a soft-second mortgage immediately, but Hillary Frank Pizer, MAHA's lead organizer, told her it would be a few weeks before the program was in operation. Fearing that she might lose the house on Jones Hill if she waited for the soft-second program, Florence applied for a different mortgage. As she sat in her living room the day after being denied, Florence received a call from MAHA telling her that the new soft-second affordable mortgage program was now up and running. She completed her application on a Sunday night, with a loan originator from Shawmut Bank sitting at her kitchen table.

At the informational session a few weeks earlier, Florence had joined MAHA, thinking that membership in MAHA might improve her chances to get a soft-second mortgage. Now, after being denied a standard mortgage and applying for a soft-second, she was on the verge of buying a home of her own. Joining groups did not come naturally to Florence, in spite of her childhood experience of watching her mother fight community battle after battle. As she got older, she thought that community activism was not for her. But her mother had died recently, and she had begun to think about what she had to give to her community.

Florence was impressed by the other women at the MAHA meeting. Diana Strother was not yet ready to buy a house, but she argued forcefully that it was up to the people in that room to show that this program—almost two years in the making—could succeed. A woman named Adrianne Anderson who made too much money to qualify for the soft-second program also pushed the others to apply. "They were there," Florence reflected. "They were the ones who got this started. Here these women spent the last two years negotiating this deal and for it to happen and not benefit them at all—well, I felt like I got it, so I need to do something. That's why I felt that I should keep coming to the meetings."

On January 29, 1991, Florence Hagins closed on the home of her dreams. As it turned out, her loan application won an important victory for affordable housing right off the bat. While banks, MAHA, and MHP had agreed in principle that the program would be available for two- and three- as well as single-family homes, the program opened for business with loans for only single-family homes. Florence's application for a two-family home forced the issue right away, and Shawmut made an exception for the very first soft-second loan, thus setting an important precedent. To the banks' surprise, the organizing did not stop, did not move on to other issues. They had not counted on a group like the HBU—a single-issue group dedicated to home-buying issues. When, after a year, BayBank had made only a handful of soft-second loans, the HBU did some research. They called BayBank loan officers. They walked into branches. They clipped newspaper ads. Nowhere could they find evidence that BayBank even offered the soft-second loan program. The group then invited the president of BayBank Boston to a meeting in Dorchester, where they presented these findings. And, like magic, the number of BayBank soft-second loans suddenly increased. HBU members were learning an important lesson. They had the power to change the banks. "We were very well prepared when we went to meetings. We always knew what we were talking about. If one of us didn't know, the other one would chime in. Many times we would be better prepared than the bankers we were meeting with," Florence recalls.

MAHA next asked Shawmut's president to renew Shawmut's agreement on soft-seconds, an important moment for the program. "It was kind of intimidating," said Florence of negotiating with Boston's leading bankers.

> We had to deal with a heavy dose of attitude at many of these meetings. The bankers would seem to be saying "I don't want to be here, you know, all you black women or whatever, I don't want to do this mortgage, I'm just doing it because I have to"—you know, that type of attitude.
>
> I wasn't intimidated by the titles of these bankers but I was originally worried that they might have more knowledge than I did about various banking products. I never thought that we would be negotiating for millions of dollars across the

table from bankers, but there we were—in both dingy, cramped community rooms and in boardrooms with the fanciest china and silverware.

Fleet Bank, now the nation's seventh-largest bank but then just a brash upstart from Rhode Island, acquired the failed Bank of New England and agreed to honor its commitment to the soft-second program. Fleet, too, came to Dorchester to announce an $8 million commitment at MAHA's office.

Adrianne Anderson, HBU cochair and MAHA board president, came up with the next idea. By the end of 1993 MAHA had added Fleet, Citizens, U.S. Trust, and Boston Safe Deposit and Trust to the original list of three banks that offered the program. Seven banks, seven agreements, and many negotiations. What if, Adrianne wondered, we could get all of the banks in the same room at the same time and reach multiyear agreements with them?

Florence was skeptical. "That ain't gonna work," Florence thought at the time. "They didn't want to do one year, never mind three or five years."

While nervous about its chances of success, HBU members embraced the idea and invited Boston's banking elite to Roxbury's Morgan Memorial building. There the bankers were met by an overflow crowd of three hundred MAHA members and supporters and a huge scoreboard designed to track the evening's action. "I got so excited when people started coming in. We were all running around getting extra chairs and everything. I was scared to death at that meeting. So many people. I got nervous—I'm not sure I had ever spoken in front of three hundred people before that night," Florence later recalled.

Adrianne's plan worked to perfection. By the end of the evening, MAHA had won commitments for $93 million in Soft Second Program (SSP) mortgages and many banks had made five-year commitments. Bank of Boston officials had told MAHA organizers just hours earlier that the bank would make a three-year promise, but the bank increased its commitment on the spot after seeing competitors make five-year pledges. At the conclusion of the meeting MAHA members knew that this "one-shot" mortgage program would last at least until the end of the decade.

Florence and her daughter Andraea brought fifteen or twenty people to the meeting. "I told people that this meeting was important to me and they came. My neighbors came, my friends came, my aunt came. I wasn't sure if they would come, but they did. And they all thought 'Wow, what a great meeting.' No one had ever seen $93 million put on the table in our community before."

The Numbers Add Up

The SSP compiled some pretty impressive numbers in its first ten years (Campen and Callahan 2001; all statistics in this section are from this paper unless otherwise indicated). Affordability was an important goal of MAHA members from the beginning. Diana and other HBU members sought a mortgage-lending program that would make homeownership possible for those with incomes as low as $15,000. The SSP's remarkable success in achieving this goal can be viewed from three perspectives.

First, an examination of the income levels of all SSP borrowers during the ten-year history of the program shows that 32 percent had incomes of $25,000 or less, 60 percent had incomes of $30,000 or less, and 94 percent had incomes of not more than $40,000. Even Diana's ambitious goal of making home-ownership possible for those with incomes of $15,000 was met—twenty-four SSP homebuyers had incomes between $10,000 and $15,000.

Second, more than half of the 2,100 Boston SSP loans during the ten-year period have gone to low-income homebuyers, or people with incomes at or below 50 percent of the median family income of the greater Boston area; the low-income ceiling has risen from $25,100 in 1991 to $32,750 in 2000.

A third perspective on the affordability provided by the SSP comes from comparing the monthly payments required to buy a house under each of four major targeted mortgage programs operating in Boston. With its minimum payment between $207 and $311 lower than that required by the other targeted mortgage programs, the SSP is by far the most affordable mortgage program in the city.

Reaching Minority Homebuyers

The 1989 Federal Reserve Bank study found that Boston's "housing and mortgage credit markets are functioning in a way that hurts black neighborhoods" (Bradbury, Case, and Dunham 1989). Since its enactment, the SSP has done its part to reverse historic patterns of redlining. Both banks and community groups have targeted their marketing and outreach efforts to neighborhoods of color. These efforts have contributed to the fact that minority homebuyers—who constituted just one-third of Boston's households in 1990—received three-quarters (74.3 percent) of all SSP loans in the city during the program's first nine years.

By the year 2000 blacks and Latinos received percentages of Boston's SSP loans more than twice as great as their 1990 shares. Blacks received 44.5 percent of the city's loans while accounting for 20.6 percent of Boston households, while Latinos, who made up 8.1 percent of the city's households, obtained 21.0 percent of all SSP loans.

An examination of the geographical distribution of Boston's SSP loans shows that the program has been successful in financing affordable homeownership in the city's most underserved neighborhoods. Low- and moderate-income census tracts with more than 50 percent black and Latino residents, which contained just under 16 percent of the city's mortgageable housing units in 1990, have received 37 percent of Boston's SSP loans.

At the same time, however, many minority buyers have been provided with the opportunity of moving out of predominantly minority neighborhoods into predominantly white, moderate-income neighborhoods such as Hyde Park and Roslindale. These two neighborhoods had 28 percent and 21 percent minority residents, respectively, and had the fifth- and sixth-highest income levels among Boston's sixteen major neighborhoods. Although they were home to only 11 percent of Boston's population in 1990, 20 percent of the city's SSP loans were for homes located within their borders. Of these loans, 76 percent went to black or Latino borrowers.

Sustainable Homeownership

When BayBank executives called SSP mortgages at interest rates 0.5 percent below market sustainable, MAHA's Homebuyers Union members recognized that they had a chance to make a long-lasting impact on the city. As MAHA members well understood, there are no real benefits to home*buyers*—and their neighborhoods—unless they are able to remain home*owners*. MAHA members encouraged the staff to initiate a full-fledged homebuyer counseling program in 1991–92. The program would enable MAHA to reach three goals: 1) help promote the fledgling soft-second program; 2) educate buyers with critical and unbiased information about the home-buying process; and 3) assist in organizing neighborhood residents into a strong grassroots constituency for affordable housing.

In 1996 MAHA established its HomeSafe Resource Center, again at the urging of its members, to help low- and moderate-income families succeed as homeowners. When SSP homebuyers become homeowners, they are automatically enrolled as members of HomeSafe and encouraged to participate in free homeowner education classes. Since 1996 more than 2,100 homeowners have graduated from the three-session "Homeowner 201" course, cosponsored by the city of Boston, thereby becoming eligible for discounts from property insurance companies, oil suppliers, home-supply centers, and alarm companies. All HomeSafe members are encouraged to take advantage of assistance with rehab, repair, and maintenance matters and consultation on landlord-tenant issues. SSP homeowners are especially encouraged to make use of MAHA's comprehensive foreclosure prevention program if and when they experience— or even anticipate—difficulties in making their monthly mortgage payments.

The effectiveness of these measures to promote sustainable homeownership for SSP borrowers is reflected in the program's low delinquency rates. Since 1996 delinquency rates for SSP loans have generally been somewhat lower than the rates for all Massachusetts mortgages. Recently, the SSP delinquency rate was 2.5 percent in Boston (and 2.9 percent statewide), compared to a delinquency rate of 2.9 percent for all mortgages in the state. Furthermore, foreclosures on SSP loans have been rare. By the end of 2000, only five of the 2,112 loans originated by the Boston SSP had ended in foreclosure—a rate of one in 422, or 0.24 percent.

"I lived through a failed mortgage program. This was not going to be another BBURG," said MAHA's Florence Hagins of the ill-fated and ill-conceived Boston Banks Urban Renewal Group mortgage program of the late 1960s and early 1970s (Levine and Harmon, 1992). "We were determined to show the banks that our neighborhoods were good for business and the soft second program has done that."

CRA for Insurance Companies?

For years MAHA and other community-based organizations had also been engaged in a campaign to require insurance companies to do a better job of meeting the needs of lower-income and minority communities in Massachusetts. The success of the SSP and other bank initiatives in low-income and minority Boston neighborhoods lent credibility to these efforts. In 1995 MAHA hired HBU member Sonia Alleyne to direct its efforts to increase insurance company accountability. While efforts to establish insurance counterparts of HMDA and the CRA at the state level fell short, the campaign did result in the enactment of two precedent-setting laws.

MAHA's studies of property-insurance redlining and its community organizing—motivated in part by difficulties that SSP homebuyers had in obtaining homeowners insurance—set the stage for the 1996 passage of the country's most comprehensive property insurer disclosure law. The top twenty-five property insurers in Massachusetts are now required to report on the number of policies, cancellations, and nonrenewals by zip code. Each year, in October, the state then makes this data, as well as industry aggregate loss-ratio data by zip code, available to the public. As a result, property/casualty insurance companies began to provide start-up financial support for MAHA's HomeSafe program. In addition, MAHA has negotiated agreements with ten of the state's top property insurance companies to offer graduates of these classes discounts of 5 to 15 percent on homeowner insurance premiums. MAHA is now able to track property insurer activity in low-income neighborhoods by producing an annual report ranking the top twenty-five companies on how well they are serving the state's underserved zip codes.

MAHA and the Massachusetts Association of Community Development Corporations led the campaign that called attention to the life insurance industry's extremely limited investments in affordable housing, small businesses, and community development in the state—either directly or through financial intermediaries that had been established for that very purpose. Although this campaign did not bring about a full insurance CRA for Massachusetts insurance companies, it did result in significant legislation and increased investment.

This effort first bore fruit for MAHA members in 1997, when the initial securities backed by SSP first mortgages were sold. Packaged by Fannie Mae, the securities offered a rate of return fifty basis points below the market level. Robert Sheridan, CEO of Savings Bank Life Insurance (SBLI), announced at a 1997 MAHA community meeting attended by five hundred people that his company would buy $20 million of these securities over the next ten years. SBLI had already fulfilled 40 percent of that commitment by the end of 2000 by purchasing $8 million of securities backed by SSP first mortgages originated by Citizens Bank. Sheridan equates SBLI's investment in affordable housing with the company's own mission—established by its founder Louis Brandeis—of providing affordable insurance. "This is not charity, this is a sound economic decision," he told a community newspaper after announcing the SSP commitment (Forry 1997).

Three other life insurers were invited to attend this meeting but refused. The MAHA members in attendance each signed a postcard to senior executives of the three missing companies. These postcards, along with cuddly stuffed ostriches from FAO Schwartz were sent to the homes of the executives with their "heads in the sand."

In 1998 the Massachusetts legislature passed a bill that required, as a condition of receiving long-sought tax relief, that the state's life insurance industry and property/casualty insurance industry each establish an investment fund, capitalized at $100 million, to make CRA-type investments throughout the state. One of these funds, the Life Insurance Community Investment Initiative (the Life Initiative), purchased $6 million of SSP mortgage-backed securities—the fund's largest single investment to date.

Since the passage of the 1998 law, life insurers have become more engaged in promoting affordable homeownership. John Hancock Financial Services became the first sponsor (that was not also a mortgage lender) of MAHA's homebuyer classes. SBLI has supplemented its purchases of SSP-mortgage-backed securities with financial support for MAHA's efforts to reach out to more low- and moderate-income homebuyers.

Powerful Action

In a reprise of its successful multibank community meeting five years earlier, MAHA moved into action again in May 1999. This time, with nine banks and two thousand loans on the line, Boston mayor Thomas M. Menino and twelve hundred residents filed in to the Reggie Lewis Athletic Center at Roxbury Community College to see if MAHA could convince banks once again to extend this "one-shot deal." New leaders like Henry Crawford, Gerthy Lahens, and Iolanda Miranda joined Florence Hagins on stage to ask the bankers to make five-year commitments.

Mayor Menino, who earlier had written at MAHA's behest to each of the city's banks asking them to come and make a commitment, summed up the evening perfectly when he took the microphone. "What you have tonight in this room, that's power." Power recognized by the city's financial and political leaders. Power wielded by individuals and neighborhoods not accustomed to winning. Power speaking to power.

The odds are long in each new fight, but the power of organized groups to win meaningful victories for themselves and their communities is what helps keep financial giants accountable to some of the nation's most underserved neighborhoods. With the rise of predatory lending, the consolidation of the financial services industries, and an increasingly technology-driven mortgage market, new challenges abound. Community groups will have to rely on organizing campaigns to force businesses to realize that they often overlook and misunderstand low-income and minority neighborhoods.

Florence Hagins reflected recently on why a group like the Homebuyers Union has been so successful against some of nation's most powerful financial interests. "I think it is because we do what we say we are going to do. Banks and insurance companies can respect that even when they disagree with us. And we have never asked them to give us anything. We are asking them to do business—to make loans. These are things that our neighborhoods deserve. And they know they can't pay us to be quiet."

References

Bradbury, Katharine L., Karl E. Case, and Constance R. Dunham. 1989. Geographic Patterns of Mortgage Lending in Boston, 1982–1987. *New England Economic Review*, Sept./Oct., 3–30.

Campen, James T. 1992. The Struggle for Community Investment in Boston, 1989–1991. In *From Redlining to Reinvestment: Community Responses to Urban Disinvestment*. Ed. Gregory D. Squires. Philadelphia: Temple University Press.

Campen, James T., and Thomas M. Callahan. 2001. *Boston's Soft Second Program: Reaching Low Income and Minority Homebuyers in a Changing Financial Services Environment*. Paper delivered at the Federal Reserve System's Conference on Changing Financial Markets and Community Development, Washington, D.C., April 6. Available online at <www.mahahome.org> and at <www.chicagofed.org/cedric/>.

Community Investment Coalition. 1989. *Community Investment Plan, A Plan to Build and Preserve Affordable Housing and Improve Banking Services in North Dorchester, Roxbury, and Mattapan*. August.

Devine, Kevin. 1989. The Luck of the Draw: Not Many Can Afford "Affordable" Housing. *Boston Ledger*, April 6.

Forry, Ed. 1997. Savings Bank Life Sets a Bold New Standard for Insurers. *Dorchester Reporter*, Sept. 20.

Levine, Hillel, and Lawrence Harmon. 1992. *The Death of an American Jewish Community: A Tragedy of Good Intentions*. New York: Free Press.

Marantz, Steven. 1989a. Inequities Are Cited in Hub Mortgages: Preliminary Fed Finding Is "Racial Bias." *Boston Globe*, Jan. 11.

———. 1989b. Bank of N.E. Official Urges More Community Lending: Driscoll Says "Abandon Old Ideas" about Bank's Roles. *Boston Globe*, June 23.

Stanley A. Lowe and
John T. Metzger

6   A Citywide Strategy:

       The Pittsburgh Community
       Reinvestment Group

The Pittsburgh Community Reinvestment Group (PCRG) was formed in 1988 as a multiracial advocacy coalition for Pittsburgh's neighborhoods. Made up of black and white staff and board members from twenty-seven community organizations, PCRG's goal is to unify Pittsburgh's community advocacy groups and establish working relationships and lending partnerships with bankers through the Community Reinvestment Act (CRA). These financial institutions make investments in low- and moderate-income and African American neighborhoods that promote homeownership, housing rehabilitation, historic preservation, commercial district revitalization, and other real estate and business development implemented or endorsed by the community development corporations (CDCs) and neighborhood organizations that join PCRG.

The Pittsburgh Community Reinvestment Group uses the CRA to expand the base of nongovernmental resources for community-based development. Its emphasis on research increases its ability to negotiate CRA partnerships with financial institutions. These lending partnerships generate credit-eligible mortgage-loan applicants, and have resulted in more than $3 billion in loans so far to Pittsburgh's neighborhoods. The PCRG also helps develop leadership skills in the city's community organizations. The coalition forms political alliances that minimize confrontation over lending practices and promote collaborative relationships between lenders and community groups (Schwartz 1998). Some of the CDCs use the corporate business linkages established by PCRG to create strategic plans for their neighborhoods, but other neighborhoods are not following this path. PCRG is not yet organizing countywide and statewide coalitions to expand its power, as out-of-state financial companies acquire Pittsburgh's banks, high-interest subprime and "predatory" lenders expand their market share, and government and foundation funding for housing and community development diminishes.

This chapter reviews the history and accomplishments of the PCRG, and the lessons learned, from the perspective of the founding organizer and spokesperson (Stanley Lowe), and the first staff member (John Metzger).

Economic Exclusion in Pittsburgh

Pittsburgh is a regional, national, and global financial center, anchored by the headquarters of the interstate financial companies PNC and Mellon Bank. As Pittsburgh's manufacturing base eroded during the 1970s and 1980s, symbolized by the decline of the steel industry, the banking sector boomed. In 1976 Pittsburgh's banks held 2 percent of the deposits in the 250 largest U.S. commercial banks (Noyelle and Stanback 1984, 272–78). By 1993 Pittsburgh's banks controlled $94 billion of the assets in the hundred largest commercial banking companies, with 4 percent of the total, ranking fifth behind New York, San Francisco, Charlotte, and Chicago (Sassen 1994, 63). The concentration of bank deposits per capita in Allegheny County (the urban core county that includes Pittsburgh) was second only to Manhattan (Bangs and Hong 1994).

By the 1980s it was clear that the Pittsburgh economy was generating unequal patterns of employment and wealth. According to the 1990 Census, the city of Pittsburgh had the highest poverty rate for blacks aged eighteen to sixty-four, among fifty of the largest U.S. cities selected in a comparative survey. Pittsburgh also had the highest percentage of unemployed black males between the ages of twenty-five and fifty-four, and the highest racial disparity in this workforce participation rate (Bangs and Hong 1995). The poverty rate for African American female-headed families in the city of Pittsburgh was 56 percent. The racial disparity in this poverty rate was greater than that in any of the forty-eight largest cities in the United States (Bangs and Weldon 1998).

The PCRG was organized in 1988 to leverage investments by these financial institutions into low- and moderate-income and African American neighborhoods in the city of Pittsburgh (Metzger 1992). PCRG was formed because blacks in Pittsburgh were excluded from the financial mainstream, and there were dramatic disparities in lending, financial services, and homeownership between blacks and whites. A national analysis of home loan applications to savings institutions between 1983 and 1988 (before the 1989 amendments to the Home Mortgage Disclosure Act) found that the Pittsburgh metropolitan area had the second-highest racial disparity in home loan rejection rates (Dedman 1989). Pittsburgh's biggest commercial banks were joining the Pittsburgh Partnership for Neighborhood Development, an intermediary organization formed by national and local foundations and Mayor Richard Caliguiri to fund community development corporations (Lurcott and Downing 1987; Metzger 1998). But the banks were reluctant to lend money directly to the city's lower-income and African American neighborhoods (Metzger 1992). The 1990 Census reported that the black homeownership rate in the city of Pittsburgh was only 34 percent, compared to the white homeownership rate of 59 percent. African Americans made up 24 percent of all households but only 15 percent of all homeowners.

The mortgage revenue bonds issued by the Urban Redevelopment Authority (URA) financed below-market-rate home-purchase and renovation loans within the city of Pittsburgh. The tax-exempt revenue bonds were backed by the mortgage insurance of the Federal Housing Administration (FHA) and sold to investors. But these housing finance programs were not reducing racial disparities. From 1987 to 1989 the URA allocated 77 percent of its single-family homeowner financing through the bond-funded and FHA-insured Pittsburgh Home Ownership Program (PHOP). Only 13 percent of PHOP homebuyers during these three years were black, less than the 15 percent of all black homeowners and 24 percent of all black households in Pittsburgh. The URA allocated another 10 percent of its single-family homeowner financing through the bond-funded Home Improvement Loan Program (HILP), which used FHA insurance or HUD Community Development Block Grants (CDBGs) to reduce the risk for bond investors. Again, only 13 percent of HILP homeowners were black.

This racial pattern in tax-exempt mortgage revenue bonds was exacerbated by a geographical shift. After 1987 the URA targeted the PHOP to white middle-income neighborhoods. During the five-year period 1988–92, the dollar volume of PHOP lending surged to $98 million. Fifty-eight percent of this amount was lent to the twenty-eight neighborhoods of the city with a black population of less than 5 percent. During the previous nine years, when the URA had targeted PHOP to racially mixed neighborhoods, these white neighborhoods (mostly in outer locations) had received only 13 percent of PHOP funds.

PHOP financed $56 million in home-purchase loans in the period 1979–87, with nearly two-thirds of this dollar volume in seven racially mixed neighborhoods: a cluster of six on the North Side plus South Oakland, near the University of Pittsburgh. Most of the PHOP loans on the North Side were linked to the Neighborhood Housing Services program, a HUD Urban Development Action Grant, and historic districts (Metzger 1992, 2000a). In South Oakland the PHOP loans were part of the Oakland Plan, a collaborative neighborhood plan (Weiss and Metzger 1987). In two of the seven neighborhoods (historic Manchester and South Oakland), PHOP lending increased the number of homeowners between the 1980 and 1990 Censuses, countering the citywide trend.

The racial and geographical shift in the Pittsburgh Home Ownership Program after 1987 was caused by the biases of secondary-market investors in URA mortgage revenue bonds, and the changing politics in Pittsburgh resulting from the death of Mayor Caliguiri in 1988. The Pittsburgh Community Reinvestment Group was organized that year to reduce these racial and neighborhood disparities in capital access through the Community Reinvestment Act (CRA).

A Multiracial Advocacy Coalition
for Neighborhoods

The catalyst for organizing the PCRG was the Manchester Citizens Corporation (MCC), a leading nonprofit community housing developer based in a predominantly African American historic neighborhood on the city's lower North Side. During the 1960s and early 1970s, MCC and the Pittsburgh History and Landmarks Foundation (PHLF) contested the plans of the Urban Redevelopment Authority to demolish and redevelop blocks of historic homes. The population of the neighborhood was increasingly African American and included households displaced by the URA's massive redevelopment project in the lower Hill District, adjacent to the downtown "Golden Triangle" planned by Richard King Mellon's Allegheny Conference on Community Development. Manchester worked with PHLF to preserve and restore the neighborhood as a historic district and prevent the displacement of residents. The historic preservation foundation provided research assistance, financial programs, and technical support to design and implement rehabilitation plans for Manchester (Kidney 1989; Moe and Wilkie 1997, 119–38). This strategy was replicated in adjacent neighborhoods such as the Central North Side, where the first Neighborhood Housing Services (NHS) program in the country was established after the 1968 riot in Pittsburgh (Metzger 2000a).

The Manchester Citizens Corporation was part of the Northside Leadership Conference, an umbrella advocacy organization that advised the North Side Civic Development Council on housing and economic development activities. In addition, MCC was connected to CDCs in other neighborhoods through its executive director, Stanley Lowe (the coauthor of this chapter), who also directed the Preservation Loan Fund of the Pittsburgh History and Landmarks Foundation. This loan fund (capitalized by the profits from the Station Square historic adaptive reuse project) financed strategic interventions by the CDCs to acquire and preserve buildings threatened by demolition, redevelopment, or abandonment. The CDCs collaborated through the Pittsburgh Partnership for Neighborhood Development, organized by the Ford Foundation in 1983 as the first locally based CDC intermediary in the country. By 1989 the Partnership intermediary network was formalized with its own staff and development fund. The Partnership hired Sandra Phillips, the CDC director in Oakland, as its first executive director. The Federal Reserve Bank of Cleveland then named her to the board of its Pittsburgh branch; previously, Phillips had served on the national consumer advisory council to the Federal Reserve. Meanwhile, the CDCs were creating interorganizational networks with each other ("peer-to-peer" networks), and with local businesses, community groups, government agencies, and institutions ("hub-spoke" networks), to advance strategies for employment training and job placement (Metzger 1998; Harrison and Weiss 1998).

The largest Pittsburgh banks—Mellon Bank and Pittsburgh National Bank (later known as PNC)—had joined the Partnership intermediary as funders and board members. The Partnership was the counterpart to Richard Caliguiri's 1980s downtown development program (known as Renaissance II), and the banks made grants to help fund the operations of the CDCs (Metzger 1998). But neighborhoods such as the Hill District and Homewood-Brushton, where many of the city's African Americans lived, were still redlined by financial institutions and neglected by the URA. In 1988 the holding company for Union National Bank, a large bank headquartered in Pittsburgh, requested approval from the Federal Reserve for its merger with Pennbancorp. Union National Bank operated a branch in Manchester but did not lend money in the neighborhood. Unlike the city's other large downtown commercial banks, Union National was not part of the Partnership intermediary.

The Manchester Citizens Corporation and Stanley Lowe of PHLF convened a citywide coalition to invoke the CRA during the regulatory application process. With technical assistance from the National Training and Information Center, the PCRG was organized to replicate a strategy used in Chicago (U.S. Senate Committee on Banking, Housing, and Urban Affairs 1988). MCC and PHLF analyzed the Home Mortgage Disclosure Act statements and annual reports of the banks; recruited nineteen other CDCs and neighborhood groups through the Northside Leadership Conference and the Partnership; organized committees and scheduled informational meetings; and gathered credit needs assessments from each member of the coalition, combining these into a CRA lending program. The PCRG overlapped with the other interorganizational networks created by the CDCs. After a series of meetings and neighborhood tours, Union National Bank agreed to implement PCRG's five-year, $109 million CRA lending program and to join the Partnership CDC intermediary (Metzger 1992).

The Union National Bank lending agreement stimulated competition among the banks in Pittsburgh to make loans and expand their services in low- and moderate-income and African American neighborhoods, creating demand and strengthening the real estate and business ventures of the CDCs through direct investments in their key projects and supplemental investments in homes and businesses. This competition also generated more resources for the neighborhood historic preservation activities of the Pittsburgh History and Landmarks Foundation, after the Tax Reform Act of 1986 reduced the federal tax incentives for historic investors (Lowe, Kidney, and Metzger 1991; Moe and Wilkie 1997, 119–38). The Pittsburgh CRA strategy demonstrates how financial institutions can form partnerships with community development corporations and neighborhood groups to rehabilitate historic buildings and districts in redlined areas (Blake and Lowe 1992; Holland 1998).

The financial institutions consult with the PCRG to assess credit needs, identify business opportunities, and develop marketing and loan counseling strategies, contributing annual grants to pay for PCRG's operating expenses. The CDCs use PCRG as a citywide advocacy coalition for reducing financial disparities by race, class, gender, and place through the CRA. The PCRG also generates competition in the financial services sector by informing community leaders, elected officials, and regulators about the CRA performance of Pittsburgh's lending institutions. In this way PCRG is developing leadership for community-based development (Jones 2001). Meanwhile, new advocates and leaders for the city's neighborhoods emerge from the homeowners, tenants, and business entrepreneurs financed and assisted through the CRA lending partnerships.

Organizing Lending Partnerships

Flexible Underwriting

The Union National Bank lending agreement established lending goals in low- and moderate-income census tracts (those with a median household income equal to 80 percent, or less, of the median for the Pittsburgh metropolitan area), and in other eligible census tracts selected by PCRG. Through flexible loan underwriting, the agreement created an affordable conventional home-purchase mortgage product for homeownership in PCRG neighborhoods. Union National reduced the interest rate on these loans by at least one-half of one percent below their prevailing rate; waived points, mortgage insurance, and minimum loan amounts; and increased the loan-to-value and qualifying debt-to-income ratios. To avoid the conservative underwriting preferred by secondary-market investors, Union National agreed to keep these home mortgages in portfolio. The bank consulted with PCRG to resolve any loan defaults. Borrowers without a credit history were not disqualified. With the exception of the rate discount, this flexible underwriting was extended to home improvement loans and second mortgages. The agreement also established lending goals for small businesses—including minority- and woman-owned businesses and nonprofit organizations—and real estate projects by nonprofit CDCs and their for-profit developers. The bank expanded its community development grant-making and internal CRA training programs, and made deposits in a credit union and a black-owned savings and loan, both located in the Hill District (Metzger 1992).

The Union National agreement created a more competitive environment for CRA lending in Pittsburgh. In 1989 Pittsburgh National Bank worked with PCRG and the Urban Redevelopment Authority to redesign the URA's Housing Recovery Program to leverage flexible conventional (non-FHA) loans for home purchase and rehabilitation in PCRG neighborhoods. The gap between the rehabilitation costs and the appraised value of the property upon completion was subsidized by a deferred second mortgage funded by the Pennsylvania Department of Community Affairs. The Housing Recovery Program was more successful at financing black homebuyers than were other URA programs constrained by bond investors. In the pilot program, 69 percent of these combined purchase-rehabilitation loans were made to African Americans, and 51 percent financed households headed by women. Union National Bank (later renamed Integra Bank) responded with its own conventional home-purchase-rehabilitation mortgage, and then extended its multiyear agreement with PCRG, increasing the annual lending goals and expanding the lending area to include low- and moderate-income census tracts outside the city of Pittsburgh but within the metropolitan area. Meanwhile, Pittsburgh National Bank executive Edward Randall became chairman of the Pittsburgh Partnership for Neighborhood Development intermediary, and his bank financed CDC real estate and business development projects (Metzger 1998).

Community Development Advisory Groups

An important aspect of the Union National lending agreement was the establishment of a Community Development Advisory Group (CDAG) to monitor the agreement. The CDAG included the president and senior executives of Union National, a representative from the community development committee of the bank's board of directors, and representatives from the member organizations of PCRG. This CDAG oversight structure was then replicated with each bank that formed a CRA partnership agreement with PCRG. The CDAG advises the CRA lending programs developed with the bank. Through the CDAG, PCRG assesses credit needs, develops loan products and marketing strategies, and refers neighborhood residents for jobs with the financial institution. The bank contributes funds to pay for the operating expenses of research and coalition organizing.

Using the CRA

To initiate the lending partnerships, the PCRG followed the guidelines of the 1989 interagency CRA policy statement by the federal financial regulators, which encouraged proactive negotiations with lending institutions in advance of regulatory applications. But the regulators were notified when financial institutions (outside the Partnership intermediary network) initially resisted the efforts of PCRG to increase their CRA lending. PCRG submitted studies of Home Mortgage Disclosure Act data and branch locations and testimony from neighborhood residents. The coalition advised the city of Pittsburgh and the Pittsburgh Board of Education to put their money in the banks with the strongest CRA lending records and withdraw funds from financial institutions that engaged in redlining (Metzger 1992). Local hospitals and nonprofit institutions also agreed to link their banking accounts to CRA.

The Community Reinvestment Act was amended in 1989 to publicly disclose the regulators' CRA ratings of financial institutions. The Home Mortgage Disclosure Act was also amended to disclose annual loan application registers reporting the race, income, and gender of each loan applicant, the disposition of their application, and the census tract of the property (Fishbein 1992). Previously, the law had mandated disclosure of only the total annual loan originations in each census tract by the reporting institution. These changes caused more competition among the banks. By 1991 PCRG had CRA partnership agreements with nine commercial banks and savings institutions headquartered in the Pittsburgh area.

Fair Lending and Credit Counseling

The disclosure of HMDA loan application registers exposed widespread racial disparities in loan approvals and rejections by income group and neighborhood location, significantly expanding the scope of PCRG's research activities. At the coalition's request, the attorney general of Pennsylvania investigated the racial lending practices of Lincoln Savings Bank, before it was sold to Integra Bank (Massey 1993). Through the CDAGs, PCRG worked with the lenders to reduce the home loan denial rates for African Americans. The financial institutions agreed to establish and fund the Community-Lender Credit Program, a nonprofit credit counseling organization, to qualify disadvantaged households for home-purchase loans in Allegheny County. The CDCs and neighborhood groups in PCRG referred prospective homebuyers to this program. It was later merged into Neighborhood Housing Services (also funded by some of the financial institutions) after NHS formed closer ties to the Northside Leadership Conference and PCRG. Some of the smaller banks joined to create the "Ain't I a Woman" homeownership initiative (named in honor of Sojourner Truth) to assist low-income African American women with the purchase of a home. As a result of these efforts, the PCRG lending institutions increased their home loan approval rates in the city of Pittsburgh. PCRG lenders increased their combined approval rate for African Americans with incomes below $18,000 from 37 percent in 1992 to 56 percent in 1995. In census tracts with an African American population of 50 percent or more, these lenders increased their approval rate from 39 percent in 1992 to 57 percent in 1994. Union National/Integra Bank reported to PCRG that their annual number of home-purchase loan applications (conventional and FHA) from African Americans increased from 68 in 1990 to 340 in 1994, and the denial rate for these applications declined from 53 percent to 17 percent.

Advocacy and Implementation

The lending partnerships generated measurable increases in community loans. Table 6.1 shows the lending by Integra Bank from 1988 through 1994, reported under the partnership agreement with the PCRG. The bank invested $651 million during these seven years in low- and moderate-income census tracts and other areas and borrowers targeted by PCRG. Fifty-eight percent financed small business development during an economic recession, 35 percent was

TABLE 6.1. Integra Bank Lending Partnership with PCRG, 1988–1994

Year	Amount Lent	Small Business	Real Estate	Home Loans
1988	$ 10,281,925	$ 7,701,575	$ 402,400	$ 2,177,950
1989	32,593,910	15,365,098	7,980,000	9,248,812
1990	28,402,455	13,936,089	1,525,000	12,941,366
1991	84,515,636	61,964,614	4,704,900	17,846,122
1992	123,987,299	68,260,724	14,367,900	41,358,675
1993	179,788,734	105,382,002	5,359,900	69,046,832
1994	191,511,543	106,841,841	9,528,005	75,141,697
7-Year Total	651,081,502	379,451,943	43,868,105	227,761,454

Source: Partnership for the Future between Pittsburgh Community Reinvestment Group and Integra Bank of Pittsburgh (Nov. 1995).

home lending, and 7 percent financed real estate projects by CDCs and for-profit developers. The bank's lending increased dramatically after the federal disclosure amendments took effect in 1990. PCRG and the Pittsburgh History and Landmarks Foundation also designed small business and community development lending programs with Mellon Bank, and organized a consortium of eleven banks to finance existing small businesses in low- and moderate-income historic neighborhoods (Holland 1998). In addition to creating these lending partnerships, PCRG worked with the banks to preserve and expand their system of neighborhood branches during the financial mergers of the early 1990s. The number of branches operated by the PCRG financial institutions in low- and moderate-income census tracts in Pittsburgh increased from forty-four in 1988 to fifty-seven by 1994. For the CDCs, the branches serve as anchors for revitalizing neighborhood commercial districts.

The CRA lending partnerships leveraged construction and longer-term financing for the housing and economic development projects of the CDCs in PCRG neighborhoods. But the implementation of these projects required greater cooperation and support from the Urban Redevelopment Authority of Pittsburgh. In 1992 Mulugetta Birru, a CDC director, was named the executive director of the URA. Birru was from the Homewood-Brushton Revitalization and Development Corporation—an important CDC in the PCRG and the Partnership intermediary—and was on the national consumer advisory council to the Federal Reserve. The following year, state representative Thomas Murphy was elected mayor of Pittsburgh. During the 1970s Murphy had been a community organizer on the North Side, where he worked with Thomas Cox, a North Side CDC director who later headed the CDC intermediary organization in Cleveland. Murphy named Cox deputy mayor and then chairman of the URA. PCRG's organizer and spokesperson (a coauthor of this chapter) was named director of neighborhoods and planning policy and then executive director of the Housing Authority of the City of Pittsburgh (HACP), where Murphy became board chairman. The new mayor held sixty-seven meetings across the city's eighty-eight neighborhoods to improve government service delivery, signed a memorandum of understanding between PCRG and Integra Bank, and in 1995 spoke at the "Save the CRA" public hearing in the Pittsburgh city-county building, when Congress was debating proposals to weaken the federal banking law. The new CRA regulation had been completed earlier that year, replacing the twelve assessment factors with three performance-based ratings of lending, investments, and services.

The Murphy administration created a public-private development finance fund and formed citywide housing and industrial development corporations to plan and implement real estate projects with developers and CDCs, outside the foundation-funded Partnership intermediary. HACP secured federal grants from the HUD HOPE VI program to redevelop and renovate public housing, forming partnerships with CDCs in Manchester and the Hill District. The Murphy agenda created tension within PCRG, when the foundations and the city reduced their financial support for CDCs (Metzger 1996, 1998). Meanwhile, the holding company for Integra Bank was acquired by National City Corporation, an out-of-state banking company headquartered in Cleveland. National City executives did not renew the Integra lending agreement but instead formed a CDAG to work with PCRG. The holding company for Mellon Bank began to divest its consumer and retail banking activities, shifting its focus to financial services for the wealthy. In 2001 Mellon Financial Corporation sold most of its bank branches to Citizens Financial Group of Rhode Island, owned by the Royal Bank of Scotland.

By then thirteen banks and savings institutions had CRA partnership agreements with the Pittsburgh Community Reinvestment Group. The four largest (with assets of more than $2 billion) had CRA performance ratings of "outstanding"; the other nine had CRA ratings of "satisfactory." From 1996 through 1999, these thirteen institutions and their affiliates combined to originate more than $50 million in home loans each year in the low- and moderate-income census tracts of Allegheny County, and more than $20 million in home loans each year in the African American census tracts.

One of the PCRG's key goals is to increase affordable conventional home-purchase lending in the city's low- and moderate-income and African American neighborhoods. Many of these areas remain underserved by the bond-funded mortgage programs of the Urban Redevelopment Authority. CDCs such as the Bloomfield-Garfield Corporation organize against the "fast foreclosure" policies of the Federal Housing Administration and other FHA program abuses by realtors, contractors, and mortgage companies. HUD foreclosures accelerate public-private disinvestment and depopulation in lower-income urban neighborhoods (Metzger 2000b). Through the CRA lending partnerships, the CDCs and neighborhood groups gain more control over home-lending practices in their communities. The thirteen PCRG lenders account for three-fifths of the conventional home-purchase lending in the low- and moderate-income and African American census tracts of the city of Pittsburgh.

The Secondary Mortgage Market

The PCRG lending institutions are attempting to develop a stronger secondary mortgage market for their CRA loans, to replenish the sources of funds. During 1995–96, only 6 percent of the single-family home-loan purchases by Fannie Mae and Freddie Mac in the Pittsburgh metropolitan area were in low- and moderate-income census tracts. In 1998 the PCRG and its lending partners worked with Fannie Mae to design an affordable home-purchase mortgage product. But the Fannie Mae loan underwriting for Pittsburgh is not competitive with the more flexible terms offered by the conventional home-purchase programs created through PCRG. Instead, Fannie Mae is securitizing the URA's bond-funded loans for sale to secondary-market investors (Boxall and Silver 2001).

Problems with the New CRA

In addition to these secondary-market problems, Mellon Bank has not been competitive with the other PCRG lenders in originating home loans, despite its size advantage. Mellon has been originating home loans through its national mortgage subsidiary based in Texas (Mellon Mortgage Company). In the low- and moderate-income and African American census tracts of Allegheny County, Mellon's home-loan denial rate has far exceeded the combined rate of the twelve other PCRG lenders each year from 1996 through 1999. Despite this HMDA evidence, the Office of the Comptroller of the Currency (OCC) assigned Mellon a CRA rating of "outstanding" in its 1997 examination, the same rating that the bank received in 1993 and 1995. The frequency of CRA examinations is reduced for banks with "outstanding" ratings.

Mellon's multistate performance evaluation did not discuss HMDA loan-denial statistics from 1996 or 1997. The OCC's fair lending review concluded that "there was no evidence in the fair lending examination to indicate any discriminatory practices had occurred against protected classes in Mellon's lending activities." According to the PCRG's analysis, however, Mellon received more home-loan applications than any other financial institution in the city of Pittsburgh in 1996. But the OCC warned of less loan demand and more lending risk in the city: "Pittsburgh has a declining population, and housing activity is subdued. The demographic trends suggest that the city's economy will not perform as well as the rest of the nation."

In 2001 Mellon sold its branches to Citizens Financial, a Rhode Island banking company with an "outstanding" CRA rating despite its questionable fair lending record. The Inner City Public Interest Law Center and the Delaware Community Reinvestment Action Council have both challenged this CRA rating.

These regulatory enforcement problems undermine the CRA lending partnerships organized by the PCRG. The OCC regulates the other two large downtown commercial banks, PNC and National City. Both have received "outstanding" CRA ratings since the mid-1990s. PNC is substituting a Freddie Mac secondary-market home-purchase loan (used by its national mortgage company) for the conventional loans in Pittsburgh that are kept in portfolio (Boxall and Silver 2001). After acquiring Integra, National City Bank of Pennsylvania closed seven branches in low- and moderate-income census tracts in the Pittsburgh metropolitan area, its primary CRA assessment area. In the bank's 2000 performance evaluation, the OCC used PCRG as the source of community contacts: "Although Pittsburgh has been successful in moving towards a service-based economy, numerous pockets of high unemployment and poverty continue to plague lower-income neighborhoods. Community groups noted a lack of basic services, e.g., grocery stores, dry cleaners, hardware stores, and banking facilities in these neighborhoods." But the OCC rated National City as "outstanding" on the CRA service test, despite the branch closings and community concerns reported in the performance evaluation.

The revised CRA regulation emphasizes a metropolitan "performance context" of market information and business strategy, over institutional market share comparisons. After the new regulation was released in 1995, CACI Marketing Systems announced its CRA compliance software contract with the Federal Deposit Insurance Corporation. CACI is a leading federal contractor that designed the ACORN system of neighborhood cluster profiles, using race-based stereotypes of consumer lifestyles and spending behavior to guide the investment and location decisions of financial institutions and national real estate investors (Metzger 2001). The racial typologies of CACI disadvantage African American neighborhoods such as Manchester, where PCRG was organized in 1988. In its 1996 book on national demographics, CACI Marketing Systems classified the Manchester zip code (15233) as "Low Income Southern Blacks." CACI's estimates of median household income ranked Manchester eighty-fourth out of ninety-one zip codes in Allegheny County. But Manchester was ranked at the bottom (ninety-first) on CACI's spending potential index for home loans and home repairs (CACI Marketing Systems 1996). The federal information contractor ranked historic Manchester at the bottom for home-loan demand in Allegheny County, despite the increase in owner-occupied units within the neighborhood during the 1980s (reported by the Census), and the CRA lending programs leveraged by the Manchester Citizens Corporation, the Pittsburgh History and Landmarks Foundation, and PCRG.

The Importance of Research

To organize and sustain its CRA partnerships with financial institutions, the Pittsburgh Community Reinvestment Group prepares research studies of HMDA reports and other corporate filings with regulators. This research analyzes the lending patterns, branch locations, loan products, and business strategies of the bank. After the disclosure of CRA ratings and HMDA loan-application registers began in 1990–91, PCRG published an annual report summarizing the lending activity of its partner financial institutions. PCRG uses the annual studies to disclose racial and neighborhood disparities in capital access, assess community credit needs, monitor the progress in lending through the CRA partnership agreements, and report on the changing dynamics of home finance in low- and moderate-income and African American neighborhoods, such as the growth of mortgage banking and subprime lending. In recent years the geographic scope of the study has expanded to include Allegheny County.

The CDCs in PCRG use the annual report as a reference in negotiating loans. The financial institutions use the annual report to inform their loan-marketing programs and competitive strategies. PCRG audits HMDA-loan application registers by analyzing the mortgage records of the Allegheny County recorder of deeds, which exposes and corrects HMDA reporting problems. The annual lending studies are an educational tool for elected officials and government agencies that provide political and financial support for community-based development. The reports also generate media coverage, spotlighting lending disparities and the work of the CDCs.

This research allows PCRG to place its CRA lending partnerships in the larger context of the home-finance market in Allegheny County. In the county's low- and moderate-income census tracts, the PCRG financial institutions originated $67–70 million in home loans each year in 1996, 1998, and 1999, and $53 million in 1997. But the PCRG market share of all home loans in these areas declined from one-half in 1996 to less than one-fourth by 1999. This is explained by the home refinancing boom of the late 1990s. In the city of Pittsburgh, the dollar volume of home refinancings in low- and moderate-income census tracts reached $70 million during 1999. Mortgage companies and subprime lenders originate most of these loans, as well as an increasing number of home purchase and improvement loans. There is a similar pattern in the African American census tracts of Allegheny County, where the PCRG lenders originated $20–24 million in home loans each year during 1996–1999. In the city of Pittsburgh, home refinancings in these areas reached $38 million by 1999.

Through targeted marketing strategies, high-interest subprime and "predatory" lenders solicit applications from lower-income and African American neighborhoods, where Fannie Mae and Freddie Mac are reluctant to buy loans. The subprime companies have higher loan rejection rates and are more likely to foreclose on the homes they finance. These lenders require homebuyers with inadequate credit scores to pay an interest rate surcharge, in addition to buying mortgage insurance and pledging their home as collateral. Their targeted marketing is guided by the race-based neighborhood cluster profiles created by national demographics companies and the leading credit bureaus, such as Equifax and Experian (Metzger 2001). During the late 1990s the subprime lenders captured a growing market share of home-loan applications in low- and moderate-income and African American census tracts in Allegheny County. In the African American areas, subprime home loan applications were one-half of the total. Through research, PCRG can organize to reverse these trends by strengthening the housing finance regulatory system to support the marketing and origination of more affordable CRA home loan products with flexible underwriting.

Strategic Neighborhood Planning

PCRG's CRA advocacy work establishes linkages between the CDCs and Pittsburgh's corporate world, leveraging private resources to fund and finance the implementation of neighborhood plans. The banks grant CDC operating funds and purchase low-income housing tax credits through the Pittsburgh Partnership for Neighborhood Development intermediary (Metzger 1998). The CRA advocacy of PCRG led the Partnership intermediary to collaborate with the Urban Redevelopment Authority to plan the Crawford Square redevelopment in the lower Hill District, an African American neighborhood. PNC Bank and the other large downtown commercial banks joined to finance Crawford Square with loans and tax credits. This neighborhood redevelopment— built by a for-profit developer with CDC marketing support—includes more than three hundred units of mixed-income housing and a shopping center with a PNC branch. The comprehensive neighborhood plan uses new urbanism design principles (Deitrick and Ellis 2001).

The public-private implementation strategy for Crawford Square serves as a model for the housing construction program of the Murphy administration. PCRG works with Mayor Murphy to secure additional public and private funding for neighborhood plans, beyond the foundation monies of the Partnership intermediary and the resources of the Urban Redevelopment Authority. These funds include HOPE VI public housing community revitalization grants from HUD and state tax credits to business corporations in exchange for their long-term operating support of a CDC (Metzger 1996, 1998). The PCRG organizations receive strategic planning assistance from the Pittsburgh History and Landmarks Foundation (which sponsors the annual lending studies), and the National Trust for Historic Preservation. For the Bloomfield-Garfield Corporation, the CRA lending partnerships are key in implementing plans for the Penn Avenue commercial corridor, an area in which the historic foundation finances building preservation, Integra/National City has opened a new branch and also finances housing and commercial development, and Allegheny Valley Bank maintains a branch and finances mixed-use commercial rehabilitation (National Community Reinvestment Coalition 1997; Holland 1998). But other neighborhoods represented by PCRG have not yet developed strategic plans.

Lessons from Pittsburgh

Since 1988 the CRA strategy of the Pittsburgh Community Reinvestment Group has catalyzed the expansion of bank lending, investments, and services in low- and moderate-income and African American neighborhoods of Pittsburgh. But economic disparities persist, both within Allegheny County and across the metropolitan area. From 1982 to 1997 the population of the metropolitan area declined by 8 percent, but the developed land area increased by 43 percent (Fulton et al. 2001). Pittsburgh's financial institutions are reluctant to invest in the low-income communities of the Monongahela River valley. But in the suburban North Hills highway corridor, Mellon Bank financed the corporate headquarters and industrial park of Fore Systems Inc., a rapidly growing computer switch manufacturing company formed by computer scientists at Carnegie Mellon University. The bank provided a $70 million long-term loan at a below-market rate, and the Allegheny County Department of Economic Development lent another $10 million in below-market funds for the balance of the project cost (Bull 1995). Meanwhile, Mellon was rejecting six out of ten home-loan applications in the low- and moderate-income and African American census tracts of Allegheny County. These bank investment patterns exacerbate the disparities created by suburban sprawl.

The ability of PCRG to organize countywide and statewide advocacy coalitions is undermined by staff turnover. In 2000–2001 three executive directors of PCRG resigned. Some of the CDCs continue to suffer from high staff turnover (a problem that began in the early 1990s), and public-sector partners such as the Housing Authority have financial management problems. The CDCs are not developing enough replacement apartments to accommodate the households displaced by public housing redevelopment in Pittsburgh. Instead, HUD vouchers are converting single-family homes into absentee-owned rental properties.

To implement the CRA lending partnerships, CDCs must acquire technical skills in loan underwriting, real estate development, and public-private financial packaging. Renewed efforts are needed to build and sustain the capacity, skills, and leadership of the CDCs and of PCRG, their CRA advocacy organization. PCRG can benefit from research and technical assistance collaborations with universities and continued involvement in national advocacy coalitions.

The Pittsburgh case is a leading example of CRA advocacy by a citywide community development coalition. With HMDA research, the Pittsburgh Community Reinvestment Group focuses attention on racial and geographical lending disparities in Pittsburgh and Allegheny County. Its emphasis on research supports the negotiation and implementation of the CRA partnerships. The Community Development Advisory Groups are a collaborative forum with financial institutions to design and monitor lending programs and related initiatives. The Community Reinvestment Act advocacy of the PCRG coalition requires a supportive regulatory environment, and strategic political alliances, to produce the collaborative partnerships with financial institutions. But PCRG will have to revisit the confrontational tactics of the past in order to respond effectively to the growth of subprime lending, national interstate banking consolidations, and other financial services trends that disadvantage low- and moderate-income and African American communities.

References

Bangs, Ralph L., and Jun Hyun Hong. 1994. *Economic Benchmarks: Economic Indices for the City of Pittsburgh and Allegheny County.* Pittsburgh: University Center for Social and Urban Research, University of Pittsburgh.

———. 1995. *Black and White Economic Conditions in the City of Pittsburgh.* Pittsburgh: University Center for Social and Urban Research, University of Pittsburgh.

Bangs, Ralph L., and S. Laurel Weldon. 1998. *Economic Benchmarks: Updated Indices for the City of Pittsburgh and Allegheny County.* Pittsburgh: University Center for Social and Urban Research, University of Pittsburgh.

Blake, Jennifer L., and Stanley Lowe. 1992. *Using the Community Reinvestment Act in Low-Income Historic Neighborhoods.* Information Series No. 56. Washington, D.C.: National Trust for Historic Preservation.

Boxall, Patrick, and Joshua B. Silver. 2001. Performance of the GSEs at the Metropolitan Level. *Cityscape: A Journal of Policy Development and Research* 5 (3): 145–217.

Bull, John M. R. 1995. North Hills Plant, Offices Planned. *Pittsburgh Post-Gazette.* Sept. 29.

CACI Marketing Systems. 1996. *The Sourcebook of Zip Code Demographics: 1996 Edition.* Arlington, Va.

Dedman, Bill. 1989. Blacks Turned Down for Home Loans from S&Ls Twice as Often as Whites. *Atlanta Journal-Constitution.* Jan. 22.

Deitrick, Sabina, and Cliff Ellis. 2001. The Importance of Design: New Urbanism and Community Revitalization. *Shelterforce* 116 (March/April): 18–20.

Fishbein, Allen J. 1992. The Ongoing Experiment with "Regulation from Below": Expanded Reporting Requirements for HMDA and CRA. *Housing Policy Debate* 3 (2): 601–36.

Fulton, William, et al. 2001. *Who Sprawls Most? How Growth Patterns Differ across the U.S.* Washington, D.C.: Center on Urban and Metropolitan Policy, Brookings Institution.

Harrison, Bennett, and Marcus Weiss. 1998. *Workforce Development Networks: Community-Based Organizations and Regional Alliances.* Thousand Oaks, Calif.: Sage Publications.

Holland, Dan. 1998. Historic Preservation of Pittsburgh's Neighborhood Business Districts. Paper presented to the National Town Meeting of the National Main Street Center, Pittsburgh. May 17–20.

Jones, Diana Nelson. 2001. Garfield's Aggie Brose Sees the Payoff of More Than Twenty-five Years of Activism. *Pittsburgh Post-Gazette.* July 29.

Kidney, Walter C. 1989. *A Past Still Alive: The Pittsburgh History and Landmarks Foundation Celebrates Twenty-Five Years.* Pittsburgh: Pittsburgh History and Landmarks Foundation.

Lowe, Stanley A., Walter C. Kidney, and John Metzger. 1991. The Pittsburgh Experience: Financing Preservation Projects in Low- and Moderate-Income Districts. *Historic Preservation Forum* 5 (May/June): 26–33.

Lurcott, Robert H., and Jane A. Downing. 1987. A Public-Private Support System for Community-Based Organizations in Pittsburgh. *Journal of the American Planning Association* 53 (autumn): 459–68.

Massey, Steve. 1993. Lincoln Savings' Loans Probed. *Pittsburgh Post-Gazette.* Dec. 22.

Metzger, John T. 1992. The Community Reinvestment Act and Neighborhood Revitalization in Pittsburgh. In *From Redlining to Reinvestment: Community Responses to Urban Disinvestment.* Ed. Gregory D. Squires. Philadelphia: Temple University Press.

———. 1996. Reinventing Housing in Pittsburgh: An Interview with Mayor Tom Murphy. *Shelterforce* 86 (March/April): 13–18.

———. 1998. Remaking the Growth Coalition: The Pittsburgh Partnership for Neighborhood Development. *Economic Development Quarterly* 12 (Feb.): 12–29.

———. 2000a. Neighborhood Housing Services in Historical Perspective. Paper presented to the Annual Housing Forum of the Federal Home Loan Bank of Pittsburgh, and the Pennsylvania Housing Finance Agency, Hershey, Pennsylvania. Feb. 10.

———. 2000b. Planned Abandonment: The Neighborhood Life Cycle Theory and National Urban Policy. *Housing Policy Debate* 11 (1): 7–40.

———. 2001. Clustered Spaces: Racial Profiling in Real Estate Investment. Paper prepared for the International Seminar on Segregation in the City, Lincoln Institute of Land Policy, Cambridge, Massachusetts. July 28.

Moe, Richard, and Carter Wilkie. 1997. *Changing Places: Rebuilding Community in the Age of Sprawl.* New York: Henry Holt.

National Community Reinvestment Coalition. 1997. *Models of Community Lending: Neighborhood Revitalization through Community/Lender Partnerships.* Washington, D.C.

Noyelle, Thierry J., and Thomas M. Stanback. 1984. *The Economic Transformation of American Cities.* Totowa, N.J.: Rowman & Allanheld.

Sassen, Saskia. 1994. *Cities in a World Economy.* Thousand Oaks, Calif.: Pine Forge Press.

Schwartz, Alex. 1998. From Confrontation to Collaboration? Banks, Community Groups, and the Implementation of Community Reinvestment Act Agreements. *Housing Policy Debate* 9 (3): 631–62.

U.S. Senate Committee on Banking, Housing and Urban Affairs. 1988. *Community Reinvestment Act.* Washington, D.C.: U.S. Government Printing Office.

Weiss, Marc A., and John T. Metzger. 1987. Technology Development, Neighborhood Planning, and Negotiated Partnerships: The Case of Pittsburgh's Oakland Neighborhood. *Journal of the American Planning Association* 53 (autumn): 469–77.

Allen J. Fishbein

7

Filling the Half-Empty Glass:

The Role of Community Advocacy in Redefining the Public Responsibilities of Government-Sponsored Housing Enterprises

The Affordable Housing Program is the "crown jewel" of the Federal Home Loan Bank System.

—Timothy O'Neill, Federal Housing Finance Board chairman, remarks to a Federal Home Loan Bank System conference, June 6, 2001

Our record homeownership rate, I'm convinced, would not have been reached without CRA and its close relative, the Fannie [Mae]/Freddie [Mac] [affordable housing] requirements.

—Ellen Seidman, Director of the Office of Thrift Supervision, speech before the Greenlining Institute, October 2, 2001

Effective advocacy by national community groups is directly responsible for the enactment of affordable housing requirements for three government-sponsored housing enterprises (GSEs). These are the Federal Home Loan Bank system (FHLBs or FHLB system), Fannie Mae, and Freddie Mac. Enacted a decade or more ago, these regulatory requirements are readily embraced today by the GSEs as an integral part of their public purpose. The funding and loans generated by the affordable housing requirements are mostly taken for granted by nonprofit low-income housing practitioners, who have come to regard these resources as indispensable to their work. Yet the origins of these mandates are not well known, even among the very constituencies that benefit most from them. This chapter examines how these requirements came about and the important role that community advocacy played in achieving them.

Even the most fervent proponents of these mandates probably could not have imagined the important impact they would have on expanding home ownership and rental housing opportunities for low- and moderate-income families. While each of these GSEs is publicly chartered and was established to perform a public purpose, it was only after affordable housing requirements were imposed on them that these financial institutions began to be viewed as important contributors to serving low-income housing needs. The FHLBs' requirements collectively generate between $200 million and $265 million annually in grants for low-income housing development and have helped to finance nearly 315,000 badly needed units since 1990. Fannie Mae's and Freddie Mac's affordable housing goals require them to devote at least 50 percent of their mortgage business to low- and moderate-income families, more than doubling what these companies were doing prior to the enactment of this mandate.

The GSEs and Their Missions

The FHLB system, Fannie Mae, and Freddie Mac are all considered government-sponsored enterprises, although the FHLBanks do not always refer to themselves this way. The FHLB system is organized differently from the other two and performs a somewhat different function than do Fannie Mae and Freddie Mac, the two secondary-market GSEs. However, each is chartered by Congress to perform certain functions in support of the nation's system of housing finance.

As GSEs, each receives significant public benefits and indirect advantages afforded by their federal agency status. In return, Congress has established through statute certain public purposes for the GSEs. The benefits include exemptions from state and local taxes and conditional access to a line of credit from the U.S. Treasury. But the most important benefit these companies get from their GSE status is that their borrowing costs are lower than the costs for fully private financial institutions, because the financial markets perceive an implicit federal guarantee of GSE securities.

Despite their agency status, each of these entities is owned by private shareholders and operated for profit or for the mutual benefit of their owner-members. Hence the GSEs are hybrid public-private financial institutions. The GSEs were created for the public purposes defined in their charters. While chartered for somewhat different reasons, all three are expected to promote housing finance and homeownership by bringing stability and liquidity to the housing markets. Each has been around in one form or another for years, but all three have grown greatly in size, particularly in recent years. Consequently, it is difficult to overestimate the impact of the GSEs on the nation's housing finance system or, for that matter, on the overall economy. Hence, the public's stake in their activities is huge (HUD 2000).

Notwithstanding their importance to the housing market, the GSEs' role in financing housing was not very well understood by local community groups when concerns about mortgage redlining practices first became an issue in the early 1970s. Capitol Hill insiders referred to the FHLB system at the time "as the best kept secret in Washington," and for the most part, the FHLBs liked it that way.

Even less was commonly known about Fannie Mae and Freddie Mac, which, as secondary-market institutions, tended to operate in shadowy obscurity. Nor for the most part did community groups understand or appreciate the influence wielded by these two companies, through their underwriting and appraisal guidelines, over the types of mortgage products available to would-be homeowners and rental property owners. However, local groups fighting to curb redlining soon learned that changing the way these companies treated loans made to older urban neighborhoods was critical to their efforts to promote community reinvestment.

The Federal Home Loan Banks

The FHLB system was established in 1932 to provide support for the short-term funding needs of the nation's savings and loan institutions during the Great Depression. The system consists of twelve regional wholesale banks (District Banks) that make loans to their member financial institutions (they do not make direct loans to homebuyers). The FHLBs borrow money in the capital markets and then lend that money to mortgage lending institutions that are shareholders. These shareholders, also called members, then can use this money to make housing loans to their communities.

The FHLBs are privately owned corporations that are publicly chartered. While no federal dollars are invested in them, their federal agency status enables the FHLBs to borrow money at much cheaper rates than typical private entities could. With more than $600 billion in assets, there are approximately 7,600 members of the system, including commercial banks (which now are the majority of the system's members), along with thrifts, some credit unions, and even a few insurance companies.

The funds the FHLBs lend to members/shareholders are called "cash advances." The interest charged on these cash advances generates the primary source of earnings for the system. The FHLBs operate in the manner of a cooperative financial institution. Consequently, they raise funds primarily through consolidated obligations, which are debt securities issued in the capital markets jointly by the District Banks. In 2000 the system raised more than $591 billion on the capital markets.

For most of their history, the FHLBs were supervised by a three-member public agency called the Federal Home Loan Bank Board (FHLBB, or Bank Board), which also regulated S&L institutions and ran the Federal Home Loan Mortgage Corporation (Freddie Mac). The FHLBs were originally created to provide a "bankers' bank" for savings institutions. In 1989 Congress abolished the FHLBB and established a new independent public agency, the Federal Housing Finance Board (FHFB), as the FHLBs' regulator.

Fannie Mae and Freddie Mac

Congress established and chartered Fannie Mae and Freddie Mac (the two secondary-market GSEs) as government-sponsored, privately owned corporations to enhance the availability of mortgage credit across the nation during both good and bad economic times. The Federal National Mortgage Association, or Fannie Mae, as it is now called, was chartered in 1938 as a government-held association to buy and hold mortgages insured by the Federal Housing Administration. In 1968 Congress reorganized Fannie Mae as a government-sponsored, privately owned, for-profit corporation. Congress chartered the Federal Home Loan Mortgage Corporation, or Freddie Mac, as it is now called, in 1970, and it was initially a subsidiary of the FHLB system. In 1989 Congress established Freddie Mac as a government-sponsored enterprise that is owned by private investors.

Together, the two secondary-market GSEs dominate the housing finance market, together purchasing about half of the home loans originated by mortgage lenders. The two GSEs have doubled in size since 1993.

Fannie Mae and Freddie Mac fund mortgages by purchasing conforming loans (at present, this means that the mortgage balance must be below $300,800 and the loan-to-value ratio cannot exceed certain limits) directly from the primary mortgage originators, such as commercial banks, savings institutions, and mortgage bankers. They hold these loans in their own portfolios or, more typically, package the loans and sell them to investors as mortgage-backed securities. In this way both types of GSEs provide lenders with cash they need to issue new mortgages.

The U.S. Department of Housing and Urban Development (HUD) is the mission regulator for Fannie Mae and Freddie Mac. Among other things, HUD sets annual minimum percentage-of-business goals for the two GSEs' mortgage purchases, known as the Affordable Housing Goals. To ensure that they are operating within their charters and fulfilling their public missions, these goals require that the enterprises support low-income lending and lending to underserved geographic areas. An independent office within HUD, the Office of Federal Housing Enterprises Oversight (OFHEO) serves as the financial safety and soundness regulator for the secondary market GSEs.

The GSEs: A Mission Glass Half-Empty?

Defining the GSEs' appropriate level of responsibilities for meeting the needs of low- and moderate-income families has been a challenging task since the earliest days of the anti-redlining movement in the 1970s. At the time, S&Ls were the dominant housing lenders, originating more than half of all mortgages. Yet many S&Ls were also the worst redliners. Consequently, the Bank Board, the S&Ls' regulator at the time, became an obvious target for complaints about the lending practices of these institutions.

Even prior to the enactment of the Home Mortgage Disclosure Act (HMDA) and the Community Reinvestment Act (CRA), community activists and several national civil rights organizations challenged the Bank Board to take action to stop redlining. In Illinois a coalition of community groups led by Chicago activist Gale Cincotta used a variety of tactics, including direct actions, to convince the S&L regulator to do more. These groups tied red ribbons around the offices of the Chicago District Bank and pressed the Bank Board to require S&Ls to disclose where they made their mortgages. One of the earliest anti-redlining victories came in 1973, when these local groups convinced the Bank Board to establish a pilot system of voluntary mortgage loan data disclosure for S&Ls (National Commission on Neighborhoods 1979, 81).

Putting the Bank Board on the defensive reaped additional dividends a few years later. In the late 1970s a reform-minded former S&L executive, William McKinney, became the Bank Board's chairman. Under his leadership and with support from the Carter administration, the agency took a strong stand against redlining. In 1978 the Bank Board adopted strong anti-redlining regulations that for the first time prohibited thrifts from discriminating in mortgage lending based on the age or location of a dwelling. McKinney also moved to create an interagency Urban Investment Task Force that eventually launched the Neighborhood Housing Services program. NHS worked to create local community-lender partnerships to help combat disinvestment and neighborhood decline (National Commission on Neighborhoods 1979, 82; Nader and Brown 1989, 18).

McKinney also carved out a new role, albeit a modest one, for the FHLBs when he required the system to establish the Community Investment Fund (CIF). The CIF program was launched as a five-year, $10 billion program. CIF provided $2 billion a year in special cash advances to member institutions for use in "preserving and revitalizing the nation's urban and rural communities" (Nader and Brown 1989, 18). CIF provided targeted advances to members at the FHLBs' cost of funds. McKinney also established an internal technical services infrastructure to support this initiative. An Office of Community Investment was created, along with senior community investment officers at each of the District Banks (FHLBB 1981, 2).

The Bank Board's action quickly advanced it to the head of the line among sister regulators in acting to combat redlining. And while momentum for these initiatives slowed during the two Reagan administrations, the experience with CIF served as an introduction to the FHLB system for community groups. Due to the success of the CIF program, the FHLBs were no longer a "best-kept secret."

Community group concerns about the operations of Fannie Mae and Freddie Mac can also be traced to the 1970s. These groups became convinced that the secondary market GSEs' policies, whether intentional or not, reflected an anti-urban bias, and led to discriminatory effects for minorities and residents of these areas. The closer they looked at the underwriting and appraisal policies and the marketing practices of Fannie Mae and Freddie Mac, the more they became convinced that these two companies contributed to redlining. National Peoples Action (NPA), a national coalition of community groups, the Association of Community Organizations for Reform Now (ACORN), and others complained that Fannie Mae and Freddie Mac practices discouraged conventional lending by banks and thrifts. Of particular concern to these groups was that the secondary-market GSEs' loan-purchase criteria presented obstacles to purchasing mortgages from older urban dwellings, especially when the housing consisted of mixed-use properties located in neighborhoods not exclusively residential or with relatively high vacancy rates. Locational factors such as these, the groups believed, meant that Fannie Mae and Freddie Mac further encouraged the discriminatory practices responsible for the disinvestment of their neighborhoods.

Community groups pushed hard to force Fannie Mae and Freddie Mac to revise their practices, and the two GSEs appeared to make amends. While still denying that they discriminated, the two GSEs undertook reviews and made modifications to their business practices. In 1979 the final report of the National Commission on Neighborhoods, a federally created body whose membership included anti-redlining leader Gale Cincotta, noted this progress and concluded: "The underwriting guidelines used by FNMA and FHLMC initially reflected many of the traditional discriminatory underwriting assumptions used by private lenders," but in recent years, "many of these discriminatory factors had been removed" from the enterprises guidelines (National Commission on Neighborhoods 1979, 104).

The removal of many of the offending provisions, however, was not enough to reverse decades-old patterns of disinvestment. The proliferation of CRA agreements between community groups and local banks and thrifts in the late 1970s and 1980s revealed that other aspects of Fannie Mae's and Freddie Mac's guidelines still got in the way. Community groups succeeded in getting lenders to apply more flexible underwriting standards in an effort to increase mortgage approvals for low- and moderate-income families. These groups believed, and their experience seem to confirm, that the use of more flexible loan terms and conditions (for example, lower down payments, higher debt-to-income ratios, and counting nontraditional sources of income) did not adversely affect loan performance for borrowers with modest incomes. But Fannie Mae and Freddie Mac guidelines at the time did not account for these features. Consequently, mortgage originators found they were unable to sell these loans to the secondary-market GSEs and instead had to hold them in portfolio (risk-based capital standards made portfolio loans more costly to lenders). As one key community organizer put it, "it is becoming increasingly clear that the secondary mortgage market has been a hidden officer at the loan origination table" (U.S. Senate Committee on Banking, Housing, and Urban Affairs 1991, 92). Community advocates thus continued to call for the secondary-market GSEs to change their practices and procedures.

The FHLBs' Affordable-Housing Requirements

The Home Loan Banks' CIF program during its first five-year period (1978 to 1983) extended a cumulative volume of $7.9 billion in special cash advances. By the early 1980s, however, the FHLB system seemed to have lost interest in the CIF program, and it was not extended. Instead, authority was delegated to the individual District Banks to continue or abandon the program at their option. Consequently, the program continued on a vastly smaller scale. For example, from 1986 through 1988 the cumulative volume of CIF funds was only $720 million (Nader and Brown 1981, 18).

Yet by the late 1980s the federal bank regulators and most Washington lawmakers were not thinking about the CIF program, or about what additional steps the GSEs could take to support low-income housing finance. The burgeoning S&L debacle grabbed most of the attention, as doubts surfaced about whether the thrift industry and the FHLB system could even survive.

In many respects the S&L crisis was the direct result of the deregulation pushed by Congress in the early 1980s. Until then, S&Ls were restricted to originating mortgages. Deregulation allowed them to move into risky commercial real estate and energy investments, with the government-backed Federal Savings and Loan Insurance Corporation (FSLIC) obliged to cover any losses. A downturn in the Texas oil patch and deteriorating regional economies spelled doom for many of the S&Ls. As a result, there was talk in Washington about a bailout of the nearly insolvent FSLIC fund, as well as of the restructuring of the system regulating these institutions. Estimates at the time projected that the S&L cleanup would cost taxpayers upwards of $100 billion (Brumbaugh and Litan 1989, 3; Greider 1988, 41; *Nation* 1989, 75).

Many community reinvestment advocates feared that the S&Ls' demise might also set back the gains in lending they had worked so hard to achieve. Others were concerned that a massive government bailout would divert already dwindling federal resources from low-income housing. At the same time, some key community advocates wisely anticipated that a bailout might provide new opportunities to push for expanded support for affordable housing and community development, at least in some areas.

ACORN, a leading national community advocacy group, announced the creation of the Financial Democracy Campaign (FDC), a new coalition to press for progressive solutions to the S&L mess. The FDC was launched in late 1988 with important backing from civil rights leaders, including Rev.

Jesse Jackson, representatives from organized labor, and many national and local consumer and community groups. The Southern Finance Project, Bank Watch (a Ralph Nader monitoring group), the Center for Community Change (CCC), and Consumers Union lent expertise to the new coalition (*Nation* 1989, 76).

The FDC circulated "A Call for Action on the S&L Crisis" to enlist the widest possible support for its efforts to influence the shape of the legislative bailout package. Early in 1989 the coalition put forth its agenda, which, among other things, called upon Congress to develop a fair plan for paying for the cleanup, earmark public funds to address the "nation's unfinished housing agenda," take needed steps to reform the regulatory system to prevent a recurrence of the debacle, and ensure that, in return for assistance, S&Ls and the lending industry live up to their public obligations. As part of this agenda, the FDC urged that the FHLBs target more of their funds to affordable housing initiatives.

The efforts of the FDC and other community and affordable-housing advocates drew the attention of Rep. Henry Gonzalez (D-Tex.), the new chair of the House banking committee. Gonzalez had already held hearings on the crisis and was viewed as an outspoken critic of the crony system that had contributed to the S&L industry's demise. An old-fashioned populist, he was eager to link affordable-housing concerns to the bailout legislation being developed. Gonzalez signaled in early March 1989 his intent to offer amendments to address these concerns. He also announced that he would push to revamp the FHLBB and to make the FHLBs more responsive to affordable-housing needs (Gonzalez 1989).

Bolstered by Gonzalez's statement, several community reinvestment and consumer advocates expressed interest in developing the details. The Washington, D.C.–based CCC, a leading community support organization, convened a meeting of interested national groups to try to develop a consensus on an affordable-housing agenda to present to Gonzalez. Organizations attending the meeting in late March included ACORN, Bank Watch, the National Low Income Housing Coalition, the Planners Network, Enterprise Foundation, and two consumer organizations, Consumers Union and the Consumer Federation of America. These organizations followed up the meeting with a letter that praised Gonzalez for his leadership but also urged him to tailor his proposals to the needs of low-income families, and not to limit legislative proposals to homeownership exclusively but also address the substantial need for affordable rental housing.

Several of the attendees—Bank Watch, CCC, and Consumers Union—also continued to develop the specifics of an FHLB reform proposal they could support. What emerged was a proposal to earmark a portion of the FHLB system's funds for subsidized financing that nonprofit community groups could use to build low-income housing. The groups also advocated the establishment of a Community Investment Program (CIP), patterned after the original McKinney-era CIF program. The CIP would require the District Banks to offer cheaper, long-term cash advances to member institutions to finance targeted affordable housing and community development activities.

This proposal was presented to Rep. Gonzalez and his staff and subsequently adapted and offered as an amendment at a May Banking Committee mark-up on the pending S&L bill. Finding the necessary congressional support for this amendment was challenging, however. With two notable exceptions, the Seattle and Cincinnati FHLBs, all of the District Banks steadfastly opposed the Gonzalez amendment. They particularly objected to what they viewed as "taxing" the system's earnings for this purpose (the legislation also required the FHLBs to transfer $2.5 billion in retained earnings and make a $300 million annual payment to help the federal government pay for the cost of the industry bailout). But Gonzalez vowed to fight for his affordable housing proposal. ACORN and the National Neighborhood Coalition, an umbrella alliance of housing and neighborhood organizations, joined with the other proponents to push for adoption. Proponents effectively activated their local members and generated support from other community groups to contact their congressional representatives (Hill 1989; Harney 1989).

Proponents of the Gonzalez amendment were aided by a U.S. General Accounting Office study that found that cash advances were used predominantly by large, aggressive S&Ls, not the smaller ones, which lacked the ability to issue their own debt securities (S&Ls at the time made up most of the system's members). The study also found that many of the most poorly managed S&Ls were using the FHLB system as a cash-generating machine not to make housing loans but to fund speculative investments (Nader and Brown 1989, 17). Another study issued by CCC, based on research conducted by the Bank Watch organization, showed that the use of cash advances by S&Ls bore little relationship to the level of mortgage lending being conducted by those institutions. These findings provided additional support for the view that the FHLBanks had strayed quite a bit from their public purpose.

The Gonzalez "cash advance" amendment, as it became known, garnered sufficient support and passed the House Banking Committee by a narrow vote of 27 to 23. The provision was included in the bailout bill sent to the House in June. But FHLB opposition to the amendment continued. The cash advance provision survived another close vote, this time on the House floor, when an amendment to delete the provision lost by a margin of only two votes (206–208).

The Gonzalez amendment was one of two key votes won on the House floor by community advocates on the S&L bailout bill. Rep. Joseph Kennedy (D-Mass.) also won by a narrow vote an amendment requiring bank regulators to disclose CRA ratings and expanded HMDA; Kennedy's amendment was accepted and added to the House passed bailout package. The Gonzalez and Kennedy provisions made it into the final legislation enacted in August and signed into law as the Federal Financial Institutions Reform, Recovery, and Enforcement Act of 1989 (FIRREA). Inclusion of the cash-advance provision in FIRREA represented a significant victory for community advocacy and for expanding resources for financing affordable housing. The unique aspect of this provision, especially at the time, is that the Affordable Housing Program (AHP) it created is funded entirely through system earnings, rather than relying on appropriations from the federal budget. FIRREA required the FHLBs to contribute AHP funds equaling 10 percent of the preceding year's net income or at least $100 million a year (initially 5 percent or at least $50 million annually). It was estimated at the time that about $78 million would be available for AHP. However, as the FHLB system has rebounded from the S&L crisis and increased membership to include commercial banks, system-wide earnings have grown and so, therefore, have the dollars earmarked for AHP. Last year about $264 million was generated for this program.

The CIP provision provided cash advances made at a discount from the FHLBs' regular advances. These loans are priced to just cover costs and allow the District Banks to break even on the loan. CIP's purpose is to encourage member institutions to make special efforts to increase their involvement in affordable housing and community development. CIP advances may be used to support long-term financing for the construction, rehabilitation, or acquisition of residential or commercial property that benefits low- and moderate-income areas or families up to 115 percent of an area's median income. From 1990 to 1999, almost $23 billion in CIP funds were provided to member institutions (Federal Housing Finance Board 2002). But the law's enactment did not end the need for continued vigilance. Many of the organizations closely associated with the provision's development participated actively in the development of regulations implementing both the AHP and CIP. For example, CCC coordinated a follow-up effort with eleven other national housing and community organizations and local government agencies that resulted in submission to HUD of a joint "Citizen Concept Paper on Implementation of Low Income Cash Advance Programs for the FHLBs." (FIRREA established HUD as the interim regulator until the FHFB could be constituted.) Among other things, the paper stressed the importance of targeting AHP funds to nonprofit low-income housing sponsors and urged that very-low-income households and rental housing receive high priority in project selection. Such emphasis was necessary, the cosigners believed, because of the FHLBs' traditional focus on single-family mortgage lending and relative noninvolvement with nonprofit community developers. These and other concepts promoted by the advocates were reflected in regulations adopted by HUD.

The FIRREA affordable-housing requirements helped to broaden the FHLB system's overall commitment to affordability, which has now become a more significant part of the justification for its GSE status. Today, for the most part, the FHLBs are viewed by low-income housing providers as more accessible and responsive to providing resources. Investments in housing and community development by the FHLBs, apart from AHP, have grown substantially in recent years. Yet some tension still exists about how much of this subsidy should be dedicated to the lowest-income families and to rental housing.

Fannie Mae and Freddie Mac Affordable Housing Goals

In the wake of multibillion S&L cleanup, some lawmakers expressed concern about the federal government's potential exposure should Fannie Mae and Freddie Mac encounter financial difficulty. Wall Street views the GSEs as being implicitly guaranteed by the government. Concerns that the government could be left holding the bag in the case of default led Congress in 1991 to pass legislation tightening financial oversight of these two GSEs. Once again, however, some community reinvestment advocates saw this move as opening an avenue to raise complaints about the affordable-housing performance of Fannie Mae and Freddie Mac.

A Senate banking subcommittee hearing on "Secondary Mortgage Markets and Redlining" provided an early opportunity to spotlight what community groups believed to be inadequacies in the GSEs' record, namely, their hampering community reinvestment. Testimony presented at the hearing revealed that although Fannie Mae and Freddie Mac served the needs of middle-class homebuyers, they were much less successful in meeting the needs of low- and moderate-income families. The standardization and dominance the GSEs had brought to the home-mortgage market, and the development of mortgage-backed securities, actually worked against lower-income and non-suburban borrowers' ability to obtain mortgage loans, according to the community groups testifying. Support for this view was provided by a report from the Advisory Commission on Regulatory Barriers to Affordable Housing, " 'Not in My Back Yard': Removing Barriers to Affordable Housing," which concluded:

> Fannie Mae's and Freddie Mac's underwriting standards are oriented towards "Plain vanilla" mortgages. The standards encourage lending in the suburban, growing, homogenous and high-income areas, where housing and zoning requirements result in the production of "cookie cutter" new homes in uniformly single-family neighborhoods. These standards work against more diverse building types and mixed-use neighborhoods, which are more difficult to assess and to underwrite. (U.S. Senate Committee on Banking, Housing, and Urban Affairs 1992, 30)

Lenders' increasing emphasis on CRA and community reinvestment provided fresh evidence of the obstacles posed by the secondary-market standards. Lenders complained to community groups about the difficulties in selling these loans to Fannie Mae and Freddie Mac. NPA's Cincotta, who also testified, said that the standardizing influence of the GSEs' underwriting guidelines directly contributed to fewer loans being made in urban neighborhoods.

"Lenders will respond to the most conservative standards unless [Fannie Mae and Freddie Mac] are aggressive and convincing in their efforts to expand historically narrow underwriting." This point was reinforced over and over again by other witnesses (U.S. Senate Committee on Banking, Housing, and Urban Affairs 1991, 78).

A GAO study of secondary-mortgage market activities in the Atlanta area released the previous year provided further evidence that GSE performance was poor. The statistics showed that the number of mortgage loans purchased by the GSEs declined as the percentage of minorities in a neighborhood increased and the income level of the neighborhood declined (U.S. Senate Committee on Banking, Housing, and Urban Affairs 1991, 33).

The charters of both enterprises specified that "a reasonable portion of the mortgage purchase of the corporation be related to the national goal of providing adequate housing for low and moderate income families, but with a reasonable economic return for the corporation" (HUD 2000). Since the late 1970s HUD had set a nonbinding goal that 30 percent of the conventional mortgages purchased by Fannie Mae be directed to this goal. A separate goal, also nonbinding, specified that 30 percent of such mortgages be on homes located in central cities. (The standard did not apply to Freddie Mac because it was not a GSE when HUD first developed the goal.)

The Senate banking committee found that HUD had not monitored adequately the GSEs' success at meeting these goals. The committee released information showing that the limited monitoring HUD did was based on a proxy measurement tied to home price that inflated the activities of Fannie Mae and Freddie Mac in low-income areas. In other words, the basis HUD used to assess the GSEs' performance was inadequate (U.S. Senate Committee on Banking, Housing, and Urban Affairs 1992, 33).

HUD later proposed new regulations to codify the so-called "30/30" requirements and also apply them to Freddie Mac. The regulations also sought to beef up the HUD's monitoring and enforcement for affordable housing purposes (*Inside Mortgage Finance* 1991, 5). But the rules were never finalized and were superseded by the passage of the new GSE legislation.

The hearings proved useful to community reinvestment advocates, nevertheless, as they documented a record of inaction by HUD and the GSEs. These groups also used this forum to propose ways to toughen the GSEs' existing requirements; and the committee later considered some of these approaches.

In the aftermath of the Senate hearing, an array of community reinvestment and low-income housing advocates came forward with proposals for stiffening the GSEs' regulatory requirements for low-income housing. Most called for the establishment of statutorily prescribed performance requirements, along with GSE loan data disclosure and better HUD oversight. However, there were some differences in emphasis.

ACORN, which had played an effective role in the S&L bailout legislation, advocated that a portion of Fannie Mae's and Freddie Mac's earnings be set aside annually to support low-income housing. This approach was similar to the one that had been applied to the FHLB system. Some federal lawmakers also supported such an approach. NPA took a different tack, however, and sought to have existing HUD housing goals incorporated into legislation.

Meanwhile, the House banking committee prepared to take up GSE legislation. At the urging of CCC, the National Low Income Housing Coalition convened a "working group" of major affordable-housing stakeholders, including ACORN and Consumers Union, along with the major community development intermediaries: the Enterprise Foundation and the Local Initiatives Support Corporation (LISC). This group explored prospects for developing a consensus on legislative strategies. The National Council of State Housing Finance Agencies, a key association of public agencies doing business with the GSEs, soon joined the ad hoc group.

Meanwhile, Rep. Gonzalez's banking committee was preparing to mark up a GSE bill aimed at establishing capital standards and toughening financial oversight of the companies. Aware that key members of his committee were divided over what requirements, if any, to support, Gonzalez informally deputized the working group of housing advocates to develop workable provisions that would also be broadly acceptable to Fannie Mae and Freddie Mac.

The working group could not agree on a "tithing" approach along the lines of the FHLB system's provisions in FIRREA. It focused instead on provisions it hoped would help change the culture within the two companies and thereby expand their appetite for financing low-income housing. In the course of several marathon meetings held in July 1991, the working group reached consensus among its own members and then hammered out a proposal with the participation of officials from Fannie Mae and Freddie Mac.

The working group's proposal called for a completely new affordable housing goal, in addition to the 30/30 goal already established. The new goal was targeted to low-income housing needs for borrowers under 80 percent of an area's median income, with a portion directed to very-low-income families (less than 60 percent of area median income). In contrast, HUD's nonbinding low- and moderate-income goal targeted borrowers at or below area median income. The proposed goal required the two GSEs to purchase $3.5 billion in mortgages for 1993–94, to be split equally between single-family and multifamily loans. After this transition period, a percentage requirement would be established, with both companies required to purchase not less than 1 percent of these targeted loans, as measured by their total loan volume for the prior year (Lehman 1991).

Fannie Mae and Freddie Mac agreed to support this new goal after many hours of negotiation. The proposal was then translated into legislative language and quickly adopted and incorporated into the GSE bill that passed the House committee. The bill was eventually adopted by the full House of Representatives in September 1991.

Some key community reinvestment advocates, however, would not support the new provision (which became known as the Special Affordable Housing

Goal) by itself. These groups were particularly concerned that the Special Affordable Housing Goal would replace the two existing 30/30 goals in the GSE bill that was going forward.

NPA urged that the HUD goals also be included in the House bill. After it was clear this would not happen, the coalition focused its attention on the Senate. ACORN and CCC also urged the Senate to go further, while Fannie Mae and Freddie Mac opposed this approach. They argued instead that requiring that 30 percent of GSE business be devoted to low- and moderate-income housing in central cities was unreasonable and arbitrary. They also claimed that these levels were above the proportion of total demand for conventional mortgages that such households make up, and that they could also compel the companies to curtail lending on behalf of other households.

Fortunately, the compelling evidence of the GSEs' weak performance in serving low-income housing needs proved out. The Senate version of the bill ultimately directed HUD to establish three annual affordable-housing goals: a low- and moderate-income goal, a geographically targeted goal, and the Special Affordable Goal approved by the House. The GSE legislation was enacted in its final form as the Federal Housing Enterprises Financial Safety and Soundness Act of 1992 (the GSE Act). The act gave HUD general regulatory authority over Fannie Mae and Freddie Mac in all areas other than that of their financial safety and soundness. Specifically, HUD was directed to set the three annual affordable-housing purchase requirements, monitor compliance with fair lending laws, and collect loan-level data and provide for a public-use data base. Both community reinvestment and affordable-housing advocates felt they had achieved a victory.

The GSE Act required HUD to set the annual housing goal levels after consideration of certain prescribed factors, such as the estimated size of the market that the GSEs could be serving. The goal levels were set at 30 percent and the interim Special Affordable formula applied for the first two years, after which time HUD was authorized to readjust the goals through rulemaking, which it did.

In October 2000 HUD revised these rules significantly, increasing the GSEs' affordable-housing goals. For each year from 2001 through 2003 the goal levels were set as follows: for the Low- and Moderate-Income Goal, at least 50 percent of the GSEs' business was directed to families with incomes under the area median income (up from 42 percent for 1997–2000); for the Underserved Areas Goal (formerly the Central Cities goal), at least 31 percent of GSEs' business was directed to underserved areas, that is, low-income and high-minority census tracts, (up from 24 percent for 1997–2000); and for the Special Affordable goal, at least 20 percent of GSEs' business was directed to very-low-income families (under 60 percent of area median income) or to low-income families (those with incomes under 80 percent of AMI) in low-income areas, (up from 14 percent for 1997–2000) (HUD 2000).

The GSE Act's affordable-housing requirement helped generate significant improvements in the performances of Fannie Mae and Freddie Mac. Fannie

Mae's performance on the Low- and Moderate-Income Housing Goal rose from 34.2 percent in 1993 to 45.9 percent in 1999. Freddie Mac's performance also increased, from 29.7 percent in 1993 to 46.1 percent in 1999. Moreover, both GSEs have launched an array of special initiatives aimed at generating enough business from the affordable-housing sector to enable them to meet their annual goals. As their shares have increased, so have Fannie Mae's and Freddie Mac's images improved with community and affordable-housing groups.

There is more progress to be made, however. The revised rule HUD adopted in 2000 was premised on the finding that the GSEs' "share of the affordable housing market is substantially smaller than their share of the total conventional market" (HUD 2000). HUD explained this disparity by citing the GSEs' underwriting guidelines and their relatively low level of activity in low-income mortgage markets. The new goal levels were issued in an effort to reduce these disparities. This suggests that there is a role for ongoing monitoring and advocacy to ensure that the secondary-market GSEs fulfill these higher goals and better serve certain segments of the affordable-housing market.

Lessons Learned

The establishment of affordable-housing requirements for the GSEs represents an important triumph for community group advocacy. Unquestionably, these rules have helped to generate billions of dollars in low-income housing lending that would not otherwise have been available. Important lessons can be drawn from these experiences that may guide future community advocacy efforts.

Matching the power of these large financial giants required developing the broadest possible grassroots and organizational base. Community advocates consciously reached out to other constituencies, such as labor, civil rights, and consumer organizations. These alliances were crucial to developing the necessary political support. The S&L bailout precipitated the development of a new coalition, albeit a temporary one. By contrast, advocacy on the GSE bill was conducted on an ad hoc basis. Both efforts, however, involved community advocates finding common ground with other constituencies. The success of future community reinvestment policy advocacy will require the development of similar ad hoc and short-term alliances.

The magnitude of the historic S&L bailout created an unprecedented situation. The entire S&L industry, much of the regulatory structure, and even the broader lending community were very much on the defensive. No legislator in 1989 wanted to be associated with the S&L debacle. This unusual situation provided community advocates with an important advantage and helped offset the inside lobbying advantages normally enjoyed by powerful institutions like the FHLBanks. Even so, this was a hard-fought battle, and victory was not guaranteed.

No such crisis atmosphere was present for the GSE legislation. Fannie Mae and Freddie Mac wield much influence on Capitol Hill. But community advocates made good use of the legislative hearing process. That other powerful financial industry interests tacitly supported or at least did not oppose the effort also helped. And it was important that Fannie Mae and Freddie Mac wanted to be seen as cooperative in working to fulfill their public mission. All of these factors contributed to the success of this effort.

It may come as a surprise to some, but the views of community advocates are far from monolithic. Community advocates in both campaigns discussed here started out with seemingly irreconcilable views about the agenda to push and the way to go about doing it—but the lack of consensus in the early stages was not crucial. Priorities may have differed, but so long as these differences motivated additional constituencies to become involved, competition was healthy and actually provided some synergies. Consensus was more or less achieved as the less politically feasible ideas dropped away.

Past experience with advocacy campaigns also contributed to the success of these efforts. The community advocates who won the GSE victories had been seasoned by earlier battles to stop redlining, enact HMDA and CRA, and then by fighting to preserve those laws. All of their victories defied the odds and bested conventional wisdom about the futility of fighting powerful, organized industry interests. Future advocacy efforts can build on these gains and find ways to enlarge them.

References

Brumbaugh, R. Dan Jr., and Robert E. Litan. 1989. The S&L Crisis: How to Get Out and Stay Out. *Brookings Review* (spring).

Citizen Concept Paper on Implementation of Low Income Cash Advance Programs at the FHLBs. 1989. Joint proposal submitted by twelve national nonprofit organizations and associations of local public officials. Oct.

Federal Home Loan Bank System and Federal Home Loan Bank Board. 1981. Reaching Out: A Thrift Industry Initiative. Washington, D.C.: Federal Home Loan Bank Board.

Federal Housing Finance Board. 2002 Affordable Housing Statistics. Information available at <www.fhfb.gov>.

Financial Democracy Campaign. 1989. Call for Action. March.

Gonzalez, Henry B. 1989. Statement of the Chairman of House Committee on Banking, Finance and Urban Affairs, U.S. House of Representatives. March.

Greider, William. 1988. The Growing Crisis in Our S&L Industry. *Rolling Stone.* Aug. 11.

Harney, Kenneth R. 1989. The S&L Bailout Bill: Home Buyers' Bonanza? *Washington Post,* May 20.

Hill, Gwen 1989. Affordable Housing and S&L Bailout: Clash of Priorities. *Washington Post,* May 24.

Inside Mortgage Finance. 1991. New Regs for Fannie, Freddie. June 21.

Lehman, H. Jane. 1991. Housing Plan to Aid Poor Is Studied. *Washington Post*, July 27.

Nader, Ralph, and Jonathan Brown. 1989. Report to U.S. Taxpayers on the Savings & Loan Crisis. Washington, D.C.: Bank Watch.

Nation. 1989. S&L Time Bomb. Jan. 23.

National Commission on Neighborhoods, 1979. People, Building Neighborhoods. Final Report to the President and the Congress. Washington, D.C.: U.S. Government Printing Office.

U.S. Senate Committee on Banking, Housing, and Urban Affairs. 1991. S. HRG. 102-78, Hearing on Secondary Mortgage Markets and Redlining, Feb. 28. Washington, D.C.: U.S. Government Printing Office.

————. 1992. Federal Housing Enterprises Regulatory Reform Act of 1992, to accompany S.2733. S.Rep. No. 102-282. Washington, D.C.: U.S. Government Printing Office.

U.S. Department of Housing and Urban Development (HUD). 2000. Final Rule Establishing New Affordable Housing Goals for Fannie Mae and Freddie Mac, 65 Federal Register 65044, Oct. 31.

Maude Hurd and Steven Kest

8   ## Fighting Predatory Lending
     from the Ground Up:
     ### An Issue of Economic Justice

Maria and Enrique R—Oakland, California

Two years ago, the Rs qualified for a special low-rate home loan of
5 percent and monthly payments of $746 through ACORN Housing
Corporation. They heard about Beneficial through a relative and ended
up taking out a second mortgage with them in January 2001. Their
house was appraised at $175,000.

The Rs' second mortgage was structured as an open-end loan with
a credit limit of $35,000 and an initial advance of $36,800, which included an origination fee of $1,840 (plus an annual fee of $50 in subsequent years of the loan). It had a variable rate of the prime rate plus
12.9 percent, which initially left them at 22.4 percent. Their payments
on the loan were $742 a month—almost equal to the payments on their
first mortgage. These payments were extremely difficult to make on
Mr. R's monthly income of $1,800 as a janitor at a country club and
the $546 the Rs receive from SSI to help care for their daughter, who
is hearing-impaired.

Given their difficult financial situation, the Rs felt they had no
choice but to get out of the Beneficial loan by selling that house and
buying another one, which they did in April. But because their Beneficial loan had a five-year prepayment penalty for six months on all principal beyond 20 percent of the original loan amount, they ended up
paying a penalty of more than $3,000 to Beneficial.

Since 1999 ACORN—the Association of Community Organizations for
Reform Now—has been engaging community members, policymakers, and

lenders in a nationwide struggle against predatory lending. Working at the local, state, and federal levels, our goal has been to end the predatory practices of subprime lenders. Predatory lending, which disproportionately affects low-income communities and communities of color and can leave victims in extreme financial hardship, is an issue of social and economic justice. ACORN has played a leading role in not only exposing and curbing the predatory practices of subprime lenders, but also in increasing community awareness about and arming community members against predatory lending.

As the nation's largest community organization of low- and moderate-income families, with over 150,000 member families organized into seven hundred neighborhood chapters in fifty U.S. cities, ACORN is in a unique position to engage predatory lenders and policymakers on a number of levels. We use grassroots community organizing strategies to achieve real policy change through direct action, negotiation, legislation, and voter participation.

Since 1970 ACORN members have won changes in both corporate and government policies. We have played a role in passing legislation and crafting improved federal regulations on affordable housing issues. In collaboration with other advocacy groups, we have fought abuses such as single-premium-credit life insurance, and we have successfully pressured most of the lending industry to abandon this type of policy. In a political climate that favors deregulation, we have worked hard to bring legal power and public pressure to bear on an entire industry.

At the heart of ACORN's campaign are hundreds of predatory lending victims who have been willing to share their stories with community members, political representatives, industry officials, the media, and others. Our base of predatory-lending victims has provided invaluable ammunition for the campaign. When crowds of victimized borrowers and other ACORN members rally on the steps of a city hall where anti-predatory-lending legislation is being considered, or invade the offices of a predatory lender, the effect can be extremely powerful.

A Pattern of Unfair Lending Practices

Predatory lending is not, of course, the banking industry's first assault on low-income communities and communities of color. For more than two decades, dozens of community organizations and coalitions, including ACORN and the ACORN Housing Corporation (AHC), have worked to combat redlining and increase access to credit in low-income and minority neighborhoods. Using the Community Reinvestment Act (CRA), ACORN and AHC have entered into agreements with more than fifty banks and have won significant changes in bank lending practices, including radically revised underwriting standards that have made homeownership possible for low-income families. Indeed, AHC's mortgage counseling program has helped nearly forty thousand low- and moderate-income families become homeowners for the first time.

Despite these accomplishments, the banking industry as a whole has continued to ignore inner-city neighborhoods, leaving the door open to abuse by predatory lenders. Through its door-to-door organizing efforts in the 1990s, ACORN encountered a growing number of homeowners who had been taken advantage of by predatory lenders and were at risk of losing their homes.

Predatory loans turn the dream of homeownership into a nightmare, in the worst instances ending in foreclosure. The damage is increased by the fact that predatory loans are made largely in low-income and minority neighborhoods that have been deserted by mainstream banks, so that borrowers are easy prey for predatory lenders. The loss of equity and foreclosure can be especially harmful to already struggling communities.

Predatory lending occurs in the subprime loan market. Subprime loans carry higher interest rates and fees in order to cover the risk of lending to borrowers with imperfect credit. However, a Freddie Mac study suggested that about one-third of the borrowers of subprime loans could have qualified for prime loans (HUD-Treasury 2000), while the chairman of Fannie Mae has estimated that the number is closer to half (*Business Wire* 2000). In other words, borrowers with good credit are being given high-priced loans—loans that lenders justify making by citing the need to extend credit to those with bad credit records. Giving a subprime loan to someone who qualifies for a prime loan is itself predatory. Moreover, many subprime loans contain abusive terms and conditions that are unfair and harmful to any borrower. These predatory lending practices include:

- Charging and financing excessive points and fees;
- Making loans based on the value of a property, when it is evident a borrower will be unable to repay;
- Charging excessive interest rates not justified by the risk involved;
- Selling financed single-premium credit insurance, which the Consumer Federation of America has called "the worst insurance rip off" in the United States (Consumer Federation of America 1990, 1992, 1995). (Credit insurance is overpriced insurance used to pay off a loan in the event of a borrower's death or injury. "Single-premium" means that the total price of the insurance is financed into a loan, resulting in a thirty-year schedule of interest);
- Charging high and extended prepayment penalties, which trap people in high-interest loans;
- Flipping, or repeated refinancings with no benefit to the borrower;
- Packing loans with additional products such as club memberships;
- Conspiring with home-improvement contractors to solicit loans on damaging terms, and/or paying contractors directly, leaving the borrowers no way to ensure that work is done;
- Inflating home appraisal values;

- Using "mandatory arbitration" clauses that deny borrowers rights in court;
- Misrepresenting the terms and conditions of loans;
- Using harassing and intimidating collection techniques;
- Targeting high-cost loans to vulnerable borrowers, including the elderly and low-income and minority families.

ACORN has encountered victims of predatory lending in communities across the United States. While each story is unique, they share many features and often have the same unfortunate ending. Two examples illustrate the point.

A California woman went to one of the country's biggest lenders, Household Finance (which also does business under the name Beneficial), to refinance a small loan. She originally had no desire to refinance her home loan, made at 8.25 percent interest, but Household talked her into it. She ended up with two loans from Household, the first at 11 percent, the second a revolving line of credit at 20.9 percent. This woman has an excellent credit record and should have been able to refinance at an interest rate of close to 7 percent, which would have saved her about $400 a month. But between the two loans, including origination fees of more than $10,500 and credit insurance of more than $9,000 that she did not want or need, she has been lent more than the value of her home, and banks will not make her a loan for more than her house is worth. As a result, she is stuck with a high interest rate and must make monthly payments of $1,403 on a monthly income of about $1,650. With ACORN's help, this woman, like many other borrowers, was able to cancel her credit insurance and get a refund—in her case $5,381. But she is stuck with the other bad terms of her loan.

A St. Louis woman held a mortgage with an interest rate of 9.5 percent and monthly payments of $340. She had fallen behind occasionally on those payments, lowering her credit rating, but she needed cash to fix her furnace, chimney, and other items. Household repeatedly assured her that a refinanced loan would provide the extra money she needed but not differ from her old loan in any other respect. In reality, the new loan of $46,983 increased her interest rate to 12.5 percent and included $3,874 in fees and closing costs and $3,704 for a single-premium credit life insurance policy. She was never told about a mandatory arbitration clause that was slipped into her loan, limiting her rights to file any claims against Household. Though the paperwork said it was optional, she was also told that she must take out a $1,349 home and auto membership plan in order to get the loan. Together these additional points, fees, insurance, and memberships totaled 19 percent of her loan value. In addition, she was wrongly informed that her new loan covered taxes and insurance, as her old one had. When she called to speak to her loan officer, she was told he no longer worked there. After she complained about being lied to about her loan terms, Household offered her a loan to pay her taxes, which she refused. Now, with monthly payments of $483.28 for the next thirty years, she has been forced to cut back severely on other expenses.

Documenting the Damage

In October 2000 ACORN released a national report titled "Separate and Unequal: Predatory Lending in America," which documented the increase and concentration of subprime lending in low-income and minority communities. Based on analysis of data released by the Federal Financial Institutions Examination Council about the lending activity of more than 7,800 institutions covered by the Home Mortgage Disclosure Act (HMDA), as well as HUD data on subprime lenders, the report found that:

- The number of subprime loans made in the United States grew 900 percent in seven years, increasing from just over 100,000 home-purchase and refinance loans in 1993 to almost a million loans in 1999. During the same period, all other home-purchase and refinance loans declined 10 percent.
- Fully 82 percent of subprime loans were refinance loans; most subprime loans refinance existing homeowners rather than create new ones.
- Subprime lenders account for 51 percent of refinance loans made in predominantly African American neighborhoods, compared to 9 percent in white neighborhoods. In 1999, African Americans were 3.7 times more likely than whites to receive subprime loans, and Latinos 1.6 times more likely.
- Although African American borrowers are much more likely to receive subprime loans, the large majority of subprime loans are made to white borrowers.
- More than 61 percent of conventional refinance loans made to low-income African Americans (excluding manufactured housing) were from subprime lenders, as were over 30 percent of those made to low-income Latino borrowers.
- Upper-income African Americans were more likely than low-income whites to receive subprime loans when refinancing.
- While refinance loans make up the greatest portion of subprime lending, subprime lenders have made a serious entry into the home-purchase market. In 1993 subprime lenders made just 24,000 home-purchase loans, which was 1 percent of all the conventional home purchase loans made in the country. In 1999 this number jumped to almost 250,000, or 6.6 percent.

ACORN's Campaign against Predatory Lending

These findings suggest that subprime lending, with its higher prices and attendant abuses, is becoming the dominant form of lending in communities of color. Unless it is strongly resisted, it is likely to continue growing at an alarming rate. In response, ACORN has built and activated a strong constituency of predatory-lending victims and their neighbors, and has employed a variety of techniques to pressure lenders, investors, and policymakers to halt this abusive practice. ACORN has worked to change the policies of individual lenders and to pass legislation affecting the whole industry. We have also sought to change the practices of mainstream lenders and their subprime subsidiaries through the CRA. ACORN's community mobilization has helped to put a spotlight on the practice of predatory lending nationwide and to increase media coverage and raise public awareness. Many other community organizations and CRA advocates, as well as the AARP, have been active participants in the fight against predatory lending.

ACORN's core philosophy is that lasting progressive change will not occur in this country until low- and moderate-income people are organized on a large scale. Our primary strategy to curb predatory lending has been to identify and mobilize predatory-lending victims and their neighbors to demand change and accountability from the institutions, governmental and financial, that affect their lives and harm their communities. ACORN organizers have gone house to house, held house and block meetings, and organized neighborhood meetings to educate community members about how to identify and avoid predatory loans. We have also published articles in community papers, posted flyers, and done outreach to other organizations.

Community organizing has proven exceptionally effective in identifying victims who might otherwise be reluctant to share their stories with strangers or "authority figures." Local ACORN block captains, neighborhood chapter leaders, and organizers are trusted figures in the community who are able to engage victims on a personal level. As ACORN's campaign against predatory lending has heightened the visibility of the issue in the communities where we organize, victims have increasingly begun to come to ACORN neighborhood meetings or call the ACORN office to tell their stories.

Community organizations like ACORN have used decades of experience to hone the ability to generate the media attention critical to raising the visibility of an issue like predatory lending to the level where policymakers feel compelled to take action. ACORN's campaign against predatory lending, which has combined in-depth research with creative forms of "direct action," has made this an issue that the press has been unable to ignore. ACORN's research staff has developed studies and reports on the industry, providing concrete documentation for community members, the media, and policymakers. We have worked closely with reporters in many cities, providing them with victim stories for their articles and television spots. These media reports, in turn, have been extremely influential in moving policymakers.

To support our campaigns and meet our constituency's immediate needs, ACORN has also built a network of community service and legal organizations to assist the victims identified through community organizing. In many cities we have worked closely with local legal services organizations, which can represent victims in negotiation and litigation with lenders. Our sister organization, the ACORN Housing Corporation, a HUD-certified loan-counseling agency with offices in most ACORN cities, provides victims with loan counseling and helps many to refinance their loans with better terms and at better rates.

Targeting Lenders

ACORN recognizes that lasting policy change must occur on many levels, from community to industry to local, state, and federal government. By targeting predatory lenders directly, while also working to pass anti–predatory-lending legislation, our goal is to hold lenders accountable for their unfair practices. Since launching our campaign in late 1999, we have targeted three of the nation's largest lending institutions: Ameriquest, Citigroup, and Household. Using direct action, shareholder strategies, coordinated complaints to federal and state regulatory and consumer-protection agencies, and negotiation, we have pressured individual predatory lenders to change their practices. ACORN's actions have been aimed both at winning restitution for individual victims and at pushing lenders to change their practices and make credit available to low-income borrowers on equitable terms. We have also chosen individual lenders to serve as "poster children" of bad lending.

Ameriquest

One of the nation's largest stand-alone subprime lenders, Ameriquest, was the first subprime lender with which ACORN negotiated directly. ACORN members organized an active campaign of demonstrations, pickets, and sit-ins at Ameriquest offices throughout the country and at the offices of the Wall Street firms who finance Ameriquest; the filing of complaints with state attorneys general, the Federal Trade Commission, and the Justice Department; and aggressive lobbying with members of Congress, federal regulators, HUD, and the Treasury Department.

Ameriquest finally agreed to negotiate with ACORN and in July 2000, after three months of difficult negotiations between the principal owner and CEO of the mortgage company and ACORN's senior national leadership, Ameriquest and ACORN signed an agreement to make subprime loans available to borrowers on fair terms. The agreement had three major components. First, Ameriquest agreed to invest $360 million in an ACORN pilot program, to be implemented in ten cities. In these cities, Ameriquest agreed to make subprime loans with no prepayment penalties, no credit insurance, a limit on points and fees at 3 percent of the loan, interest rates below the market standard, and AHC loan counseling for every potential borrower. Second, the company adopted a set of corporate best practices to apply to all of its business operations. Finally, Ameriquest agreed to join with ACORN in developing and supporting federal and state legislation to set new standards throughout the rest of the industry. The first of its kind, the agreement created a clear alternative to predatory loans.

Citigroup

ACORN's second targets were the Associates and Citifinancial, subsidiaries of Citigroup. In 1999 ACORN released a study condemning Citigroup for its pattern of making high-cost subprime loans in minority and low-income communities, while ignoring these borrowers when it came to lower-priced A credit (ACORN 1999). When Citigroup acquired the Associates in late 2000, ACORN was already in the midst of a campaign against the Associates' predatory practices and therefore opposed the acquisition because of concerns about both parties. While Citigroup claimed that it would "clean up" the Associates' practices, ACORN and many allied organizations argued that its own subprime subsidiary, Citifinancial, had long practiced the same abuses. To back up its position, ACORN used HMDA data showing that Citibank and Citicorp Mortgage made 92 percent of their loans in middle- and upper-income census tracts in 1998, while rejecting African American applicants almost three times as often, and Latinos almost twice as often, as whites. Meanwhile, ACORN found that Citigroup's subprime subsidiaries, which charge higher rates and fees, did 5.5 times more lending in majority/minority neighborhoods and 6.5 times more lending in low-income neighborhoods than did fair-priced Citibank lenders.

Not long after Citibank acquired the Associates, the FTC charged the Associates with predatory lending practices. ACORN was able to provide the FTC with firsthand information about problem loans made by both the Associates and Citifinancial. Under pressure from the FTC, ACORN, and numerous community and consumer groups around the country, Citigroup announced that it would make certain improvements in its practices in conjunction with the Associates purchase. Citigroup's improvements were inadequate, however, and pressure on the company continued to increase, especially from groups like the North Carolina–based Coalition for Responsible Lending. In June 2001, as a result of this continuing pressure and a growing national focus on predatory lending, Citigroup agreed to stop selling single-premium credit insurance. ACORN and its allies considered this a major victory and urged other lenders to follow Citigroup's example.

Household

Household International, which includes the subsidiaries Household Finance and Beneficial, is the second-largest subprime lender in the country (after Citigroup), and one of the most abusive. In part because it had failed to report its HMDA data, revealing how many loans it was making and where, Household had been able to stay off the radar screen until ACORN launched its campaign to build public pressure for reform. Household's and Beneficial's abusive lending practices include:

- Charging high fees—typically 7.25 percent on first mortgages—and high interest rates unrelated to borrowers' credit risk;
- Refinancing loans and collecting excessive points and fees, when these refinancings leave borrowers worse off than they were before the loan;
- Including mandatory arbitration clauses and costly prepayment penalties in their loans;
- Trapping borrowers in high-cost Household loans by making loans for more than the value of borrowers' homes;
- Financing over-priced single-premium credit insurance into borrowers' loans, often without the borrowers' understanding what they have been sold or how much it costs, and sometimes without the borrowers' knowing it has been included at all. (Household announced in July 2001 that it would end single-premium credit insurance sales on mortgage loans beginning with five cities in August 2001.)

ACORN's campaign against Household has included a range of tactics, from direct action to shareholder strategies to regulatory action. A key element of the campaign has been our organizing work in low-income neighborhoods, where we have mobilized Household victims and other community residents to hold demonstrations at the company's offices around the country. These actions have in turn helped to generate media coverage, which has served to raise awareness of the issue generally and to warn borrowers about Household in particular. ACORN's campaign against Household has also included pressure on secondary targets such as Best Buy, whose credit card is managed by Household. ACORN members have demonstrated at Best Buy headquarters and at local stores, warning shoppers that their credit information was being turned over to Household, which would then try to sell them credit insurance or high-priced loans, and encouraging Best Buy to end its relationship with Household. When Household International announced that it would hold its 2001 annual shareholders' meeting in an obscure suburb of Tampa, Florida, we saw a unique opportunity to complement our direct-action campaign with a shareholder strategy. ACORN members traveled from Miami and New Orleans to greet the shareholders with posters, chants, and giant sharks as they arrived. In addition, we supported a shareholder resolution on predatory lending sponsored by Responsible Wealth and United for a Fair Economy. Domini Social Investments allowed ACORN to use its proxy to get an ACORN leader into the meeting to add her voice to the debate. The shareholder resolution, which asked that executive compensation be tied to efforts to combat predatory lending, garnered 5 percent of the vote; this is considered a high level of support for such a resolution the first time out, and guaranteed that it would be on the proxy statement the following year. At Household's 2002 annual meeting in the isolated town of London, Kentucky,

ACORN succeeded in getting an unprecedented 30 percent of shareholders to vote in favor of our resolution.

Media coverage of the action in Tampa and of other activities around the country strongly favored ACORN's case. *St. Petersburg Times* columnist Robert Trigaux's positive coverage of ACORN's campaign set off a series of written exchanges between Household and ACORN. Recounting the story of Margaret Dickens, a Household victim from St. Louis who was persuaded to take out a large loan with excessive fees and unnecessarily high interest rates and is now "stuck in a spiral of increasing debt" (Trigaux 2001), Trigaux documented Household's harsh, inequitable loan practices and contrasted these with the cushy treatment given Household executives such as chief executive William Aldinger, who made $32 million in total compensation in 2000 (Trigaux 2001). Gary Gilmer, Household's CEO, responded with a letter to the *St. Petersburg Times* protesting Trigaux's column and arguing that it was "both misleading and factually inaccurate.... [Trigaux] used blatantly false statements and generalizations from an unreliable source to paint a 'David and Goliath' story that, in this instance, simply does not exist" (Gilmer 2001). Maude Hurd, ACORN's national president and coauthor of this chapter, responded with her own letter, emphasizing that Gilmer's attack on Dickens's credibility "sinks to the same level of deception regularly used by Household to push homeowners into abusive mortgages" (Hurd 2001). While this was one of the most public exchanges between ACORN and Household, mainstream newspapers such as the *Chicago Sun Times*, the *Philadelphia Daily News*, and the *Tampa Tribune*, and industry journals like *American Banker*, also ran sympathetic stories on ACORN's campaign against Household and predatory lending in general.

ACORN's shareholder action in Tampa kicked off a series of actions across the country. Within two months, resolutions calling on their pension fund managers to divest from Household were passed by city councils in St. Louis, Los Angeles, and Chelsea, Massachusetts, and proposed in Household's hometown of Chicago. Council members in Washington, D.C., Boston, and Minneapolis–St. Paul also pledged to support such resolutions. In New York, City Comptroller Alan Hevesi, a trustee of the city's millions of dollars in pension funds, added his voice to the demands that the company change its practices. ACORN also stepped up the regulatory pressure on Household, filing complaints with state regulators and attorneys general in ten states and holding public meetings to allow regulators to hear directly from borrowers about the problems with these loans. Complaints to such agencies often result in little or no action, and to prevent that outcome here ACORN has followed up aggressively, holding officials accountable for taking action wherever possible. In our campaign against Household, we used our strong labor connections to encourage the AFL-CIO, which uses Household for its union privilege credit cards, to put significant pressure on the lender to clean up its practices. In addition, we have worked with local unions who have members on pension boards to advance this part of our strategy. To illustrate the devastating impact of Household's practices on union members themselves, we have identified current and former union members who have been victimized by predatory lenders. We have met with national union leaders and with local unions to encourage them to support our predatory lending and Household campaigns. In the months following the Tampa shareholders' meeting, for example, the Greater Baton Rouge Central Labor Council, the Arkansas AFL-CIO, the Central Arkansas Labor Council, and the St. Paul Trades and Labor Council all passed resolutions asking the AFL-CIO to investigate Household and urging divestment from Household if the company refused to change its practices.

By the end of June 2001 media coverage of Household's predatory lending and of opposition to it had increased dramatically, and public pressure was increasing by the day. In the face of this pressure, and despite earlier statements that it would not do so, on July 12 Household announced that, like Citigroup, it would no longer sell single-premium credit insurance on mortgage loans. In 2000 alone Household had sold $355,320,000 worth of single-premium credit insurance, interest payments on which, at 12.5 percent, will cost borrowers $546,073,000 over the next thirty years (Household 2001). In effect, the single-premium credit insurance policies sold by Household in 2000 will strip more than $900,000,000 in home equity from the people who can least afford to pay it. Though Household's decision was a breakthrough that will benefit thousands of borrowers, it did not signal the end of the company's predatory practices. ACORN's campaign continued. In the summer of 2002 more than two thousand ACORN members traveled to Chicago and rallied in the front yards of the homes of Household's CEO and four of its board members, passing out flyers to the neighbors warning them of "loan sharks in your community." Then, on October 11, 2002, in a step that ACORN members viewed as a significant victory in their multiyear fight for justice for Household borrowers, a consortium of state attorneys general announced a $484 million settlement with the company. The settlement was by far the largest ever awarded in a predatory lending case. In addition to money for restitution, it included injunctive relief committing the company to improved lending practices for the future.

Working with Bank Partners: The Community Reinvestment Act

In addition to targeting predatory lenders, ACORN and the ACORN Housing Corporation, along with other community organizations, have also used the CRA and existing relationships with banks to pressure mainstream lenders to develop fairly priced and marketed subprime products.

Because predatory lenders operate in neighborhoods that have been abandoned by banks, a crucial component of ACORN's campaign is to use the CRA to encourage banks to lend in previously redlined communities. This is especially true of banks that own subprime affiliates—and that operate what is essentially a two-tier, separate-but-unequal lending program, with the bank offering decent loans in white and middle- to upper-income neighborhoods, and the subprime affiliate operating in lower-income and minority neighborhoods.

ACORN has worked to persuade bank regulators to issue precedent-setting rulings that would take into account—and deny CRA credit to banks that engage in—two-tier lending programs. We have used the CRA to seek agreements with national banks such as Bank One, Bank of America, and Washington Mutual to develop fairly priced subprime lending programs for people with impaired credit, including provisions for counseling by the ACORN Housing Corporation. The goal of such agreements has been to push for adoption of such practices throughout the banking industry—and to encourage banks to see that they can make profitable loans to people with impaired credit at terms more favorable than those of predatory lenders.

Changing Regulation and Passing Legislation

ACORN has worked at both the state and federal levels to improve regulations governing the banking and lending industry, and at the local, state, and federal levels to push for legislation against predatory lending. This work has been accompanied and amplified by the federal legislative and regulatory efforts of other groups, such as the National Consumer Law Center, the North Carolina Coalition for Responsible Lending, Consumers Union, and AARP. By working to change both regulations and legislation on multiple levels we have been able to pressure predatory lenders to change their practices and have taken crucial steps toward reforming the entire industry.

Regulation

ACORN has demanded, and made some progress on, governmental action against predatory lending on many fronts. In our push to strengthen industry regulations, we have taken the issue to top officials at HUD, the Treasury Department, the Justice Department, the FTC, and bank regulatory agencies. In early 2000 ACORN pressure helped in the formation of a HUD/Treasury Task Force on Predatory Lending that examined the federal government's laws and regulations on the issue. The task force held regional hearings, and ACORN members and predatory-lending victims testified in New York, Los Angeles, Chicago, and Baltimore. The four federal banking agencies—the FDIC, OTS, OCC, and Federal Reserve—jointly sent out a letter of guidance to banks and thrifts about what standards agency examiners would use in inspecting institutions' subprime lending programs for evidence of predatory practices.

ACORN also held a number of actions, including a march in June 2000 on the Federal Reserve Board's Philadelphia office attended by one thousand people, to press the Board to use its statutory authority to write regulations curbing predatory lending. After holding hearings in early fall, the Board issued a proposed rule that included some modest but useful regulatory steps. ACORN submitted detailed comments in support of the proposal and lobbied members of Congress to send in their own comments.

ACORN has also pushed for the reasonable enforcement of existing regulations, calling on state and federal officials to investigate lenders and take appropriate measures, such as revocation of licenses and prosecution, in response to deceptive and abusive lending practices.

Legislation

Too often policymakers are hampered by incomplete or cursory knowledge, often gleaned from press accounts, of predatory practices and as a result the policies they develop are inadequate to deal with the problems. ACORN has been able to work closely with policymakers to craft proposals designed to eliminate the specific predatory practices encountered in the affected communities. At the same time, we have been able to mobilize large numbers of neighborhood residents (and voters) whom policymakers have to take into account. Not only predatory lending victims but also their neighbors (many of whom have only narrowly escaped becoming victims themselves) have participated in our broad-based campaigns to win policy changes.

After decades of fighting for policy changes, we have learned to be strategic about our mobilizations, targeting specific politicians who are critical to the success of a policy initiative and mobilizing constituents in that member's district. Our broad community alliances have enabled us to establish relationships with influential institutions (such as churches and unions) and formulate collaborative campaigns.

ACORN's first anti–predatory-lending ordinance was passed in Philadelphia after more than a year and a half of campaign work. In April 2001 the Philadelphia City Council passed the country's toughest predatory lending legislation by a vote of sixteen to zero. The ordinance not only prevented city government from doing business with predatory lenders but actually prohibited abusive lending anywhere in the city and required loan counseling for borrowers of high-interest loans. Philadelphia ACORN and its allies began this groundbreaking campaign by defining the problem, issuing reports, generating publicity, and working with a member of city council to draft a bill. For weeks we produced almost daily press on the topic, exposing abuses and urging city council members and the mayor to "do the right thing" in the face of intense opposition by the lending industry. In the end, however, the outcome of Philadelphia's ordinance was determined not by the city council or the mayor but by the state legislature, which responded to pressure from the banking industry and Household and enacted legislation preempting the city's ability to regulate loans—in effect invalidating the ordinance.

Though no longer in effect, the Philadelphia bill has served as a model for legislation elsewhere. The ACORN chapter in Oakland, California, helped pass a citywide ordinance that would prohibit single-premium credit insurance, excessive prepayment penalties, and repeated refinancings with no benefit to the borrowers; require loan counseling on very-high-cost loans; ban excessive points and fees; ban loans that borrowers will clearly be unable to repay; and prevent the city from investing in or doing business with predatory lenders. We are confident that the industry will not be able to pass preemptive legislation in California as they did in Pennsylvania. ACORN members are lobbying for local legislation now in many other cities, and the movement has spread to places where ACORN is not active, including DeKalb County, Georgia, and Dayton, Ohio. ACORN has also been at the forefront of efforts to move state legislation, most notably in California and New York.[1] After a huge effort both in Sacramento and in the field, in which ACORN was joined by the AARP and Consumers Union, California passed a modest but useful bill regulating some of the worst predatory abuses.

At the same time that we have worked to pass ordinances on the local and state levels, we have consistently pushed for federal legislation. Our federal strategy aims to force the industry to choose between accepting meaningful federal legislation or dealing with numerous state and local policies across the country. ACORN's work on local and state ordinances both protects borrowers on the local level and plays a crucial role in a national strategy to move federal legislation forward. Indeed, local activity has filled the banking trade press with discussions of federal legislation as a tool to head off local action. In July 2001 the Senate banking committee held hearings on predatory lending, moving the debate forward several steps and putting the issue of predatory lending squarely on the national agenda.

Making Predatory Lending an Issue That Policymakers Can't Ignore

When Federal Reserve chairman Alan Greenspan testified before Congress in July 2001, he was grilled about his efforts and plans to combat predatory lending—an issue that was not even in Congress's vocabulary a mere two years before. Clearly, in order to make policy changes that improve conditions for low- and moderate-income communities and communities of color, community organizations like ACORN must first raise public awareness of the issue. ACORN has been very successful in this respect. On March 23, 2000, more than a year before the senate hearings, the *Los Angeles Times* reported:

Federal Reserve Chairman Alan Greenspan added his voice Wednesday to the mounting criticism of so-called predatory lending practices by mortgage companies that target low-income borrowers, primarily minorities. Greenspan's remarks, his first on the subject, came as community activists descended on Capitol Hill to complain about Wall Street's role in financing such lenders. Led by the grass-roots Assn. Of Community Organizations for Reform Now, or ACORN, the protesters say those lenders are charging excessively high fees, as much as 10% of the loans, to people who have poor or no credit. (*Los Angeles Times* 2000)

Increasing awareness of the issue is the first step to making it something that must be dealt with by people in power—whether it be the CEO of Household or the chairman of the Federal Reserve. Creating an environment in which predatory lending is talked about and challenged on all levels is also a first step in achieving real policy change. Furthermore, challenging predatory lending is fundamentally part of a larger fight to achieve economic justice for low-income people. Only by holding lenders accountable and ensuring that there are no longer two separate but unequal lending and banking structures in the United States can we begin to equalize homeownership and economic opportunity for low-income communities and communities of color.

Note

1. While New York and Massachusetts have already enacted regulations banning a limited number of predatory practices, low-income and minority borrowers in these states continue to be targeted by predatory lenders.

References

ACORN. 1999. Fact Sheet/Report on Citigroup. Washington, D.C.: Association of Community Organizations for Reform Now. Oct.

———. 2000. *Separate and Unequal: Predatory Lending in America.* Washington, D.C.: Association of Community Organizations for Reform Now. Available at <www.acorn.org>.

Business Wire. 2000. Fannie Mae Has Played Critical Role in Expansion of Minority Homeownership. March 2.

Chicago Sun-Times. 2001. Group Pickets Household in Florida. May 9. Available at <www.acorn.org/acorn10/household/press/picket.htm>.

Coalition for Responsible Lending and Eric Stein. 2001. Quantifying the Economic Cost of Predatory Lending. Durham, N.C.: Coalition for Responsible Lending.

Consumer Federation of America and National Insurance Consumer Organization. 1990, 1992, 1995. *Credit Life Insurance: The Nation's Worst Insurance Rip Off.* June 4, 1990; updated May 20, 1992, and July 25, 1995.

Davies, Paul D. 2001. Drop City Stock in Predators. *Philadelphia Daily News.* May 9. Available at <www.acorn.org/acorn10/household/press/drop.htm>.

Gilmer, Gary. 2001. Household Is a Responsible Lender. *St. Petersburg Times.* May 12. Available at <www.acorn.org/acorn10/household/press/letter.htm>.

Household International. 2000. *Annual Report*. Prospect Heights, Ill.: Household International. Jan. Available at <www.household.com/ffacts.html>.

HUD-Treasury Task Force on Predatory Lending. 2000. Curbing Predatory Home Mortgage Lending. June 20. Washington, D.C.: U.S. Department of the Treasury, U.S. Department of Housing and Urban Development.

Hurd, Maude. 2001. Lending Looks Predatory. *St. Petersburg Times*. May 30. Available at <www.acorn.org/acorn10/household/press/response.htm>.

Julavits, Robert. 2001. Protests at Household's Shareholders' Meeting. *American Banker*. May 9. Available at <www.acorn.org/acorn10/household/press/protests.htm>.

Los Angeles Times. 2000. Greenspan Joins Critics of Mortgage Fee Gouging. March 23.

Stockfisch, Jerome R. 2001. Protesters Say Lenders Prey. *Tampa Tribune*. May 9. Available at <www.acorn.org/acorn10/household/press/lenders_prey.htm>.

Trigaux, Robert. 2001. Florida Newest Turf in Lending Hostilities. *St. Petersburg Times*. May 9. Available at <www.acorn.org/acorn10/household/press/newfla.htm>.

Matthew Lee

---

9   Community Reinvestment
in a Globalizing World:

To Hold Banks Accountable,
from The Bronx to Buenos Aires,
Beijing, and Basel

The Community Reinvestment Act, a quarter-century after its relatively quiet enactment by the U.S. Congress, provides a model for the emerging and much needed architecture of global financial regulation. The banking industry is subject to supervision and regulation in every modern state, not only because it is government-insured (in the United States and many other counties), but also because of the government-like function it performs—the creation of money and fueling of development projects, both positive and negative. The question, of course, is "regulation for what," or, more directly, "for whom"?

The CRA mandates that banks have a duty to the communities from which they draw their deposits. It is at once simple and potentially radical, particularly in our rapidly globalizing, increasingly digital world, where more than a trillion dollars a day pass through the currency exchange markets, where banks and others hold the sovereign debt of developing countries (and the power inherent in being a creditor), and where, at the neighborhood level, people cannot buy houses, apartment buildings cannot be constructed or maintained, and businesses cannot be started or expand, without access to credit. Financing defines the limits of what is possible for the individual, for neighborhoods, for nations and even supranational regions. The lessons of the CRA should be part of the global debate on how, and for whom, the new transnational financial conglomerates should be regulated and supervised. What follows is an account of the lessons learned by one organization, Inner City Press/Community on the Move, from 1987 through 2001.

Banks and The Bronx

The Bronx is one of the five counties that make up New York City. Since the 1960s it has been the lowest-income county in New York State. Due in part to a refusal by banks and insurance companies to lend or write policies in The Bronx, the county lost more than a third of its population in the 1970s. In 1977 President Carter visited the South Bronx to stand before abandoned buildings and assess, he said, the extent of urban decay (Walsh 1977). Ronald Reagan repeated the trip in 1980 and declared that Carter's and the Democrats' policies had failed (Kneeland 1980). Little investment followed in the wake of these announcements. In 1987, when South Bronx residents joined together to form Inner City Press/Community on the Move (ICP), there were still hundreds of abandoned buildings in The Bronx, and whole neighborhoods, tens of thousands of people, without a bank branch.

ICP's first mission was to reclaim and repair abandoned buildings. The group's membership, which grew from a dozen to several hundred in the first year, systematically staked claim to two dozen vacant and tax-delinquent buildings in The Bronx and Upper Manhattan. The work of homesteading—clearing rubble out of apartments, repairing roofs and stairways, reconnecting water and electricity—raised questions. Why had these buildings been abandoned in the first place? And why did neighborhood residents find it so difficult to get loans to buy, repair, and maintain the housing stock? I was one of the founders of ICP and had spent hundreds of hours tarring roofs and plastering walls when I was nominated by the group to look into a law we'd heard mention of, the Community Reinvestment Act.

Banks, the CRA says, have a continuing and affirmative obligation to serve the credit needs of their entire communities, including low- and moderate-income neighborhoods. But an initial inquiry into the policies at least five major banks in New York City found that they had defined their communities as excluding the South Bronx. Three of the banks excluded Bronx County in its entirety. A fourth—the Bank of New York, a $50 billion institution founded by Alexander Hamilton—defined its community as Manhattan to 96th Street (the beginning of East Harlem), picking up again in suburban Westchester County, just north of The Bronx. This seemed, to ICP's members, to constitute explicit redlining. We met with Bank of New York representatives, but nothing changed. In 1992 Bank of New York applied to acquire sixty branches from Barclays and we filed a protest (Associated Press 1992). More meetings followed, and two days before the Federal Reserve Board was slated to vote on Bank of New York's application, the bank announced that it was expanding its definition of its community to include The Bronx, Brooklyn, and Harlem (*Real Estate Weekly* 1992).

Emboldened, ICP approached the four other banks, which similarly excluded the South Bronx from the areas they acknowledged a duty to serve. But not one of these four banks voluntarily changed its map. So in 1994 we challenged expansion applications by each of these banks. The first, Nat West, settled the protest by agreeing to open a new branch in the South Bronx, the first new-construction bank branch in the South Bronx in forty years (Stancavish 1994). Three others—First Fidelity (later bought by First Union), Marine Midland (later renamed HSBC), and Republic National Bank (later bought by HSBC)—expanded their maps, and each agreed to lend $15 million in the South Bronx over the next three years (Dugas 1994). ICP's advocacy was celebrated in some quarters but reviled by corporate law firms and bank trade associations and also by some large nonprofits that had been comfortably working with the banks that excluded The Bronx. In retrospect, it is possible that even larger commitments could have been won. But what did we know? In our next challenge the inside/outside conflict would become explicit.

Inside Versus Outside Strategies: Dime and Anchor

In the fall of 1994 Dime Savings Bank announced that it would apply to acquire Anchor Savings Bank, which had barely survived the savings and loan industry crisis. Anchor had bought near-failing thrifts in the Southwest and Florida, while lending less and less in its original community in and around New York. Home Mortgage Disclosure Act (HMDA) data showed that fewer than 5 percent of Anchor's loans in Bronx County were in the South Bronx, the lower-income half of the county, where more than 95 percent of the residents are African American or Latino. ICP filed comments with the Office of Thrift Supervision, the primary federal regulator of both Anchor and Dime. The OTS granted ICP's request for a formal hearing, declaring the protest to be "substantial." This ruling was reported on the Associated Press newswire and in newspapers beyond New York; the *Chicago Tribune*'s headline on November 12, 1994, was "Bias Charges Stop Deal," while the *National Law Journal*'s headline read "Dime to Face Federal Hearings on Bias." Corporate lawyers told the *American Banker* that ICP's challenge had "the potential of stopping the merger in its tracks" and that "the hearing could take several months, then be delayed" (Seiberg 1994a). Dime and Anchor declared that they stood behind their lending practices and were preparing for the hearing at which Dime's chief executive, Richard Parsons, would represent them.

Behind the scenes, the banks asked community development groups that they had previously funded to write a joint letter to the OTS supporting the banks' lending records, and to release this letter to the media. A number of the groups refused to sign on, but twenty-two did, stating that "both institutions have long and positive working relationships with the city's infrastructure of nonprofit housing and community development groups." Contacted by the press, ICP was at first somewhat belligerent, then characterized Dime's strategy as "unfortunate" and urged reporters to ask the signatory groups if they had even read ICP's comments to the OTS or its analysis of Anchor's and Dime's actual lending records. The coordinator of the letter, the head of the New York City Housing Partnership (an affiliate of the city's chamber of commerce, which had been founded by Chase Manhattan Bank's David Rockefeller) admitted to the *American Banker* that she had not read ICP's filings (Seiberg 1994b). Nevertheless, she wrote an op-ed piece for *New York Newsday* denouncing ICP's challenge; *Newsday* asked ICP to respond. This spat between big nonprofits and grassroots groups threatened to blur the focus and let the banks off the hook.

The OTS hearing was scheduled for November 29, 1994, the Monday after Thanksgiving. The day before Thanksgiving Dime's chief executive telephoned ICP and asked to meet. At this meeting—at which the impending hearing was repeatedly cited as a deadline, a point of no return after which no resolution could be reached—Dime agreed to open a new branch in the South Bronx and to increase its lending by $15 million in the South Bronx and $5 million in Upper Manhattan over three years. Dime offered to include in the agreement a grant to ICP, but ICP declined. The agreement was faxed to the OTS, a joint press release was issued, and the hearing was cancelled.

This CRA agreement was reported in newspapers from Atlanta to Orlando. Ironically, the op-ed piece by the coordinator of the pro-Dime community groups, now moot, appeared on the day the agreement was released. It appeared to argue that opening a bank branch in the South Bronx might be a waste of money that professionalized housing development groups could put to better use (Wylde 1994). ICP's response, published in Newsday on November 30, called it

> tragic that community groups would give their seal of approval without even knowing the banks' lending records. A bank that provides grants, while commendable, is still not complying with the CRA if it does not lend directly. The CRA, however, did its job. Yesterday, Dime, Anchor and Inner City Press reached a settlement: After the merger, Dime will open a full-service branch in the South Bronx. Even if the merger is never completed, each bank will make $15 million in housing, consumer and commercial loans in the South Bronx, and $5 million in loans in upper Manhattan. (Lee 1994)

Many community groups, and even some bank CRA officers, off the record, called to congratulate ICP on the agreement, and on the proactive (some called it "abrasive") CRA enforcement strategy that ICP had adopted.

Superficially, this episode illustrated the quintessentially American axiom, "You can't argue with success." But more substantively, the Dime-Anchor "spin war" reflected a rift that still exists between professionalized service-providing groups, which are reluctant to criticize the banks that fund them, and organizations still rooted in community organizing and advocacy. Both are needed. To use a baking analogy, someone has to get the wheat, and someone has to turn it into bread, to structure housing investments through which the banks can meet their commitments. It's a classic good cop/bad cop dynamic. But when the good cop publicly denounces the bad cop's actions while happily using the bad cop's results, there is a problem. Given the power imbalance between low-income communities and the mega-banks that increasingly dominate local and global economies and regulators, a strategy that does not involve ongoing monitoring and challenging of industry developments, including mergers, will be ineffective. That the banking industry would seek to discourage oversight and advocacy is understandable. But *community* groups? And those who purport to speak in their name, or to be part of the "community development" movement (Lindsey 2000)?

Following these five successful campaigns in late 1994, ICP committed more and more of its time and meager resources to CRA enforcement, to attempting to reverse the decades of redlining suffered by residents of The Bronx and communities like it. Through these CRA campaigns, ICP's membership expanded beyond homesteaders and tenants to include the proprietors of local small businesses, homeowners seeking to refinance their mortgages, and families seeking to buy their first home. It was an exciting and somewhat mystifying time. Bank lawyers were venturing to the South Bronx in limousines to sign lending agreements; the local press was lauding this burst of CRA enforcement; the banks began to suggest that ICP should conduct loan counseling for them or otherwise join the more professionalized, less contentious world of "bank-community collaboration." But there was more serious trouble on the horizon.

The Chase: Community Reinvestment in the Courts

ICP's members, becoming more comfortable with analyzing HMDA data to assess banks' lending, identified Citibank and Chase Manhattan as among the least active lenders to low- and moderate-income people. Since the CRA, as written, is enforced only in connection with banks' applications for approvals to expand, we focused first on Chase, once it applied for regulatory approval to merge its New York and Connecticut banks. We filed a hundred-page comment; Chase filed a response nearly as long (Hansell 1994). It became apparent to us that since Chase didn't much care *when* its application to merge banks it already owned was approved, it had decided to "draw a line in the sand"—Chase's phrase—and simply wait for the inevitable Federal Reserve Board approval and declare themselves vindicated. The bank's CRA officer made it clear: Chase would not commit to opening a new branch in the South Bronx; Chase would not make a race-specific lending commitment. None of the ICP agreements had referred to race, specifying only that the properties or small businesses be in low- or moderate-income areas. But the fight with Chase had become ideological and, in terms of the Fed's batting average for approving protested applications, the odds were stacked against ICP. It appears in retrospect that this non-time-sensitive merger was the wrong one to challenge, especially as the first action in a Chase campaign.

While the application was pending, Chase announced that it was buying part of the business of U.S. Trust, an institution that proudly advertised its focus on "affluent individuals and their families." This was a substantive merger proposal—tactically, it was more time-sensitive than Chase's application to merge banks it already owned. ICP submitted even longer, updated comments, and the legal pleadings flew (Troshinsky 1995). When the Fed approved the deal in mid-1995, ICP decided to ask a court to review the Fed's approval order, and sought a temporary restraining order against Chase's "consummating" its U.S. Trust acquisition. We were learning the language of bank mergers if nothing else.

Chase's and U.S. Trust's legal defense function shifted from its in-house CRA lawyers to an outside firm, Cravath Swaine and Moore. This firm filed a hundred-page objection; a court clerk called ICP and said there were a dozen lawyers milling around in the hallway of the U.S. Court of Appeals for the Second Circuit, demanding to see the judge who would rule on ICP's request for an injunction. Part of the case, for review of the Office of the Comptroller of the Currency (OCC)'s approval, was dismissed "without prejudice"— we had filed the OCC claim in the wrong court. We refiled in the federal district court and combined the action with a request to review the OCC's and FDIC's approval of another application, GreenPoint Bank's proposal to acquire sixty New York branches from Home Savings of America. The district court judge granted ICP's request for a temporary restraining order. Now the stakes had been raised again, at least in the banks' view (Hansell 1995). GreenPoint's and Home Savings' lawyers called the judge at his home and demanded a hearing the next day. At this hearing GreenPoint claimed that it had already reprogrammed the Home Savings branches' ATM machines, that if the deal didn't close, tens of thousands of consumers would be left without cash over the weekend. After an hour's argument the judge removed the restraining order. He did, however, grant ICP's request for the release of many documents that the banks, the OCC, and FDIC had sought to withhold (*Lee v. FDIC* 1996).

Back in The Bronx, we regrouped. What had been learned in this chaos in the court district in Lower Manhattan? It seemed clear that CRA issues would be taken more seriously by banks and regulators if community groups could get courts to review the regulators' routine approvals of protested applications. The flaw appeared to be that such review was difficult to obtain, since banks could defeat requests that the underlying mergers be stayed, pending review, by claiming that their customers would be harmed, and that the petitioning community group would have to post a bond to reimburse the bank for its expenses in halting a deal's closing. ICP couldn't afford to post such a bond. The phrase "pay to play" came to mind; only the titans could litigate with each other. The CRA is one small law in a wider statutory spider web over which corporate America has far more sway than do low-income communities.

Citigroup: From Branch Closings to "Technically Illegal" Mergers

Other lessons about the CRA, its promise and its weaknesses, were being hammered home in The Bronx and elsewhere. In 1996 Citibank quietly announced that it would be closing six branches in The Bronx. Neighborhood residents, who had seen the number of local bank branches dwindle for two decades and be replaced by check-cashing and payday loan stores, asked Citibank to reconsider (Kappstatter 1996). A picket line was organized around one of Citibank's remaining branches in The Bronx. Letters were written to Citibank's regulators, the Federal Reserve and the OCC (Kraus 1996). The regulators explained that Citibank needed no one's approval to close the branches. The bank had only to give ninety days' notice by posting an announcement inside each branch. Already posted inside each branch was a framed legal notice reading, "This bank is subject to the Community Reinvestment Act of 1977, and its regulators are required to consider the bank's record of service in low- and moderate-income neighborhoods in connection with its applications to merge or expand."

The irony was not lost on the community residents. The regulators were required to "consider the bank's record of service" but could do nothing to stop a branch from closing. There had been a flurry of bank mergers, the largest of which was Chase Manhattan's merger with Chemical Bank in late 1995, resulting in the closure of twelve more branches in The Bronx (Seiberg 1996). What were the regulators "considering" when they approved all of these mergers? The most straightforward way to find out—and to attempt to further disrupt the insular relationships between banks and their regulators—would be to get courts to review the bank regulators' decisions. But if you had to post a multimillion dollar bond to get "pre-consummation" review of a regulator's merger approval—if you had to pay to play—the legal enforcement of CRA broke down.

During this time, while serving as executive director of ICP, I was going to law school at night. Between classes I would hit the law library, reading volume 12 of the U.S. Code (Banking), the regulatory agencies' implementing regulations, and past approval orders of the Federal Reserve Board. Another incongruity in the CRA process had become clear: the CRA is a law, enforced only during the period to contest banks' applications for approval to expand. The banks and their lawyers were well versed in the process; many of the banks' lawyers had worked previously at the regulatory agencies. Community groups, on the other hand, were only part-time participants in the bank regulation process, and were often treated condescendingly and dismissively by the regulators.

ICP's local victories in winning new bank branches in the South Bronx had been reported by the Associated Press and Reuters. Community groups elsewhere in the country began calling ICP, seeking advice on how to put together comments, where to file them, even how to negotiate. ICP decided to expand its work beyond The Bronx, beyond New York. We filed a joint protest to an application by Bank One to expand in Louisiana (Wolf 1995). We collaborated with grassroots groups in northern New Mexico when then-NationsBank applied to buy the largest bank in that state (Troshinsky 1996). Grassroots activists in these states, and then others, began formally to join ICP and create ongoing projects to monitor the banks. If the CRA process required a "good cop/bad cop" approach, ICP would play, or bolster, the "bad cops" and try to hold the regulators to their legal duties to review applying banks' lending records thoroughly and to study the prospective effects of mergers and their attendant consequences of branch closings, layoffs, and increased cost to consumers. By this time I had graduated from law school and passed the New York bar exam. With funding from the National Association for Public Interest Law, ICP formed a spin-off, the Inner City Public Interest Law Project, to further expand its work. The Law Project's arguments were strengthened by reports that the banks that had reached settlements with ICP to open new branches in the South Bronx had all found the branches to be profitable (Rohde 1997). Students from several law schools began to volunteer with ICP, which allowed for more research not tied to any particular pending merger application.

ICP's frame of reference had expanded one level out. Banking is a government-insured and regulated business that affects nearly everyone in society. Public comment periods on mergers were a brief window for discussion about community lending, discussions in which the full impact of the mergers should and could be considered, and through which grassroots housing groups should and could collaborate with other types of organizations (consumers and labor, for example) to try to hold the banks accountable. Perhaps the limitations of the CRA statute could be surmounted by such collaborations.

In April 1998 Citicorp—which had been confirmed, in ICP's view, at least, as one of the least consumer- and community-friendly banks in New York—announced that it would merge with Travelers Insurance, which also owned the Salomon Smith Barney investment bank and which ICP had previously opposed (Lee 1997). Industry pundits and the journalists who quoted them noted that the merger was "technically illegal" under the Glass-Steagall Act of 1933 but that the Federal Reserve Board would probably approve it anyway. Communities might be constrained by the law but the titans were not. It was worldwide news: Travelers' Sandy Weill, who had begun by buying a high-interest-rate lender in Baltimore (Commercial Credit), had returned to embrace Wall Street. Citicorp's chairman, John Reed, winced uncomfortably in a photograph that ran in the tabloid newspapers sold in The Bronx. In a county where overcrowded high school classrooms were thinned each year as students, mostly male, were arrested and imprisoned, this creatively cavalier approach to the law—"technically impermissible under current law," is the way one newspaper put it—made people take notice.

Among the things that most interested ICP was Sandy Weill's claim that he had presented the deal to the Federal Reserve before announcing it, and that he had every reason to believe that the merger would be favorably viewed by the Fed. ICP filed a Freedom of Information Act (FOIA) request with the Fed, asking for all documents about these communications. But the Fed responded that the notes its staffers had taken at the meetings with Citigroup in March 1998 were not available under FOIA, that they were not "records of the Board" but rather the personal property of the Fed staffers, akin to their shopping lists or notes from their spouses. The Fed claimed that it had only offered "guidance," and not pre-approval, to Mr. Weill and his lawyers, and promised that all public comments, including ICP's, would be considered closely (Rehm 1998). The Federal Reserve Board noted that the New York Fed had just announced that it would hold a public hearing in its auditorium near Wall Street; Citibank's "record of service," the Fed's press release said, would also be considered.

At the hearing, held in an air-conditioned amphitheater in the Fed's castle-like building on Liberty Street, a number of elected officials praised Citibank's record of service to their districts and to New York's economy. The "technical illegality" of the merger was hardly mentioned; John Reed, who was allowed to speak first, did not mention it. Residents of low-income New York City, including ICP members, and of Rochester and Buffalo, related their experiences of Citibank's branch closings and of Travelers Insurance Company's unwillingness to write policies in low-income neighborhoods. The two companies, now calling themselves Citigroup and adopting Travelers' red umbrella as their logo, announced that they would lend $115 billion in low- and moderate-income communities over the next ten years. But as ICP and many others noticed, a large part of this pledge consisted of credit card lending, a category of lending that no other bank had ever included in a CRA pledge. The Fed, however, seemed convinced of the merits of the Citigroup merger, for reasons that had nothing to do with CRA. Bigger is better, the Fed seems to think, easier to supervise and better able to compete with the Japanese and European universal banks.

After the hearing ICP filed a lawsuit asking the federal District Court for the Southern District of New York to order the Fed to release the documents about its meetings with Sandy Weill and his lawyers, and to extend the comment period. The Fed responded that while the court had jurisdiction to consider the FOIA issues, it had no power to order the Fed to extend the comment period. The court agreed, and the Fed closed its comment period (Seiberg 1998). Soon thereafter the Fed approved the merger, giving Citigroup a two-year grace period in which to either "cure" the illegality of combining banking and insurance or have the Glass-Steagall Act repealed. The financial press called the repeal likely, even moreso now that the largest U.S. bank would be focusing its lobbying and campaign contribution budget on this one inconvenient law. It was becoming clearer to ICP that the Community Reinvestment Act and the communities it was meant to benefit were now more than ever subject to wider forces, regarding which we would have to learn more.

The CRA in Congress: Deregulation, Foreign and Domestic

In November 1998 the Republican Party won control of the U.S. Senate, and Texan senator Phil Gramm became the chairman of the Senate banking committee. Almost immediately Senator Gramm began to denounce the CRA as an extortionist "tax" on banks. He compared CRA activists to *mafiosi*, proclaiming that CRA had become "bigger than General Motors." Through the legislative process surrounding the banks'—now most visibly Citigroup's—efforts to replace the Glass-Steagall Act, Senator Gramm began to call for the repeal of the CRA or, at a minimum, a "safe harbor" for the 98 percent of U.S. banks that had been awarded satisfactory or outstanding CRA ratings by their regulators. Through the National Community Reinvestment Coalition, which ICP had joined in 1995, efforts were made to counteract Senator Gramm's claims. Among other things, these "spin battles" made clear that many Americans had never *heard* of the Community Reinvestment Act, and that the banks—again, primarily Citigroup—were so committed to winning the deregulation legislation that they would increase their campaign contributions to both parties, whatever the effect on CRA.

This is not to imply that many banks were not also gunning for the outright repeal of CRA. But some banks claimed publicly that they had learned to live with the law, even that it was "good business." As noted above, each of the banks that had reached agreements with ICP to open new branches in the South Bronx had found the branches to be profitable (Rohde 1997). Senator Gramm's strategy was to insist that anti-CRA provisions had to be part of any financial modernization law or he would not allow a vote on the law. Senator Gramm almost single-handedly blocked a vote on Glass-Steagall repeal in late 1998. Throughout 1999 versions of financial modernization floated around Capitol Hill, and planeloads of bankers were flown in to lobby. Eventually most of the Democrats folded and agreed to vote for a version of financial modernization that would allow banks to get into insurance and securities without taking on any new CRA responsibilities.

"We must be allowed to compete with Japanese and German banks," a Democratic congressman intoned, explaining his support for the Gramm-Leach-Bliley Act. The banking industry had presented itself as a victim, tied up in anachronistic laws while some ill-defined "foreigners" were taking over the global financial industry. But the reality was that U.S.-based investment banks were (and are) dominating underwriting and foreign exchange trading in most of the world, and that the chieftains of the global "bulge bracket" banks, including HSBC, Deutsche Bank, BNP Paribas, and Japan's Mizuho, have more in common with each other than with the residents of the countries in which they are supposedly headquartered. Nationalism is increasingly an anachronism when it comes to global profit making. The World Trade Organization, the World Bank, and the International Monetary Fund (IMF)—even the United Nations—instruct countries to open their borders and make way for acquisitions and currency speculation if they want to be part of the global economy. Not coincidentally, the instructions continue, countries should repeal their remaining consumer-protection laws, which serve only as a burden on free trade, a drag on the brave new world of multinational financial supermarkets along the lines of Citigroup. Prior to the Citicorp-Travelers merger, the Federal Reserve had already allowed bank holding companies to own securities-underwriting subsidiaries. What was new, with Citigroup, was its involvement in insurance underwriting, both property/casualty and health and life insurance. These businesses were—and remain, as of this writing—regulated at the state rather than the federal level. While federal bank regulators can legitimately be accused of cheerleading for the institutions they supervise, the process of "regulatory capture" is often even worse at the state level. In many states the chief regulator is elected, often with campaign contributions from the insurance industry. When Travelers applied to buy Citicorp in 1998, ICP commented to several state insurance regulators and attended the required hearings in Dover, Delaware, and Trenton, New Jersey. In Dover, Travelers appeared with a dozen lawyers and contested ICP's right to comment, much less conduct cross-examination (Epstein 1998). While some cross-examination was eventually allowed, the approval order was issued soon thereafter by the state's insurance commissioner, who had reportedly accepted campaign contributions from Travelers (Otis 1996). At least in Delaware, there appear to be no conflict-of-interest standards. Worse, the Delaware insurance commissioner declared that her only duty was to residents of Delaware—despite the large number of insurance companies that have headquarters in Delaware but do business only in other states. To date, and primarily in connection with Citigroup's continued expansion, ICP has participated in proceedings before insurance regulators in Arizona, Nevada, Minnesota, Tennessee, Indiana, Texas, Delaware, New Jersey and Missouri—where, as set forth below, ICP has also litigated the Missouri Department of Insurance's refusal to allow consumer groups to conduct pre-hearing discovery, including deposing the applicant's witnesses. While always educational and providing opportunities to collaborate with consumers as well as community organizations, the state regulation of insurance is an anachronism shot full of loopholes, demonstrated in the first year of the twenty-first century by the frauds allegedly committed by insurance investor Martin Frankel (Tuckey 2001). ICP has joined with many other groups pushing for federal insurance regulation, including public reporting of insurance underwriting data, similar to the Home Mortgage Disclosure Act, and the application of the principles and legal responsibility of community reinvestment to the insurance industry, in both its policy-writing and its investment practices. Citigroup, which so lucratively broke down the legal walls between banking and insurance in 1998, and to which this narrative now returns, is an appropriate focus for this insurance accountability campaign.

Citigroup Round II: Predatory Lending and No Place to Comment

The Gramm-Leach-Bliley Act, also (mis)named the Financial Modernization Act of 1999, maintained the state regulation of insurance and provided many other benefits to the financial services industries. A provision of the GLB Act that received little press coverage but constituted another significant concession to the industry was the elimination of the requirement that companies apply for approvals of mergers with "non-banking" firms. Since the CRA is enforced only in connection with the pre-consummation review of mergers, this change seriously weakened CRA enforcement. This became clear in September 2000, when Citigroup announced that it would acquire Associates First Capital Corporation, the largest subprime (high-interest-rate) consumer finance lender in the United States.

ICP had previously opposed Associates' applications to get into banking (Coulton 1997). Associates' application for a savings bank charter was suspended, and the Justice Department filed suit against Associates' credit card bank for discrimination against Latinos. Now Citigroup proposed to acquire this company, and there would not even be a comment period before the Federal Reserve Board.

Citigroup *did* submit applications to the OCC and the FDIC to acquire Associates' credit card banks—but these agencies loudly proclaimed that the Community Reinvestment Act didn't cover these "Change in Bank Control Act" applications. Neither federal agency held a hearing on Citigroup's applications. ICP commented to several state insurance regulators and to the South Dakota Division of Banking. At a hearing in Pierre, South Dakota, in October 2000, Citigroup's representative focused on grants Citigroup had given in Rapid City and claimed that predatory lending issues were "irrelevant" (Wells 2000). The South Dakota regulator agreed and approved Citigroup's application (Baker 2000). At a hearing in Jefferson City, Missouri, Citigroup claimed that only Associates' Missouri-domiciled insurer was relevant (Lee 2000a). The Missouri Department of Insurance approved Citigroup's application in mid-November. ICP filed suit on December 1, 2000; but by then Citigroup had rounded up the remaining approvals, all within the course of a few hours on November 30, 2000, and had immediately closed the deal. Citigroup then argued that the Missouri case was moot. ICP was becoming all too familiar with this word.

It was a crash course in deregulation. The regulators had allowed, without a hearing—the Federal Reserve did not even accept comments—the largest U.S. bank to acquire the largest U.S. subprime lender, a company that was being sued for racial discrimination. Citigroup had announced some vague reforms in mid-November 2000, but ICP, along with most of the other groups who tried to opposed Citigroup's application, felt the reforms did not go far enough, and had little confidence that the regulators would even hold Citigroup to them. There were other, larger lessons that advocates in other fields, from environmental protection to trade regulation to human rights, had been confronting for years. Industry consolidation and the decades-long capture of even purported liberals by business interests, the undermining of the 1960s "Great Society" ideal, culminating in President Clinton's signing of welfare "reform" (read: repeal)—all had resulted in what some, only half-jokingly, were calling corporate anarchy. The 1994 North America Free Trade Agreement, for example, allows corporations to sue governments for "over-regulating" them. The World Trade Organization, quietly formed in 1995, has the power to overrule nations' laws and regulations if they impede free trade (and corporate profits). Citigroup, now with nearly a trillion dollars in assets and operations in over one hundred countries, was evading any meaningful regulation. The Federal Reserve, Citigroup's "home country supervisor," looked only at Citigroup's operations in the United States, and even then allowed Citigroup to buy a problematic subprime lender without so much as a public-comment period, much less a hearing (Lee 2001).

Chase Round II: Predatory Lending in Japan; Regulatory Capitulation

When Chase Manhattan and J. P. Morgan merged in late 2000, the Federal Reserve Board's approval order said that U.S. environmental issues could be addressed by the U.S. Environmental Protection Agency, U.S. labor issues could be addressed by the U.S. Department of Labor, and so on—but the Fed was entirely silent on Morgan Chase's effects on communities, workers, and the environment outside the United States. As ICP had documented to the Fed, these activities included investment in predatory lenders. For example, the *Times* of London reported on November 27, 1999:

> A former employee of Nichiei Co, Japan's leading lender to small companies, was arrested yesterday after being accused of telling a borrower and his wife to sell their kidneys to repay their debt.... "Make money by selling your kidneys. You can sell them for three million yen," he was quoted by a police official as telling the borrower and his wife, who was the guarantor.... Japanese regulators have begun questioning 13 Japanese and foreign banks that provided funds to Nichiei, including Merrill Lynch and Citibank. Chase Manhattan has a 4.7 per cent shareholding.

The (London) *Guardian* reported on November 6 that "the scandal is also embarrassing to foreign investors, who own 31 percent of Nichiei. These investors, led by Chase Manhattan Bank, have enjoyed healthy dividends from the company in recent years." To date, the Federal Reserve Board refuses to inquire into what it characterizes as "consumer issues" outside the United States. Meanwhile, U.S.-based banks are expanding into country after country.

While ICP could (and can) be criticized for not thinking strategically enough, these lessons were inescapable. Community reinvestment advocates would have to begin looking at wider issues and collaborating with the emerging movement that questioned mega-corporations' domination of regulatory processes both national and supranational, if local communities were to be able to hold the large banks accountable to those they take deposits from and those they affect.

Beyond CRA, or, Community Reinvestment by Other Means

And so ICP began expanding the scope of issues raised in its comments to regulators, and expanding the range of regulators to which it would comment. There had been some initial forays: in 1994, ICP had commented to the Federal Reserve on Republic's (now HSBC's) request to be able to deal in palladium as well as platinum. The bank claimed that these two precious metals were interchangeable. But ICP's kitchen-sink research found articles in the mining industry press that emphasized their differences, proving the speciousness (or sloppiness) of the bank's argument. Soon thereafter, Republic agreed to lend $15 million in the South Bronx (Seiberg 1994c). In 1995 ICP had commented to the Securities and Exchange Commission (SEC) in opposition to an application by Chase to be deemed an authorized custodian of securities in Russia. ICP's research found that there were not yet actual share certificates in Russia, and that a number of investors had simply had their shareholdings wiped out by the underlying companies' accountants (Pelle 1995). Responses flew until the SEC conveniently determined that Chase didn't actually *need* any approval for this new role, that it could be accomplished by a "No Action" letter on which no public comments were allowed. These proceedings led ICP to expand its research functions further and to redouble its efforts to intervene, where necessary, with the right regulator, at the right time—even on transactions the agencies claimed were not subject to public comment. Without question, the Internet allows grassroots groups to do more and better research. The balance of power, however, changes more slowly.

In 1999, when Lehman Brothers applied to the Office of Thrift Supervision to acquire a near-failing thrift, Delaware Savings Bank, ICP submitted a joint comment, along with the Delaware Community Reinvestment Action Council (DCRAC). Lehman's goal was to shift its mortgage purchasing and lending, much of it subprime, into a federal savings bank, in order to get around state laws (Harrison 1999). Although the OTS contended that Lehman's was an emergency application not subject to public comment, the issues ICP and DCRAC raised were considered and the OTS required from Lehman Brothers a letter that it would avoid, and monitor the loans that it bought for, "predatory practices." It was a promising precedent but to date has been of little practical value, as "predatory practices" were not defined by the OTS.

In another OTS proceeding, ICP raised questions about the CRA duties of the then-largest Internet bank, which E∗TRADE was applying to acquire. The institution was soliciting deposits throughout the United States but maintained that its CRA duty was limited to Arlington, Virginia, where its headquarters were located. Through its web site, the bank not only accepted deposits but also offered mortgage loans. ICP raised these issues in some detail (Fraser 1999). The bank ultimately announced that it would purchase $750 million in low- and moderate-income mortgages nationwide, and would contribute $1 million to a project to "bridge the digital divide" (a project not affiliated with ICP). This was another interim solution, however; the OTS and the other agencies have said they want to avoid "inhibiting innovation" in Internet banking, and will probably not resolve the issue in their next periodic rewrites of the CRA regulation. At some point, in some Congress, the CRA statute will be substantively debated, in light of the many industry changes since 1977. It is imperative that this debate include the full scope of issues—the ways in which banks, insurance companies, and investment banks affect low- and moderate-income communities, and, secondarily, the subsidies, safety nets, and government-coordinated regulatory regimes from which these industries benefit. These include not only FDIC insurance, the Securities Investors Protection Fund (SIPC) and state-run insurance bail-out funds, but also such things as the SEC system of centralized disclosure, which encourages transfers of funds as surely as government insurance of bank deposits does.

ICP has been expanding its scope beyond retail banks in the United States. In 2000, ICP commented to the Federal Reserve on an application by three Japanese banks to merge and form the world's largest financial institution, Mizuho (Hyuga 2000). Each of the three Japanese banks was involved with subprime lenders in the United States, either as warehouse lenders, trustees, or underwriters. The Federal Reserve required the banks to respond on these issues, and forwarded ICP's comments to other agencies. One of the subprime lenders to which the banks had issued a warehouse line of credit, PinnFund USA, was subsequently charged with fraud by the SEC and closed down (Chaffin 2001). Later in 2000 ICP commented to the New York Banking Department on Credit Suisse First Boston's application to acquire the New York trust bank of DLJ. ICP put into the record recent reports that Credit Suisse had handled funds for the ex-dictator of Nigeria, Sani Abacha. The Banking Department required responses on these issues (Analore 2000). Credit Suisse discovered a clever way to consummate the deal before obtaining banking department approval, by simply leaving its New York bank behind with DLJ's majority shareholder, AXA. Through each of these proceedings, ICP has learned more. Anti-predatory-lending advocates nationwide are increasingly aware of the centrality of investment banks in securitizing the high-cost loans made by smaller subprime lenders. Investment banks have a significant impact, both positive and negative, on low-income communities in the United States and around the world.

The Future: The Global Struggle for Fair Finance

As of this writing, ICP has been working with an array of environmental, human rights, and other public interest—or "civil society"—groups for more than a year. This collaboration had already begun before Citigroup announced its acquisition of Associates First Capital in September 2000. As a first experiment, ICP informed environmental activists of the New York banking department's November 10, 2000, public hearing on Citigroup's application to acquire Associates' operations in New York. Environmentalists came to the hearing and testified about Citigroup's destructive practices in Indonesia, Burma, and Ecuador, which harm indigenous people, rainforests, and even orangutans. In a summary ICP subsequently obtained under the FOIA, the FDIC's representative at the hearing noted dryly that he didn't find these issues "relevant" to the legal standard the FDIC had to consider. But that standard includes the "integrity" of the managers of the applicant bank and the transaction's effect on the "public interest." There is a need for new legal arguments, a new discourse, on banks' duties to the communities they are chartered to serve, to the societies they increasingly dominate.

Citigroup was and is at the forefront of these lessons. In May 2001 Citigroup announced a proposal to acquire Banamex, the second-largest bank in Mexico, and thereby to take control of more than 25 percent of the banking assets in Mexico (Kelleher 2001). A week later the Dutch insurer ING announced its acquisition of the largest insurance company in Mexico. Meanwhile, ING has chartered a non-branch bank in the United States, soliciting insured deposits over the Internet but limited its CRA duties to a small portion of the United States (Lee 2000b).

The regulators are asleep at the switch—or, many increasingly believe, in the industry's pocket. The voice of the people affected must be heard. ICP's current thinking is that the globalization of the financial services industry will require a global regulator that will impose regulation not only on financial but also on social and environmental issues, along the lines of the CRA.

As a vehicle for the next stage of this work, a Fair Finance Watch has been launched, which in May 2001 commented to this effect to the current supranational regulator, the Basel Committee on Banking Supervision. Looking at the global situation, the trends are inescapable: low- and moderate-income people in Argentina, Ecuador, and Thailand, to name only a few, are marching against what they call the IMF's predatory loans to their countries—or, in some cases, to since-deposed dictators, who simply took the loan money and laundered it through major banks like Citigroup. Bank workers in Seoul, South Korea, have protested the cost-cutting merger of that country's two largest banks—which in turn were controlled by the U.S.-based investment bank Goldman Sachs and the Dutch conglomerate ING Barings. A global demand is growing for transparency and accountability, for a slowing of (or CRA-type duty applying to) the 1 trillion dollars that currently flow every day through foreign exchange markets, through over-the-counter (that is, nonregulated) derivatives transactions, through hedge funds based in off-shore banking centers. Too much of the debate about the CRA ignores this wider context. Local communities in the United States and elsewhere are threatened with being left further and further behind. There is much work to be done in this new decade and century, and the Community Reinvestment Act and its lessons can and should play a role in this debate, in this advocacy and organizing, this awakening and linking of global civil society. Not only financing but organizing and advocacy define the limits of what is possible.

References

Analore, Andrew. 2000. Credit Suisse First Boston Working on "Approved Issuer" List to Battle Loan Abuse. Inside Mortgage Finance's *Inside B&C Lending* (Nov. 6).

Associated Press. 1992. A Bank of New York Proposal Hits a Snag (Sept. 22). In *New York Times*, (Sept. 23), D1.

Baker, Patrick. 2000. Bank Merger OK'd Despite Group's Protest. *Pierre Capital Journal* (Oct. 19).

Chaffin, Joshua. 2001. The Fund Manager and the Porn Star. *Financial Times* (April 30), 26.

Coulton, Antoinette. 1997. Activist Group Targets Ford Unit, Calling Its Card Rates Excessive. *American Banker* (January 27), 1.

Dugas, Christine. 1994. Banks to Put Up $45 Million; Bronx Group's Muscle-Flexing Leads to New Commitments. *New York Newsday* (Oct. 21), A53.

Epstein, Jonathan. 1998. Travelers Grilled on Buyout Plan. *Wilmington News-Journal* (June 5), B7.

Fraser, Katharine. 1999. Nationwide CRA Zone Urged in Telebank Deal. *American Banker* (Aug. 25), 2.

Hansell, Saul. 1994. Bronx Group Is Challenging A Planned Merger by Chase. *New York Times* (Nov. 5), 41.

———. 1995. Court to Hear A Challenge To Greenpoint. *New York Times* (Sept. 21), D4.

Harrison, David. 1999. Activists Question Lehman's Loan Record. *American Banker* (May 17), 2.

Hyuga, Takahiko. 2000. U.S. Consumer Group Protests Merger of Japan's Biggest Banks. *Bloomberg News* (April 28).

Kappstatter, Bob. 1996. Bank Won't Give In on Closings. *New York Daily News* (Jan. 24).

Kelleher, Mary. 2001. Consumer Group Challenges Citigroup's Banacci Deal. *Reuters* (June 4).

Kneeland, Douglas. 1980. Reagan Urges Blacks to Look Past Labels and to Vote for Him. *New York Times* (Aug. 6), A1.

Kraus, James. 1996. Citibank's Quiet Branch Closings and Switch to ATMs Stir Outrage. *American Banker* (Feb. 12).

Lee, Matthew. 1994. About Banks and The Bronx: Fair Is Fair. *New York Newsday* (Nov. 30), A32.

———. 1997. OTS Curbs on Travelers' Thrift a Model for CRA in New Era. *American Banker* (Dec. 10), 4.

———. 2000a. Citi-Associates Deal Proves Fin Mod Oversight Inadequate. *American Banker* (Nov. 10), 12.

———. 2000b. Revamp CRA Rules for Web Age. *American Banker* (March 10,) 9.

———. 2001. Fed: Big Talk, Little Action. *U.S. Banker* (May), 20.

Lee v. FDIC, 923 F. Supp. 451 (S.D.N.Y. 1996).

Lindsay, Lawrence B. 2000. Community Development at a Crossroads. *Neighborworks Journal* (winter): 54–55.

Otis, L. H. 1996. Delaware Commissioner's Campaign Fund Scrutinized. *National Underwriter*, Life and Health/Financial Services ed. (Nov. 4), 1.

Pelle, Wendy. 1995. Community Group Still Dogs Chase on Low-Mod Lending. *National Mortgage News* (May 15), 13.

Real Estate Weekly. 1992. Bank of NY to Expand Community Outreach (Dec. 16), 10A.

Rehm, Barbara A. 1998. Citi Merger Protester Critical of Fed Counsel's Role. *American Banker* (May 29), 2.

Rohde, David. 1997. Banks Discover the South Bronx; Forced to Open, Branches Profit and Refute Stereotype. *New York Times* (April 16), B1.

Seiberg, Jaret. 1994a. OTS Orders Dime-Anchor Inquiry after CRA Charge. *American Banker* (Nov. 8), 1.

———. 1994b. N.Y. Community Group Backs Dime in CRA Dispute. *American Banker* (Nov. 22), 3.

———. 1994c. Republic New York Agrees to $15 Million Bronx Lending Effort. *American Banker* (Oct. 25), 3.

———. 1996. Red-faced Fed Trying to Undo Damage after Releasing Chase List of Closings. *American Banker* (May 13), 1.

———. 1998. Judge Denies Extension of Citi Deal Comment. *American Banker* (July 2), 4.

Stancavish, Don. 1994. NatWest to Expand Lending to the Poor. *Bergen Record* (Aug. 24), C1.

Troshinsky, Lisa. 1995. Group Attempts New Tactic in Fighting Chase Takeover. *Regulatory Compliance Watch* (July 10), 1.

———. 1996. Finance Subs Free From Pricing Scrutiny. *Regulatory Compliance Watch* (Nov. 18), 1.

Tuckey, Steve. 2001. Frankel Prompts Rule Change. *Insurance Chronicle* (March 12), 11.

Walsh, Edward. 1977. Carter, Ending Visit, Sees Decaying South Bronx. *Washington Post* (Oct. 6), A4.

Wells, Rob. 2000. Citigroup's Purchase of Associates Challenged in State Hearing. *Bloomberg News* (Oct. 10).

Wolf, Barnet. 1995. Banc One Record "Insufficient," Says Fair-Lending Group. *Columbus Dispatch* (Nov. 2), 1B.

Wylde, Kathryn. 1994. About Banks and The Bronx: Or Is It Extortion? *New York Newsday* (Nov. 30), A32.

Malcolm Bush and
Daniel Immergluck

10   Research, Advocacy, and Community Reinvestment

Introduction

The worlds of advocacy and academic research are separate for good and well-known reasons. The time-consuming nature of academic research, and its goal of disinterested inquiry, often makes it of limited use to the legitimate needs of issue advocates for a quick synthesis of information when a political opportunity occurs. Advocacy researchers focus on doing sound, practical research that responds to the current political environment and makes a clear point to policymakers and the interested public.

Advocates who want to make a long-term difference in the lives of lower-income people have no less need than social scientists for a clear and imaginative understanding of problems and solutions. And researchers who want to be involved in current political debates know that some critical knowledge comes from participation. Sociology has a long tradition of appreciating the knowledge gained by participant-observers. In some cases, these observers participate in activities they do not particularly want to shape (Becker and Horowiz 1972). But there is another tradition of knowledge gained by research participants who want to be involved in shaping outcomes (Zuniga 1975).

Since its inception in 1973, the Woodstock Institute has deliberately brought knowledge to bear on action to promote low-income communities' access to financial resources. The institute was founded in the belief that inventing solutions that could help low-income people was more important than the endless description of problems, and that new knowledge had constantly to be brought to both activities. It is no accident that the institute was hatched in an academic research center, the Center for Urban Affairs (now the Institute for Policy Research) at Northwestern University. But, just as important, the founders, most of whom worked outside the university, all had significant practical experience in the struggle for civil rights, and they understood the importance of linking academic knowledge to practical work. As one board member put it, "Woodstock works to demystify the financial field and transfer power mindfully to its community users" (Scheinfeld 1998).

Some people argue that in a regulated industry, the presence of advocacy researchers or activists who press for the implementation of laws and enforcement of regulatory statutes is superfluous. Regulated industries have not only legislated rules of conduct but a body of full-time enforcers. But in banking, as in any regulated industry, there is a complex relationship between regulators and the regulated. The history of state and federal regulation shows that regulation can be critically weakened by the close relationships that develop between the two sides. The same relationships do not automatically exist between regulators and the citizens or consumers who are nominally the primary beneficiaries of the regulation. Moreover, the regulated often have considerable influence in the legislative bodies that establish, revise, and oversee the implementation of regulations.

Others argue that in a world of mature community development organizations with strong ties to the banking industry, advocates are increasingly less relevant. Using vivid examples of protest to characterize all community reinvestment activism, President Bush's former chief economic advisor, Lawrence Lindsey, has reflected that "one can act one way at 20 and another at 40. It is called growing up" (Lindsey 2000). But it is easy for a powerful political figure to make light of the organizing that ordinary people must do in order to be heard. The fact is that the financial services industry, more powerful today than ever before as it becomes concentrated in fewer hands, has never adequately accepted the responsibilities thrust on it by such statutes as the Community Reinvestment Act. The industry constantly seeks to weaken regulation and increase its profits, laws and regulations notwithstanding. The only way for ordinary people to check the industry's power and protect their own interests is to organize themselves effectively and use all the tools at their disposal. The nonprofit development groups that bridge the gap between applied researchers, activists, and the industry are, it is true, building the houses, the businesses, and the neighborhood economies that are the end goal of community activists. But because the developers rely on the financial services industry for loans, equity, grants, and technical help, they sometimes have to downplay their connections to community activists whose goal is to create the conditions for healthy, prosperous, and equitable neighborhoods. This chapter describes two community development projects of the Woodstock Institute and allied organizations. The success of both projects depended on research, policy development, and advocacy. Neither the finance industry nor its regulators would have contributed to either project without outside pressure, although parts of the industry were partners in both cases, while at the same time they were targets of action.

Negotiating an Extensive, Creative, and
Monitorable Community Reinvestment Agreement

One of the opportunities for influencing a bank's community reinvestment plans occurs when a financial institution makes an application to its regulator to change its bank charter (see Bush 1999, on which the first part of this section is based).[1] Banks are required to make such applications when they wish to acquire or merge with another bank or when they wish to open or close a branch. On these occasions regulators examine, among other things, a bank's community reinvestment record. In theory, the regulator can deny an application if that record is inadequate, or delay the application or attach specific community reinvestment requirements to it. In practice, the regulators rarely use any of these sanctions. In 1988, for example, ten years after the Community Reinvestment Act (CRA) was passed, the four bank regulators testified before Congress that in the previous ten years they had denied only eight out of forty thousand bank applications because of inadequate bank performance.[2]

The frequency of merger activity in the quickly consolidating U.S. banking market, and the reluctance of bank regulators to sanction banks for inadequate CRA performance in regular bank CRA exams, have led to what are known as CRA agreements.[3] These are agreements negotiated between banks and community groups in the short interval between the announcement of a bank merger and the approval of that merger by the regulators. Community groups use the slight uncertainty about the approval of a bank application to persuade financial institutions to specify and improve their goals for community reinvestment activity. Merger activity is a high-stakes, fast-moving process, and banks take seriously any perceived threat to the rapid completion of a planned merger. Some banks, therefore, are willing to negotiate with community groups to avoid protests that might delay the approval of an application.

The nature of CRA agreements varies considerably from agreement to agreement. In recent years some banks have begun announcing their own new CRA targets or commitments without negotiations with community groups. These announcements are often attempts to preempt any action by, or the possibility of negotiations with, community organizations. The absence of community analysis means that there is no independent scrutiny of whether the large amounts of money pledged in fact add up to increased commitments. In the late 1990s, for example, in the case of two large mergers, banks made such non-negotiated commitments. Citicorp promised $115 billion in community reinvestment products when it acquired the Travelers Insurance Group, and Bank America and NationsBank announced a $350 billion commitment on their merger. Both commitments were very vague on details and proved to be misleading. For example, both totals included *all* small-business lending, not just lending targeted to lower-income communities. The Citicorp agreement also included $60 billion in consumer credit, again not specifically targeted to lower-income households, while the second commitment included

$180 billion in non-targeted small-business lending. Both agreements were to hold for ten years and affected about forty states. This means that the aggregate commitment in the larger of the two cases was reduced to less than $1 billion per state per year, a figure that might or might not represent increased community lending and investments.

Neither commitment came with any provision for monitoring. The federal bank regulatory agencies do not monitor such commitments and no community group was involved with the commitments. In the view of most community reinvestment groups, such commitments are meaningless. The figures involved may not represent an increase in bank activity in lower-income neighborhoods, and even if they do, there is no mechanism, apart from the banks' own public-relations machine, to determine whether the goals are ever met.

In contrast to these paper commitments, the Chicago CRA Coalition, whose members represent more than one hundred community organizations, negotiated a detailed agreement on the occasion of the merger of First Chicago/NBD and Bank One in 1998.

The Chicago CRA coalition grew out of a long history of community organizing in Chicago and a more recent history of organizing on the issue of community reinvestment by local leaders. The later organizing came from institutions whose leaders who were trained by or affiliated with the Chicago organizer and theorist of organizing Saul Alinsky.[4] The community reinvestment movement in Chicago was born after many city neighborhoods deteriorated as a result, in part, of "block busting" (panicked home sales, spurred by real estate agents, in neighborhoods changing from white to nonwhite residents), and the disinvestment in those neighborhoods by banks and insurance companies. Two Chicago neighborhood groups, the Organization for a Better Austin and the Northwest Community Organization, hosted a national housing conference in 1972, which led to the formation of two other groups (the National Training and Information Center and National People's Action) aimed at changing bank redlining practices.[5] These organizations and groups with similar goals were instrumental in securing passage of the federal Home Mortgage Disclosure Act (HMDA) in 1975 and the Community Reinvestment Act in 1977.

The first community reinvestment agreements were negotiated in Chicago in 1983–84 with First Chicago, Northern Trust, and the Harris Banks. The Woodstock Institute was involved in analyzing HMDA data for those agreements and later in ad hoc coalitions with other groups negotiating other agreements. As discussions about financial modernization legislation that would change the face of the financial services industry heated up in Congress, the Woodstock Coalition decided to formalize its existence and recruit new members.[6] In November 1997 the coalition invited members of Chicago's community development community to join and build a permanent structure to represent community reinvestment interests. The group formed four task forces, covering housing, economic development, investments and grants, and financial services; representatives from each task force served on a steering committee.

The steering committee comprised representatives from both community coalitions and community development corporations, or CDCs. Among these were the Chicago Rehab Network, representing some forty housing organizations, and the Chicago Association of Community Development Organizations (CANDO), the country's largest local association of CDCs, representing some eighty CDCs and a number of other affiliate organizations. Also represented were individual CDCs, a county development organization, a disability rights group, a legal services organization, and Woodstock Institute itself, which convened the coalition and was its research and policy development arm.

As soon as rumors hit the press in April 1998 that First Chicago NBD (headquartered in Chicago) and Banc One (headquartered in Columbus, Ohio) were planning to merge, the coalition called another public meeting and invited representatives from both banks to clarify the details of the merger, including community reinvestment goals. (The original bank was named Banc One and the merged bank took the name Bank One.)

Dozens of community groups attended the meeting and many of them joined the coalition. Each of the four task forces agreed to develop specific CRA recommendations for the merging banks and present them to the steering committee, which would develop a coherent proposal.

At the same time, the senior CRA officer from First Chicago NBD, Mary Decker, called the Woodstock Institute to say that First Chicago was committed to working with the coalition to develop CRA goals appropriate for the new bank. On June 4 the steering committee met with high-level officials from the bank, including Decker and the CEO, Verne Istock, chairman designate of Bank One. The coalition outlined the broad issues it was interested in discussing and both sides agreed on an intensive schedule of meetings. The two sides agreed to meet roughly twice a week so that negotiations could be completed within the thirty-day public comment period, which began on June 14. The agreement was to cover the six-county Chicago metropolitan area. (Banc One refused to negotiate with groups in its other market areas.) John McCoy, the CEO and chairman of Banc One and president and CEO designate of Bank One, declared that he would honor any agreement that came out of the Chicago negotiations.

The coalition faced several challenges in drawing up goals it thought the merged banks (hereafter, the bank) should adopt. The different groups had different CRA priorities, and while the coalition initially drew up a long list of goals, it became clear that there was simply not enough time to discuss them all with the bank. The second challenge stemmed from an earlier commitment the coalition had signed on the occasion of the merger of First Chicago with NBD in July 1995. That commitment had involved what was for the time a large dollar amount, but it was plagued by some of the same problems seen in the voluntary commitments by such banks as Bank America and Citigroup, described above. Namely, it was neither based on a detailed analysis of the banks' current CRA activity nor tied to any measure of the banks' capacities.

The 1995 rewrite of the CRA regulations was intended to produce a rule that, in the words of President Clinton, was "more effective and efficient" than the existing rule. The intention was that the rule should be based on CRA outcomes rather than on processes that might lead to CRA outcomes. While there was eventual assent to that principle, the notion of what constituted an adequate outcome (for example, an adequate number of loans for a particular bank) was hotly debated. On the one hand, community organizations saw the need to tie a bank's performance to some measure of its size. On the other hand, the financial services industry labeled such an effort "credit allocation," by which they meant that setting a numerical standard for performance would amount to regulators telling the banks what particular loans they had to make. The final rule set no empirical standards but used different classes of performance as demonstrating "excellent," "good," "adequate," or "poor" responsiveness to community needs.

In the coalition's view, the lack of any empirical guide to CRA performance was likely to result in an agreement that minimized the bank's capacity for community reinvestment. To set goals for housing and small-business-lending increases appropriate for the new bank's size, the Woodstock Institute developed, and the coalition decided to use, market-share analyses. The institute argued that if a bank's market share in low- and moderate-income neighborhoods was equal to the bank's market share in middle- and upper-income neighborhoods, it was likely that the bank was making at least an equal effort in the lower-income communities. The same analysis could be used to judge a bank's record on lending to racial minorities.

The ratio of a bank's market share in different communities can be used for housing and small-business loans. One advantage of the ratio is that it adjusts for market conditions. Home-mortgage loans, particularly refinance loans, are very sensitive to interest rates. Banks sometimes argue that goal setting is difficult for this reason, although banks set their loan officers' goals every year. But a bank's market-share ratio (that is, its lower-income market share divided by middle- and upper-income market share) depends on changes in both the numerator and denominator and hence will fairly reflect market conditions.

The Woodstock Institute's analysis of the combined record of First Chicago NBD and Bank One in the six-county region showed that their market share ratios reflected a mediocre CRA record. Their best ratio, which was for home improvement loans, was 0.92, and their worst, for very small business loans (loans to businesses with under $1 million in sales) was 0.69. The banks had declared that they intended after their merger to be a CRA leader in Chicago, and the coalition took them at their word, specifying targets that would bring them, in many product lines over several years, to market-share ratios of 1.1 and higher. In line with the coalition's increasing concern about predatory mortgage lending, or home loans with excessively high fees and interest rates targeted predominantly to minority and elderly borrowers, the home-mortgage market-share ratios were to exclude subprime loans.[7]

Under the 1995 CRA regulation, banks are examined on their record of CRA investments and bank services as well as on lending. The coalition developed additional goals in these areas. In the area of bank services, one major concern was the plight of people who had no checking or savings account and instead used costly check-cashing outlets for basic banking services. Another concern was the paucity of bank branches in low-income neighborhoods. The area of investments involves several issues, including equity investments in community development projects and grants for CDCs and other community groups in lower-income communities.

In the course of six weeks, the steering committee of the coalition and senior representatives of the bank negotiated these goals intensely. Often the bank would have to check particular targets with other senior staff, and the coalition met separately to assess progress and reassess its position in light of the bank's responses.

Finally, the two sides reached a very detailed six-year agreement that the coalition thought included sufficient targets and the bank was prepared to accept. Market-share ratio goals were established for various home-mortgage products that would reach 1.1 in the last years of the agreement. Overall ratio goals of 1.5 were set for small-business lending. (In the actual text of the agreement these ratios were translated into target-loan numbers because the bank argued that it could manage only by loan totals and not by ratios.) In addition to the home- and small-business lending goals based on market share ratios, the bank set targets for increased investments and grants based on its 1998 anticipated targets and promised that the 1998 grant levels would be higher than in any previous year. It also agreed to open two more supermarket bank branches and two free-standing branches in lower-income communities. The agreement also contained provisions for increased down-payment assistance for low-income first-time homebuyers, with special provision for people with disabilities.

The bank argued that the provision of low-cost, adequately marketed accounts to people without bank accounts was too complex to be settled before the end of the official comment period for the merger. Instead, First Chicago NBD CEO Verne Istock promised that the bank would continue to work on the issue with the coalition with a view to developing a pilot program by the end of the year. The bank kept its promise and Bank One now has such a pilot program operating in six neighborhoods in Chicago.

There were several reasons for the success of the negotiations in this case. First, there was a history of productive relationships between community organizations and First Chicago, and a string of precedents for successful agreements. The history of quarterly meetings between that bank and its successors with community groups had shown that the two sides could disagree on some issues but still come to compromises on others. In addition, the bank understood that community groups could make it difficult to conduct business if bank officials failed to make good-faith efforts to reach agreement. It was clear that senior bank officials, including the CEO of First Chicago NBD, had determined to make a good-faith effort to reach a substantial agreement.

Second, Woodstock's long experience with using CRA data, and other coalition members' knowledge and understanding of community development, were vital. Woodstock was able to analyze the bank's record using public data and propose empirical guidelines for establishing new goals. (Some data that were not publicly available the bank produced on request.) Community organizations and their representatives had a good sense of potential housing, small-business and other economic development projects that were not getting adequate financing. Individual members of the coalition had many years of experience in community development finance.

The fact that coalition members had worked with each other for a long time, both informally and then more formally, made it easier for them to negotiate effectively under intense pressure. In particular, coalition members agreed that during a bank negotiation they could lobby only for aggregate six-county targets; they were not permitted to seek special treatment for their own organizations.[8] This prevented the divisive practice of coalition members seeking individual agreements from the bank.

The Bank One agreement should not be misconstrued as evidence that mainstream community groups can deal with banks without organizing and advocacy. The largest community development groups stayed out of the coalition for the simple reason that they needed to protect their daily working relationships with the banks. They very much needed the expanded community reinvestment targets contained in the final agreement to bring new debt, equity, and grant resources to their work, but they could not risk offending the banks by joining a process that was bound to be adversarial at times. Several individuals from these organizations quietly provided information on where the bank's performance should be improved, but they played no public role in the negotiations.

The bank, for its part, knew that if it failed to satisfy the minimum requirements of the coalition, the coalition would take its case to the media and the public. There was a lot of press interest in the merger. Moreover, First Chicago had developed the reputation in the 1950s of being the one bank in town that would do business with black customers, and it had a reputation to protect.

Building the Case for Action against Predatory Lending

When inner-city neighborhoods in Chicago and other U.S. cities experienced rapid racial change in the 1960s and 1970s, whites were not the only ones to flee; banks also pulled out of those neighborhoods. For many years the primary goal of community reinvestment advocates was to bring regular financial products to communities shut off from financial services. Since the early 1990s, however, home-mortgage lending has increased in disinvested neighborhoods as community activists and the Clinton administration put pressure on bank regulators to enforce the CRA. Between 1992 and 1995, for example, while overall home-buying activity increased by 54 percent, it increased by 78 percent for low- and moderate-income households and by 126 percent for African-American households (Evanoff and Segal, 1996).

Today, however, low-income people face worse dangers than the indifference of regulated financial institutions. Predatory home-mortgage loans offered by unscrupulous mortgage brokers are driving thousands of low-income and elderly homeowners into debt and foreclosure.[9] Until recently, the major regulatory check on predatory mortgage loans was the Home Ownership and Equity Protection Act of 1994 (HOEPA), which established thresholds for high-cost loans and provided for additional disclosures to borrowers considering such threshold loans. HOEPA also directs the Federal Reserve Board to prohibit unfair or deceptive mortgage lending practices. The Fed has until recently, however, taken little advantage of the provision to stop predatory lending.[10] While the Woodstock Institute and its allies have engaged in policy analysis and public education to attempt to persuade the Fed to strengthen its regulation of HOEPA, the major opportunity to restrict predatory lending has been at the state level. In 2001 advocacy groups were able to persuade Illinois state banking regulators to promulgate, and the Illinois General Assembly to approve, fairly tough anti-predatory regulation, making Illinois one of only four states with such provisions.

The Woodstock Institute routinely tracks mortgage lending trends in Chicago and around the country, and its role in the passage of the Illinois predatory lending regulation goes back a number of years. In early 1999 the institute was an active member of the Federal Reserve Bank of Chicago's predatory lending task force. This task force was one of several that were part of a project called the Mortgage Credit Access Project (MCAP), designed to bring the financial services industry and community organizations together to discuss continued barriers to equal access to homeownership.[11] Other major Chicago fair housing and housing development groups that participated in this task force included the Leadership Council for Metropolitan Open Communities, Neighborhood Housing Services of Chicago (NHS), the Legal Assistance Foundation of Metropolitan Chicago, and the National Training and Information Center (NTIC). The task force explored the problems of predatory lending and a variety of potential solutions at the local, state, and federal levels. The task force also encouraged the development of an ad hoc coalition of community groups interested in the issue.

In late 1999 the institute released its *Two Steps Back* report on the explosion and hypersegregation of subprime lending. The report received a great deal of attention both locally and nationally and sparked organizations in other cities to undertake similar analyses. The city of Chicago used the report to develop a number of possible approaches to the predatory lending problem. In early 2000 the institute was heavily engaged in policy analysis and public education on Illinois House Bill 3007, a very strong anti–predatory-lending proposal. The institute worked closely with NTIC, NHS, and other groups to support the bill, but the bill never made it out of the Democrat-controlled House, and had even dimmer prospects in the Republican-controlled Senate. Before the end of the legislative session, however, the General Assembly did pass a bill authorizing state regulators to issue regulations regarding predatory lending.

Meanwhile, in the summer of 2000, the city of Chicago passed an ordinance that required most firms bidding for city financial-service contracts to self-certify that they were not, and did not intend to become, predatory lenders as defined in the ordinance. The ordinance also required such bidders to report key lending information that would help the city's chief financial officer or the city comptroller to determine whether or not the bidders were predatory lenders. The Woodstock Institute and others had been heavily involved in conversations with city officials since the beginning of the year, particularly in debates about how strong the ordinance needed to be to avoid crippling loopholes.

Some major financial institutions worked hard to weaken the ordinance. In particular, Citigroup had hired lobbyists (including two former chiefs of staff of Mayor Richard Daley) to get a prohibition on single-premium credit life insurance struck from the measure. Citigroup's success in that effort caused the institute to oppose the final version of the ordinance because of the precedent it would set for similar debates in Illinois and other states, and in Congress. While the institute felt justified in opposing the ordinance, it understood that its colleagues who supported the ordinance were partly moved by the need to take credit for a victory that would enhance their power for their next struggle. Some organizations also felt that although the ordinance lacked this critical provision, it would still be useful in the fight against predatory lending.

At the same time that the institute and its allies were monitoring the progress of the city ordinance, they were also monitoring the development of draft lending regulations by the state regulators. In the summer of 2000, the two state regulators, the Office of Banks and Real Estate (OBRE) and the Department of Financial Institutions (DFI) issued a draft regulatory proposal that focused primarily on consumer education and had little substantive regulatory content. The institute prepared a critique of the draft and circulated it widely in conjunction with other advocates. The institute also worked closely with community organizations to help them understand the weaknesses of the draft. One of these organizations, the South West Organizing Project (SWOP) is a very influential organization in the Illinois House speaker's district in Chicago. SWOP made predatory lending a priority and engaged in intense discussions with Speaker Michael Madigan about the problem.

In July advocates met with Illinois governor George Ryan and state regulators to make the case for a substantive regulatory approach. In August the institute organized a press conference with a key state senator, Barack Obama (D-Chicago), who was cochair of the Joint Committee on Administrative Rules (JCAR), which eventually approved the state regulations, to call for stronger regulation than the state's initial draft.

This work continued through the fall. The governor had announced that he would base the state regulation on the Chicago ordinance that lacked the key provision banning single-premium credit life insurance. So the advocacy groups pressed state officials on the importance of including this provision. The institute's earlier position on this missing provision helped convince the governor to reinsert it in the state regulations, and the proposal released in December 2000 contained the ban on single-premium insurance.

When the proposal was released for public comment, the ad hoc coalition endorsed it and worked aggressively to ensure that civic, religious, and local government organizations understood its importance. Woodstock developed a boilerplate letter for other groups to use and 120 groups eventually submitted written comments supporting the proposed regulation. Support came from housing groups, townships, trade unions, and church groups.

The next step was to build editorial support, so the coalition organized a series of meetings with editors from the *Chicago Tribune*, the *Chicago Sun Times*, the *Daily Herald*, and *Crain's Chicago Business*. All of these meetings resulted in strong editorials supporting the regulations. As the institute talked to banking colleagues about the proposed regulation, it became apparent that some banks were not strenuously opposed to the ordinance. This was partly because those banks sold little or no product resembling predatory loans, and partly because they had no intention of getting into the business because of the risk to their companies' reputations.

Moreover, the banks complained about what they perceived to be an uneven playing field, and they saw that this legislation could help level the playing field. Federally regulated financial institutions are regularly examined for the safety and soundness of their operations and for their compliance with federal consumer legislation, including the Equal Credit Opportunity Act, the Truth in Lending Act, the Fair Housing Acts, and the Community Reinvestment Act. Other financial institutions, such as mortgage companies, are subject to each of those laws except CRA, but are not examined for compliance on a regular basis.

The regulated financial institutions complain that this puts them at a competitive disadvantage because they, unlike their unregulated competitors, incur costs for complying with those laws. In addition, many regulated banks felt that they could not compete with lenders who agreed to pay mortgage brokers outrageous fees. Only by putting some upper limit on fees would they have a chance to compete with these brokers and lenders. For the advocates too, the key to the proposed regulation was that it applied to all state-licensed financial institutions making residential loans in Illinois, including finance companies and mortgage brokers.

The banks were nevertheless unlikely to support the regulation publicly because of the tendency in the financial services world for groups not to oppose other groups' legislative agendas if those agendas do not directly work against their interests. But if even a few banks could be persuaded to support the regulation, the arguments of the trade associations' lobbyists would lose a great deal of their force. The institute therefore convened a series of meetings between a small number of key groups, including NHS, the Leadership Council, and SWOP, and three large financial institutions, Harris Trust, LaSalle National, and the Northern Trust banks. The community groups outlined the importance of the regulations and urged the three banks not to let the financial trade associations speak for them. The banks came back with a list of twenty troubling issues with the regulations, seventeen of which the advocates decided were technical and would not harm the regulations. The lenders agreed to concede on two of the three substantive points, and on the third issue, the advocates and the banks agreed to disagree.

As a result of these discussions, the three banks submitted a joint comment letter supporting the regulations with some minor conditions, most of which were addressed in the final regulations. In addition, an officer from one of the banks was a leader of one of the major state lending associations and testified in support of the regulations, submitting a letter identical to that of the three banks. Under pressure from other lobbyists, that lending association reversed its position and opposed the rules at a later date. The Illinois Bankers Association and other financial institutions pressured the three banks to reverse their position, but the banks held firm. In fact, the CEO of LaSalle National, Norman Bobbins, wrote a letter supporting the regulations that was published in the *Chicago Tribune* on the morning of the JCAR vote. OBRE and DFI issued the final version of Governor Ryan's proposed predatory lending regulations on March 30, 2001, and submitted them to the Joint Committee on Administrative Rules for approval. On April 17, by a vote of eight to four, JCAR approved the rules, which went into effect after thirty days. By these actions Illinois joined three other states—North Carolina, New York, and Massachusetts—in passing legislation to curb predatory lending.

The success of this campaign depended on several things. Mayor Richard Daley's support was critical, as was the support of Governor Ryan, a moderate Republican who, after some fence sitting, threw his weight behind effective regulations.[12] The House speaker, an immensely skillful politician, used his influence at key points, particularly on JCAR members before the key vote.[13] The press sensed a good story early on and gave the campaign a great deal of coverage. And the testimony of the three banks that supported the ordinance cast doubt on the protests of the trade associations and the hired-gun lobbyists.

But the *sine qua non* was the pressure of the fair lending advocates. They targeted the press, the state bank regulatory agencies, the members of JCAR, and other community groups who would support the regulation. SWOP, for example, got ten thousand of Rep. Madigan's constituents to send him post-cards supporting the regulations. Without a determined, consistent campaign of both public and private pressure, the state would have adopted the financial service industry's fig-leaf reform, a bill whose only provisions were for financial education. Only the combined and tough-minded measures of determined advocates stood a chance against the powerful financial services industry.

Independent Research and Advocacy

Both the Bank One merger agreement and the Illinois predatory-lending regulations required committed advocacy to achieve success. Both efforts improved the context in which community economic development takes place. The Bank One merger committed the bank to a more aggressive set of lending, investment and service goals, and the predatory-lending regulations provided an opportunity to reduce the devastation caused by exploitive loans.

The larger community development corporations recognized the importance of both projects; indeed, some of them were directly involved in the effort over the regulations. That some CDCs were involved might appear to validate the critique that advocates and sympathetic researchers are not necessary to these battles and that CDCs and their political representatives can succeed on their own. The record suggests that this is not the case. The community reinvestment agreement with Bank One would not have been achieved without research and advocacy of the Chicago CRA Coalition. The successful outcome of the negotiations depended on a core of organizations that were fully and intentionally committed to these outcomes as their major priority.

The state regulation fight was a different situation, in which powerful financial institutions and their trade organizations used their influence to try to block effective rules. The advocates, lacking the political and financial power of those institutions, had to use knowledge and organization to succeed. Large community development organizations can be partners in such campaigns by giving advice and occasionally taking a public role, but they cannot risk leading such a fight for fear of losing their business relationships with the financial institutions.

The future of community reinvestment will depend on independent researchers, policy developers, and advocates. As financial institutions merge (especially since the passage of the Gramm-Leach-Bliley Financial Services Modernization Act in 1999), they will become even more powerful. As the predatory-lending struggle shows, sweet reason is not going to convince powerful corporations that some of their practices are harmful to low-income and minority communities or that their community reinvestment efforts should be much more substantive. The regulatory agencies are institutionally cautious, and the current Bush administration opposes stronger regulatory action on many fronts. Only a skilled, independent, active research and advocacy community stands a chance of forcing the corporate financial services giants to consider the interests of low-income people.

Notes

1. The terms *bank* and *financial institution* are used interchangeably in this chapter, although, since the Gramm-Leach-Bliley Financial Services Modernization Act, they can be quite different entities. That legislation permitted for the first time since the 1930s the merger of banking, securities, and insurance firms into financial services holding companies.

2. In recent years examiners have agreed to hold public hearings on the community reinvestment impact of large mergers (e.g., Bank America and NationsBank and First Chicago-NBD with Bank One). Most recently, however, in July 2001, the Federal Reserve Board refused numerous requests to hold hearings on the proposed Citigroup acquisition of Grupo Financiero Banamex-Accival and its U.S. subsidiaries. The Fed's refusal was no doubt influenced by the policies of the Bush administration, which is much less favorably disposed to regulation than was the Clinton administration.

3. Ninety-seven percent of financial institutions receive either "outstanding" or "satisfactory" ratings in their CRA examinations. Only 3 percent receive the grades "needs to improve" or "substantial non-compliance."

4. For a brief history of the initial organizing around bank disinvestment, see Schwartz n.d.

5. The founding director of both organizations was Gale Cincotta, a legendary Chicago organizer who was also a major figure in the passage of the Home Mortgage Disclosure Act (1975) and the Community Reinvestment Act (1977). She remained an active figure in the fight for community reinvestment until her death in 2001.

6. Some of the information and language in the next several paragraphs is taken from Lester 1998.

7. Predatory mortgage loans are a subset of subprime loans. Currently, however, there are no publicly available data that would allow community groups to distinguish predatory from subprime loans. In December 2002, however, the Federal Reserve Board approved changes to Regulation C, which implements HMDA, to collect new information on high-cost mortgages. Unfortunately, the Fed has pushed back the implementation of the change until January 2004.

8. Grants from banks to community development organizations have come under particular fire from the former chair of the U.S. Senate banking committee, Senator Phil Gramm (R-Tex.). These grants, for the most part, are used by community groups to market banks' community reinvestment products and prepare near-bankable customers for successful loan applications. The community groups thus take on some of the transaction costs of doing business that would otherwise fall on the banks themselves.

9. In the summer of 2001, under pressure from community activists and regulators, three major financial institutions—Citigroup, Household Finance, and American General—separately announced plans to stop offering single-premium credit life insurance and replace it with insurance paid for on a monthly basis. Again, it was the activist groups who fought the public battle against this product.

10. In December 2002 the Federal Reserve Board approved changes to Regulation Z, which implements the Truth in Lending Act that HOEPA amends. The changes create a few additional restrictions on predatory lending.

11. The first such partnership was organized by the Federal Reserve Bank of Cleveland in 1993. That partnership has been described in a Woodstock Institute report (Bush and Corrigan-Halpern 1997).

12. Governor Ryan had, for example, suspended the death penalty in Illinois after a number of prisoners were released from death row in light of DNA and other evidence that proved their innocence.

13. SWOP's work was obviously critical to the speaker's efforts. Many of his constituents were retired homeowners in part of Chicago's bungalow belt and were vulnerable to predatory lenders. Moreover, according to press accounts, his daughter, Lisa Madigan, a progressive state senator and a member of JCAR, was planning to enter the race for Illinois attorney general in 2002 and supported the rules. Senator Madigan was, in fact, elected Illinois attorney general in November 2002.

References

Becker, Howard S., and Irving Horowiz. 1972. Radical Politics and Sociological Research: Observations on Method and Ideology. *American Journal of Sociology* (July 1978): 48–66.

Bush, Malcolm. 1999. The Recent Role of Community Organizing in the Implementation of the Community Reinvestment Act in the United States. Paper presented at the annual meeting of the Association for Research on Nonprofit Organizations and Voluntary Action, Arlington, Va., Nov.

Bush, Malcolm, and Paula Corrigan-Halpern. 1997. *The Cleveland Residential Housing and Mortgage Credit Project: One City's Response to the Problem of Racial Discrimination in the Home-Buying Industry.* Chicago: Woodstock Institute.

Evanoff, Douglas, and Lewis Segal. 1996. CRA and Fair Lending Regulations: Resulting Trends in Mortgage Lending. *Economic Perspectives* 20 (6): 19–46.

Immergluck, Daniel, and Marti Wiles. 1999. *Two Steps Back: The Dual Mortgage Market, Predatory Lending, and the Undoing of Community Development.* Chicago: Woodstock Institute.

Lester, Thomas. 1998. The Chicago CRA Coalition: A Lesson in Successful CRA Merger Negotiations. Unpublished manuscript. Woodstock Institute.

Lindsey, Lawrence. 2000. Community Development at a Crossroads. *NeighborWorks Journal* 18 (winter).

Scheinfeld, Sandra. 1998. Quoted in Woodstock Institute Celebrates Twenty-five Years of Promoting Economic Opportunity and Justice. *Woodstock Developments* (fall): 6.

Schwartz, Alex. N.d. Bank Lending to Minority and Low-Income Households and Neighborhoods: Do Community Reinvestment Agreements Make a Difference? Unpublished manuscript. New School for Social Research.

Zuniga, Riccardo. 1975. The Experimenting Society and Radical Social Reform: The Role of the Social Scientist in Chile's Unidad Popular Experience. *American Psychologist* 30 (Feb.): 99–115.

John Taylor and Josh Silver

---

11   The Essential Role of Activism in
Community Reinvestment

Activism is not passé; it is essential. Without activism, our society becomes less democratic and less just. This is true in many arenas, but especially in the fight for economic justice and equal access to credit and capital.

In his exhortation to community activities to "grow up," Lawrence Lindsey ignores the fact that the rich and powerful are extremely effective activists for their causes. While they do not conduct noisy demonstrations, they hire lobbyists who have the ears of influential policymakers at all levels of government. Working-class and minority people cannot afford high-priced lobbyists. They must make their opinions known through the honorable American tradition of debate and protest.

The great English philosopher John Stuart Mill asserted that the exchange of ideas and debate was essential for a healthy democracy (Mill 1975). Only through vigorous debate can a society find solutions that are equitable and efficient. Community activists in the economic justice movement provide the invaluable service of promoting ideas they believe will revitalize communities and improve the lives of poor people. On the surface, these ideas seem inimical to the corporate imperative of maximizing profit. But through debate and discussion, lending institutions have been persuaded to reform their underwriting criteria and their marketing approaches to minority and working-class neighborhoods, once they realized that they were missing out on profitable business opportunities in traditionally underserved communities.

If left to their own devices, lenders would make large loans primarily to the well-healed. Making a $10 million loan to one business is indeed more cost-effective than making ten $1 million loans to ten businesses. The incentive of easy profit will drive most lenders to the larger borrowers. In time, however, the market for larger borrowers becomes saturated. Some lenders will then turn to the low- and moderate-income market, but others will invent new products and needs for the wealthier large borrowers. Were it not for the

Community Reinvestment Act (CRA) and its advocates, neglect of the low- and moderate-income market would still be the norm.

Much more progress needs to be made, but without the forums of debate made possible by the Community Reinvestment Act, the problems of redlining and disinvestment probably would never have been addressed. The passage of the CRA and CRA-related activism show the ideals of John Stuart Mill at work.

CRA activism is why the term "redlining" is now commonly understood by the American public. It is thanks to fair lending advocates that CRA examination guidelines are now based on performance rather than process. In the preamble to the new CRA rules in 1995, the Federal Reserve System recognized the work of activist groups and the National Community Reinvestment Coalition (NCRC) in getting more community groups than banks to comment on the proposed rules. From its establishment in 1990 by sixteen national organizations, the NCRC has grown into a coalition and economic justice movement of more than seven hundred local community organizations and public agencies across the country. This chapter examines from a national perspective the need for CRA activism and how that activism has stood up to redlining and spurred a wave of reinvestment in underserved neighborhoods. We support our argument with success stories that have created win-win situations for both banks and working-class and minority communities.

The CRA Rectifies Power Imbalances

Racism, discrimination, and injustice are unfortunate realities of life. The civil rights movement and the economic justice movement have made tremendous progress in reducing bigotry in society and advocating passage of laws making discrimination illegal. Yet injustice, in its many forms, still plagues our country. Particularly insidious forms of injustice are the institutional racism and classism that prevent the working class and working poor from receiving loans and building wealth. The result is that once-thriving neighborhoods become blighted pockets of unemployment and despair.

Redlining is the refusal to make loans to creditworthy residents of minority and working-class communities even though bank branches accept deposits from these residents and invest them elsewhere. Redlining destroys neighborhoods by preventing homeowners from getting loans for home repair, and thwarts small businesspeople from maintaining their storefronts or keeping their plant and equipment current. When a neighborhood is redlined, the homeowners and small businesspeople with sufficient means move elsewhere. The poorer residents are left behind to face a community with declining property values, decaying housing stock, and high unemployment. This powerful force of economic destruction rests on the racist and classist assumption that minority and working-class people are too lazy or shiftless to be entrusted with loans (Rohde 1997).

When the CRA was passed in 1977, Congress was not in the political mood to enact a big-government solution to the scourge of redlining. The genius of the CRA rests in empowering communities to work with financial institutions to eliminate redlining and discrimination. Congress left vague the precise methods, products, and services required of banks to comply with the CRA. Even in this relatively amorphous form, it is unlikely that the CRA as passed in 1977 would become law today, given the stranglehold that the financial services sector has had on Congress during the last decade.

Most forms of injustice are due to a power imbalance. In the late nineteenth and early twentieth centuries, large corporations had the power to require twenty-hour work days and hire child labor because they faced few penalties. Only when workers formed unions, engaged in collective bargaining, and worked with sympathetic federal governments to pass labor laws did these egregious practices end.

The CRA likewise reduced the power imbalance between financial institutions and the communities they serve, in this case through accountability and disclosure, as other chapters in this volume have explained. The power imbalance between communities and lending institutions has been reduced further by the CRA's role in the merger application process, which is where the Act's greatest influence actually lies. When a lender applies to the federal banking agencies to merge with or acquire another financial institution, change its charter, or open a branch, the agencies must review the lender's CRA performance before ruling on the application. Denials of merger applications due to poor CRA performance are very rare, occurring in less than 0.001 percent of cases. Regulatory agencies do occasionally delay merger applications as they sort through community reinvestment issues, antitrust concerns, or other significant policy issues. These reviews sometimes result in "conditional" merger approvals, where the merger is subject to certain conditions, such as improvement in CRA performance.

Banks that want to grow through acquisition are particularly sensitive to CRA issues and will take pains to prevent delays in the merger application process. They will also try to avoid negative publicity as a result of lackluster community reinvestment performance. Remedying weaknesses in CRA performance in advance of the merger application process is preferable to being ordered to do so by a federal agency.

Democracy, Efficiency, and the CRA

The logic of the CRA review during mergers or other significant changes is inescapable. A financial institution's assets amount to a community's wealth. Individuals and businesses entrust banks with their savings and investments in the expectation that they, and others in their community, will have access to credit and other benefits from that institution. When another bank, from a different geographical area, with a different board of directors, and perhaps with a different reinvestment philosophy, merges with the local bank, the impact on investors and savers can be profound. The CRA protects their interests by examining the past reinvestment performance of each institution and requiring each bank to disclose future intentions, such as branch closures. Community groups expand this process by asking the bank to describe in writing their future plans for specific loan products, investments, and accounts that will be accessible to working-class and minority neighborhoods. These specific commitments are called "CRA agreements."

The democratic aspect of merger applications has created numerous win-win situations for banks and communities. When banks merge, tremendous institutional changes occur. The decision-making process for the bank may shift from a decentralized structure to a centralized one or vice versa. The CRA decisions of the bank may shift from the well-respected CRA officer in your hometown to CRA officers hundreds of miles away. The merger application process provides an opportunity for banks and communities to think through these institutional changes and develop products and strategies that will maintain or improve the CRA performance of the banks. Were it not for the give-and-take among banks and community groups during the application process, the best ideas for creating or preserving profitable business opportunities for banks undergoing structural changes might not surface, resulting in losses for all parties.

Injustice not only hurts its victims; it also hurts its perpetrators. Redlining devastates communities and it also reduces bank profits. When a bank redlines a community, it is making a blanket assumption about the residents of that community and is not thinking creatively about how to serve the community. Conventional underwriting techniques, for example, make it more difficult for people without credit histories to qualify for mortgages. Using conventional underwriting techniques, a lender may reject an applicant who does not have credit cards because the lender cannot look up the applicant's history of paying credit card bills. This type of underwriting overlooks the applicant's record of paying rent or utility bills, a record that may show several years of timely payments. The CRA merger application process allows discussions between community groups and banks that may lead the bank to reform its underwriting process in such a way that applicants who lack conventional credit histories are not penalized.

The CRA's democratic process remedies the market imperfections created by discrimination. Economic theory holds that markets will be inefficient if discriminatory barriers prevent the complete flow of information between customers and companies. In other words, a loan will not be made if a loan officer's bigoted outlook prevents an objective assessment of the qualifications of a loan applicant. The result is inefficiency from the point of view of the bank (a missed business opportunity) and inequitable from the point of view of the applicant (a loan rejection). What the CRA has made possible is a dialogue between community groups and lending institutions that has motivated lenders to make loans to applicants that formerly would not have received them.

In neoclassical economics, a solution is deemed to be "Pareto optimal" if it makes all parties better off by enlarging the economic pie. If two banks believe that their merger will create a more profitable company, communities can likewise benefit, but only if the banks make a commitment to improve their CRA performance. If the companies plan to save costs by closing branches or laying off loan officers, the typical result is that the newly merged bank makes fewer loans in its markets and considerably fewer loans to low- and moderate-income people. One party (the bank) may benefit, but the other party (minority and low- and moderate-income communities) suffers. If, however, the bank wishes to close branches but promises that loans and banking services will nevertheless increase in low- and moderate-income communities, then the outcome is Pareto optimal. If the bank delivers on its promise, it has found a less expensive system for doing so. The CRA has by no means leveled the playing field; community groups and banks remain far from equal partners. But it has created a democratic dialogue between community groups and banks. It mandates that banks meet the credit needs of all the communities in which they are chartered and from which they take deposits. Ultimately, the only way banks can do this is to listen as communities articulate their credit needs. In an imaginary world free of bigotry and mistrust, this dialogue would take place naturally and spontaneously. But in the real world, institutional mechanisms are needed to promote the kind of debate that John Stuart Mill believed was so vital to solving social problems.

What Are CRA Agreements and How Do They Work?

CRA agreements arose from the grassroots activism of community groups. The CRA and other fair lending laws do not mandate that banks must enter into CRA agreements with community groups. The CRA merger application process helped stimulate the practice of CRA agreements, but the CRA agreements are the product of a democratic, bottom-up process that encourage banks and community groups to reach agreement, through discussion and debate, on a set of lending, investment, and service goals.

Take the commitment Fleet Bank made during its merger with Bank of Boston in 1999. Community groups along the East Coast, and particularly in Massachusetts, were concerned that lending levels in low- and moderate-income neighborhoods would plummet after the merger, as these two banks overlapped considerably in many markets. In order to save costs, these groups feared, the banks might slash personnel and cut branches, particularly in Massachusetts where they both had large numbers of branches.

The community groups asked the National Community Reinvestment Coalition (NCRC) to conduct data analysis showing what happened to lending levels after Fleet's previous acquisitions, in the 1990s, of National Westminster Bank and Shawmut Bank. The NCRC's data analyses revealed significant declines in the combined lending levels of Fleet and the two other banks in the years after the merger. The drop in lending to minority and low- and moderate-income neighborhoods occurred in Massachusetts, Connecticut, New York, and New Jersey.

When the groups presented this data analysis, Fleet, to its credit, acknowledged the decline in lending. But it promised that its merger with Bank of Boston would result in increased lending to low- and moderate-income communities. Specifically, Fleet committed itself to lending and investing $14.6 billion over the next five years (starting in 2000) in several states, including Massachusetts, Connecticut, New York, and New Jersey (NCRC 2001a). Additional Fleet agreements with NCRC members such as the Massachusetts Association of Community Development Corporations, the Massachusetts Affordable Housing Association, and the treasury secretary of Connecticut described specific increases in home-mortgage lending, small-business lending, community development investments, and bank accounts. For example, the agreement with Massachusetts community organizations committed Fleet to opening forty-two thousand basic checking and savings accounts over a two-year time period (NCRC 2001a, 38).

This was a clear example of the importance of community activism. The bank, on its own, would never have acknowledged the decline in lending, because to do so would amount to self-inflicted damage in its public relations campaign during the merger application process. Without the CRA and the lending data made available by it and HMDA, community groups would not have been able to present the facts to Fleet. Without the NCRC, most community groups lack the in-house capacity to analyze lending data and assess bank reinvestment performance.

Another case in which community pressure yielded positive results was First Union's 1998 acquisition of Corestates, the last large institution headquartered in Pennsylvania. Corestates was revered by many in the Keystone state and had a proud history of serving its community. U.S. Senator Arlen Specter (R-Pa.), the attorney general of Pennsylvania, and several NCRC members (among them the Philadelphia Association of Community Development Corporations and the Pennsylvania Low Income Housing Coalition) expressed concern over how Corestates' reinvestment achievements would be preserved and strengthened after a merger with a bank based in Charlotte, North Carolina. A $13 billion CRA agreement between First Union, community groups, and the Pennsylvania attorney general promised higher levels of investment and lending than the premerger lending and investment levels of First Union and Corestates. It also promised that First Union would not close branches more than one-third of a mile apart from each other (or about four city blocks) for a period of three years. Furthermore, to allay antitrust concerns about rising prices after the merger, the bank promised to provide low-cost bank accounts to senior citizens, welfare recipients, and other low-income people.

First Union is an international corporation with many diverging interests, including overseas investments and nonbanking financial business. CRA agreements ensure that low- and moderate-income customers with deposits in the bank are not lost in the shuffle. Without the CRA agreement, how many branches in low- and moderate-income communities would have been closed? The negotiators for First Union would not have agreed to keep open branches that were not profitable or at least break-even. In addition, the negotiators for First Union realized that the community organizations now also had a stake in helping the bank make the branches more profitable by boosting the number of customers.

The branch part of the First Union agreement illustrates the mutually beneficial and sustainable nature of CRA agreements. Under this agreement, working-class communities retained access to branches and the bank gained partners in making the branches more profitable. In exchange, the community groups agreed to a three-year time period instead of demanding an indefinite time frame. If the branches proved not to be profitable for the long term, a monitoring committee made up of bank and community representatives would revisit the question of branch closures and explore other alternatives, such as opening mini-branches inside existing stores or donating the branch space to community-oriented credit unions.

In a number of instances, new branches established by CRA agreements, or existing branches kept open by such agreements, have proved to be among the most profitable in the bank's service area. In the mid-1990s, for example, NCRC board member Matthew Lee of Inner City Press/Community on the Move persuaded a number of banks to open branches in the South Bronx (see Chapter 9). The branch openings profited from pent up-demand for loans in a community that had not seen new branches in decades (Rohde 1997).

CRA agreements are sophisticated instruments that have evolved as the financial industry has changed. In the past few years, community groups have become increasingly concerned about predatory lending, a practice described in detail elsewhere in this volume. Until relatively recently, CRA agreements have focused on prime-rate lending to low- and moderate-income populations. Since many banks are commencing large-scale subprime operations, community groups have sought protections to ensure that the higher-rate subprime lending, including predatory lending, does not become the norm. In a 1998 CRA agreement with NCRC member Inner City Press/Community on the Move, Charter One and its subprime subsidiary Equity One promised to pay up to $250 in credit counseling for borrowers who were thirty-one days late on loan payments (NCRC 2001a, 28). This is a significant commitment from the lender, because it signals that Charter One has no interest in making predatory loans leading to delinquencies and foreclosures. Charter One has agreed to assess itself a financial penalty for delinquent loans.

CRA agreements have been affected by the vigorous debate now brewing over the importance of subprime lending in reaching minority and working-class populations. Incredibly, some pundits and academics believe that subprime lending has been responsible for the increase in loans during the 1990s for traditionally underserved populations (Litan 2001). Most community groups and activists, on the other hand, believe that the CRA and CRA-inspired agreements have been responsible in the surge in home purchase lending to minority and working-class populations, and that the surge in lending consists of affordable, prime-rate lending. Indeed, data analysis shows that the largest increases to working-class and minority borrowers is prime lending and that it preceded the explosion of subprime lending (NCRC 2002, 8).

Some banks with prime and subprime operations have implicitly agreed with the position of community groups. For example, in the summer of 1998 Bank One signed a CRA agreement with the Chicago CRA Coalition that promised an incredible 35,879 single-family loans to low- and moderate-income communities by the end of 2004. Bank One, which had a subprime operation at that time, promised that no subprime loans would be counted toward this commitment (NCRC 2001a, 16).

The Chicago CRA Coalition–Bank One agreement promotes a healthy choice of loan products in working-class and minority neighborhoods. Most CRA agreements have focused on home-mortgage lending, not refinance lending. Prime rate, conventional lending has been responsible for the increases in total single-family lending and increases in home-mortgage lending to minority and low- and moderate-income neighborhoods. Subprime lenders, however, have out-competed prime rate lenders in making refinance and home equity lending to minority and low- and moderate-income neighborhoods. The Chicago CRA Coalition agreement with Bank One strives to ensure that a major lender will put most of its emphasis on prime rate lending in low- and moderate-income communities and thus preserve alternatives to high-interest-rate lending in these neighborhoods.

Not all CRA agreements are equal. The durability and effectiveness of an individual CRA agreement is directly proportional to the technical sophistication of the community groups involved in negotiating the agreement. Too many agreements lack the specific goals that produce the lending results to which they aspire. Too many lack the monitoring or oversight necessary to ensure lender compliance. The largest CRA commitments are now made unilaterally by the banks during the merger application process; community groups no longer "sign" the documents as a negotiating party in many cases. These agreements pledge tens of billions of dollars for the future. But when community groups analyze them and divide their lending and investing over all the states served by the banks, the agreements end up representing modest increases in lending and investing for low- and moderate-income communities, and sometimes no increase at all. Perhaps the most egregious weakness in CRA agreements is the lack of consideration by federal regulatory agencies, particularly regarding the record of compliance with previous commitments when a bank has submitted a merger application. The NCRC is now working with its member organizations to insist that federal agencies take the CRA pledges seriously. We have insisted and will continue to insist that the agencies estimate the size of lending and investment components of the agreements. We will insist that the agencies inform the public when they believe that CRA pledges are not meaningful improvements in lending or investments. We will also be asking the agencies to scrutinize the success of banks in meeting their CRA commitments the next time they ask for approval of a merger or other type of application.

On the whole, CRA agreements have been responsible for hundreds of billions of dollars of loans and investments in America's working-class and minority communities. If regulatory agencies rigorously held lenders accountable for their commitments, the progress in lending and investment would even be higher. The Office of the Comptroller of the Currency is the only agency to state that failure to abide by a CRA commitment will be considered during the bank application process. But this is a guideline, not a regulation. Despite community group comments about lender compliance with agreements during merger applications, federal regulators, with few exceptions, have not required lenders to document their progress. But even in spite of the lack of federal banking agency oversight regarding bank promises, the impact of CRA agreements has been profound.

CRA Agreements Increase Lending

Community activism has not only improved the lending performance of individual banks, it has also had the market-wide effect of increasing access to credit for low- and moderate-income borrowers. Two teams of researchers have used the NCRC's database of CRA agreements to confirm this outcome.

The NCRC has compiled a database of approximately 390 CRA agreements made since the passage of the CRA in 1977. The great majority of these agreements have been negotiated by NCRC member community group organizations. Over the years, the NCRC has endeavored to keep its database current by conducting periodic surveys of its seven hundred member organizations and by consulting media reports and trade publications. The NCRC's database is the only systematic information available that catalogs CRA agreements by state, community group, bank, and year. The NCRC updates its publication *CRA Commitments* on an annual basis.

Since the enactment of the CRA, the agreements in the NCRC database have committed lending institutions to make more than $1 trillion in loans and investments to low- and moderate-income communities. The great majority of this money was committed from 1992 through 2000. By contrast, only $8.8 billion was committed from 1977 through 1991. It is no coincidence that most of the CRA agreement dollars were committed in the 1990s, when Congress and the federal government improved CRA and HMDA data—the main tools community groups use in their CRA activism (see the introduction to this volume).

The tremendous increase in dollars committed though CRA agreements sparked intense interest in Congress and the regulatory agencies. As part of the Gramm-Leach-Bliley Act of 1999, Congress stipulated that the Treasury Department conduct two studies documenting the benefits of the CRA and the potential impact of the Gramm-Leach-Bliley Act on the CRA. At the same time, economists at the Federal Reserve Board became interested in the NCRC database of CRA agreements.

The Treasury Department contracted with Harvard University and the Brookings Institution for the CRA study. Using the NCRC's CRA agreement database, Harvard and Brookings researchers concluded that lending to low- and moderate-income communities is higher in geographical areas in which banks and community groups negotiated CRA agreements than in other communities (Litan et al. 2001; Joint Center for Housing Studies 2002, 58–65).

Developing different econometric models, Federal Reserve economists came to similar conclusions regarding higher lending levels in geographical areas with CRA agreements. They also found that CRA agreements significantly increase conventional home-purchase lending, but not government-insured lending. This finding is consistent with the emphasis CRA agreements have placed on conventional prime-rate home mortgages. Loans to affluent borrowers as well as to low- and moderate-income borrowers increased in geographical areas with CRA agreements (Bostic and Robinson 2002, 27–31). This is yet additional evidence supporting the "Pareto optimal" outcome that CRA agreements benefit multiple parties. CRA agreements appear to motivate banks to increase their lending overall, in addition to boosting lending to low- and moderate-income borrowers. In essence, CRA agreements enlarge the economic pie, enabling all income groups to benefit.

The Federal Reserve economists also discovered that lending levels are higher in geographical areas in which community groups negotiate a series of CRA agreements than in those where only one agreement is negotiated. Another significant finding is that the lending increase associated with a CRA agreement dissipates after the third year following the agreement.

A single CRA agreement, therefore, will not guarantee long-term increases in lending. It is more likely that banks will make long-term commitments only when successive CRA agreements are negotiated. Community groups have learned that only long-term partnerships and agreements with lenders will increase access to credit. One-shot deals will not suffice, because they cannot develop the trust necessary for long-term business relationships. Nor do one-shot deals develop the infrastructure for community-based lending. CRA agreements are most likely to have a market-wide impact when a community group engages in pattern bargaining, in much the same way that large labor unions negotiate with corporations. The Treasury Department's study on the benefits of the CRA documented increases in the market share of loans of banks covered by the CRA. When the NCRC examined the study's tables on market share on a metropolitan level, we found that banks and thrifts covered by the CRA increased their market share relative to financial institutions not covered by the CRA to the largest extent in states and metropolitan areas with strong community activists. New Jersey, for example, had one of the largest market-share increases by CRA-covered institutions. From 1993 to 1998, lenders covered by the CRA increased their market share of loans by nine percentage points, on average, in New Jersey metropolitan areas. New Jersey Citizens Action has negotiated more than thirty agreements totaling $9 billion in commitments with lending institutions. The agreements have also committed the several banks to offer similar home-mortgage or home-rehabilitation loans to low- and moderate-income populations. It is easy to see how CRA agreements in New Jersey have market-wide impacts. California, with two statewide CRA coalitions that are members of the NCRC (the California Reinvestment Committee and the Greenlining Institute), is another state where CRA-covered institutions have grabbed significant increases in market share. CRA-covered lenders boosted their market share by 13 percent in San Francisco between 1993 and 1998, by 9 percent in San Diego, and by 7 percent in Riverside–San Bernandino (NCRC 2000, 6).

In addition to the organizations mentioned above, the Community Reinvestment Association of North Carolina, the Coalition on Homelessness and Housing in Ohio, the Greater Rochester Reinvestment Coalition, the Washington Reinvestment Alliance, the Pittsburgh Community Reinvestment Group, and the Delaware Community Reinvestment Action Council have engaged in sustained efforts over the years to negotiate successive CRA agreements with several different banks. Yet the NCRC recognizes that community group capacity to negotiate CRA agreements over the long term needs to be bolstered. Also, community group capacity is not evenly distributed across the country. The NCRC will be increasing its efforts to enhance community group activism in all parts of the country and will be emphasizing that the CRA works best when community groups stay engaged for the long haul.

Local governments also negotiate CRA agreements. In addition to the states of Connecticut and Pennsylvania, the city of Cleveland under the leadership of Mayor Michael White has negotiated a series of agreements with lenders that contain provisions regarding branching policy as well as promised increases in lending. NCRC board member Dean Lovelace of Dayton, Ohio, is a council member who recently wrote an anti-predatory-lending bill and works with banks through a local "community reinvestment institute." In addition, both the National League of Cities and the U.S. Conference of Mayors are active members of the NCRC, with seats on its board of directors.

It is easy to see how CRA agreements have increased lending on a market-wide basis in states with strong CRA coalitions that engage in pattern bargaining. But even in states where community groups have not negotiated agreements with a large number of banks, the increases in lending can still be market-wide. If community activists have negotiated agreements with a couple of lenders with significant market presence, other lenders will be motivated to step up their efforts in order to compete.

Comments on Merger Applications

CRA agreements have created much excitement, but they are not the only form of CRA activism. In fact, each CRA agreement achieved is cause for celebration because they are so difficult to accomplish. While nearly ten thousand banks and thrifts do business in this country, the NCRC found less than four hundred agreements from 1977 through 2000 (NCRC 2001a, 1).

CRA activists, realistic about the chances of securing CRA agreements, regularly comment on merger applications in the hope that they can achieve lending reforms short of full-blown CRA agreements. In 2001 Citigroup in particular was the focus of CRA activism on merger applications (see Chapter 9).

Through the process of commenting on merger applications, community activists have succeeded in pressuring the Federal Reserve Board and other regulatory agencies to do their jobs; significant reforms have been the result. But the war is won in increments, and the battle against predatory lending and for increased CRA prime-rate lending continues. Although significant victories have been achieved, much work remains to be done. Other easily abused practices, including prepayment penalties, have not been changed to the extent necessary. Also, Citigroup and other lenders with both prime and subprime operations refused to commit to new CRA agreements pledging faster increases in prime than in subprime lending. This is another area in which comments on merger applications can produce results short of CRA agreements. Given that big business has the upper hand in our system, the incremental reforms community groups have achieved are not to be sneezed at. In the future, community groups will push the envelope further.

Comments on CRA Exams

Approximately once every two years, examiners from federal banking agencies conduct CRA exams of banks and thrifts with assets over $250 million. (The Gramm-Leach-Bliley Act weakened CRA enforcement for smaller banks and thrifts with assets below $250 million. These institutions are examined once every four or five years.) Each quarter, the federal bank agencies invite public comment on upcoming exams and publish a list of banks and thrifts about to be examined.

Community activism has generally focused on the merger application process. The NCRC believes it is vital for community groups also to comment on CRA exams. Banks, even those that have adopted a merger acquisition strategy, may not merge for a number of years, but they undergo CRA exams on a regular basis. If a bank knows that a community group will monitor its CRA performance and comment on consecutive exams, the bank has an added incentive to strengthen its community reinvestment performance.

In one situation in New England in 1997, the Granite State Community Reinvestment Association (GSCRA), an NCRC member, charged Citizens Bank with cutting its rural staff after acquiring First New Hampshire. GSCRA documented significant declines in small-business and home-mortgage lending in its comments on a Citizens CRA exam. The FDIC downgraded the bank to a "satisfactory" CRA rating. Citizens then met with GSCRA to develop a plan for improving its CRA performance. According to GSCRA, "two years later, they were the leading rural lender, had developed an outstanding program for women in business, and were very strong partners in the rural parts of the state."

In this instance, the bank passed its CRA exam but was still motivated to improve its CRA performance. CRA ratings are an important part of a bank's public image. Many banks would rather be judged to be outstanding than satisfactory in reinvesting in the community. A high CRA rating is an important part of the bank's public relations strategy, and banks often issue press releases bragging about their "outstanding" reinvestment records. Citizens Bank may have also been motivated to improve its CRA performance because it could not counter GSCRA's charges. The bank had cut staff following the merger and was losing out on profitable business opportunities. Sometimes it takes a jolt from an outside organization for a business to overcome institutional inertia and implement needed changes. Again, the watchdog function of community activists results in a Pareto optimal outcome benefiting multiple parties.

In another instance, REDEEM, an NCRC member organization in West Virginia, was concerned about the lackluster reinvestment record of a large statewide lender called WesBanco. This bank had barely passed its previous CRA exam, earning a "needs-to-improve" score on the investment portion of the test, and a low satisfactory on the lending portion. It was also on an acquisition tear, having gobbled up one bank and embarked on another merger in the spring of 2001. The NCRC conducted data analysis for REDEEM that showed that WesBanco was making a much lower percentage of home and small-business loans to low- and moderate-income consumers and communities than its peers were. The data analysis also showed that WesBanco had not taken steps to improve its poor reinvestment performance since its previous CRA exam. In a comment letter to CRA examiners on the pending merger application, REDEEM and the NCRC stated that WesBanco had turned in poor reinvestment performance several years in a row and would respond only to penalties. The Federal Reserve Bank of Cleveland failed WesBanco on its CRA exam. The bank that was seeking to merge with WesBanco announced a halt to their planned union.

Incredibly, federal regulations allow banks to appeal failed ratings, and this is what WesBanco did. The NCRC and REDEEM protested the appeal, pointing out that the new CRA exam could have made an even more compelling case for failing the bank. The appeal was to no avail; in fact the Federal Reserve Bank of Cleveland exercised its "discretionary" authority to disregard the appeal letter of the NCRC and REDEEM. The Federal Reserve Bank revised the CRA exam and passed the bank in the fall of 2001. WesBanco proceeded with the merger.

The CRA exam process has become too easy for banks. In recent years, 98 percent of all banks have passed their CRA evaluations. While depository institutions have indeed stepped up their lending to low- and moderate-income communities, the NCRC and our member organizations believe that the failure rate should be higher than a measly 2 percent (down from 10 percent in the early 1990s). The appeal process in particular is tilted against community groups and this has contributed to the serious grade inflation. While the NCRC and our members will continue our efforts to combat this trend, we also recognize that the system, as flawed as it is, still spurs banks to improve their CRA performance. WesBanco (and many of its peer banks in West Virginia who followed the WesBanco merger process) now understand that failure to abide by their CRA obligations can entail penalties and delays in their merger plans. WesBanco itself hired a new CRA officer and announced the availability of new loan products for low- and moderate-income borrowers and communities.

In addition to commenting on merger applications and CRA exams, the NCRC urges its members to engage in regular evaluations of and dialogue with lending institutions. When a lender knows it is being watched, it will do what it can to enhance its community reinvestment performance. The community group and the bank together are also more likely to keep their attention focused on practices, strategies, and programs that will increase loans in minority and working-class communities. The fair housing officer in Norwalk, Connecticut, with the assistance of the NCRC, conducts a comprehensive data analysis of several local banks every two years. The data analysis compares the number and percentage of loans issued to minority and low- and moderate-income borrowers and communities. The banks are ranked on a series of CRA and fair lending indicators. After receiving its first report card from the fair housing officer, one of the banks implemented a first-time homebuyers program, and over the years this bank has improved from one of the lowest-ranked banks in Norwalk to one of the highest-ranked.

The CRA achieves higher loans and investments for traditionally underserved communities through a process of information sharing, evaluation, debate, and compromise. Through the disclosure of data and evaluations, banks are motivated to seek profitable lending opportunities. The CRA does not require new taxes, new federal programs, or additional budget allocations from Congress. By empowering both communities and banks to work together, it stimulates reinvestment. It extends credit and capital to hardworking Americans pulling themselves up by their bootstraps and striving for their dreams of homeownership, small-business ownership, and providing for their families. It corrects market failures and stimulates capitalism in minority and working-class communities. Attempts to strengthen it deserve bipartisan support.

The success of the CRA, however, depends heavily—too heavily—on over-burdened community groups. Where community activism is strong, the merger review and CRA exam process leverages increases in lending and investing to low- and moderate-income communities. But where activism is weak or nonexistent, CRA-related lending and investing are more likely to stagnate. The NCRC will continue to address unevenness in community group capacity. But we will also advocate that Congress do its part by making the CRA stronger and by increasing congressional oversight of CRA enforcement by the federal regulators. The responsibility to pressure CRA examiners to grade banks on the merits should not rest with community groups. Institutional mechanisms need to be established and maintained that will make this happen automatically.

Should Activists Become Dealmakers?

Despite the accomplishments of community activists, Lawrence Lindsey, former governor of the Federal Reserve and former assistant to the president for economic policy, believes that they should turn in their bullhorns and make deals with banks. Activists should stop advocating and start building homes and rehabilitating commercial areas in low- and moderate-income communities.

Lawrence Lindsey is enamored of Community Development Corporations (CDCs). He should be. CDCs are nonprofit development organizations that build and rehabilitate commercial and residential property in minority and working-class communities. Ironically, many leaders in the economic justice advocacy arena have their roots in the CDC movement. Like the NCRC's president and CEO, many learned the lesson that an individual CDC cannot compensate for the devastating effects of bank redlining. Building wealth in poor neighborhoods through increasing individuals' access to affordable credit and capital is the ultimate community economic development strategy.

Nonprofit developers have accomplished much. According to the web page of the National Congress for Community Economic Development, there were an estimated 3,600 such groups across the United States in 1998. Since the emergence of the first CDCs in the late 1960s, they have produced 247,000 private-sector jobs and 550,000 units of affordable housing.

Nonprofit developers often tackle the most difficult revitalization projects. Their efforts are vital to reinvestment in neighborhoods. But they cannot revitalize entire neighborhoods by themselves, or reach every creditworthy person of modest means who wants to buy her first home or start her first business. Consider that while CDCs have produced about half a million housing units since the 1960s, conventional home-mortgage loans for low- and moderate-income borrowers now total more than 800,000 annually. This number has almost doubled since 1993. CRA activism, as documented by Federal Reserve economists as well as Harvard University and the Brookings Institution in the Treasury Department study, is responsible for a significant part of the surge in lending to low- and moderate-income borrowers.

Nonprofit developers can show how housing opportunities in an inner-city neighborhood or rural community are possible. If lending efforts are not sustained in the neighborhood being revitalized, however, the reinvestment project will ultimately fail. Lending is much more likely to be sustained in a geographical area with CRA agreements and CRA advocacy groups than in areas that lack them.

Nonprofit developers understand the importance of the CRA for overall lending as well as for the financing of their projects. A sizable percentage of the NCRC's membership is made up of nonprofit developers, and a number of nationally renowned CDC directors sit on the NCRC's board of directors. CRA coalitions on the state and local level likewise involve a lot of CDCs. Revitalization is most successful where nonprofit developers and advocates complement each other's work.

The CRA Is Profitable for Banks

So what is the impact of CRA activism on banks' bottom lines? Are banks forced to make bad loans or marginally profitable loans, or are new business opportunities opening up?

The evidence to date strongly supports the proposition that CRA-related activities are profitable and beneficial for banks as well as communities. In their 1997 study *Community Reinvestment and the Profitability of Mortgage-Oriented Banks*, Federal Reserve economists Glenn Canner and Wayne Passmore stated, "we find no compelling evidence of lower profitability at commercial banks that specialize in home purchase lending in lower-income neighborhoods or to lower-income borrowers." They add that "our regressions for the three years [1993, 1994, and 1995] which were years of high levels of CRA-related lending suggest that the profitability of banks seems unrelated to, or perhaps slightly positively related to, the proportion of lending they extended in lower-income tracts" (Canner and Passmore 1997).

In 2000 the Federal Reserve released a survey on the profitability of CRA-related loans made by the nation's five hundred largest banks, as required by the Gramm-Leach-Bliley Act. This survey found that the great majority of banks reported CRA loans made to low- and moderate-income borrowers to be as profitable as their overall lending. In addition, the CRA loans did not exhibit higher foreclosure rates (Federal Reserve System 2000, 48). Federal Reserve economists followed the release of this survey with supplemental analysis showing that so-called marginal CRA loans were five times more likely to be reported as profitable than as unprofitable (Avery et al. 2001, 49–53).

The Treasury study found that CRA-covered lenders and their affiliates increased mortgage lending to low- and moderate-income borrowers and areas by 39 percent from 1993 to 1998, while these institutions increased their lending to other borrowers by only 17 percent. If CRA-related lending was unprofitable, it would not have increased twice as much as lending to other borrowers.

The NCRC's own members have likewise documented great success with CRA-related lending. Chapter 5 of this volume shows that the "soft-seconds" CRA lending program in Massachusetts had lower delinquency rates than did lending overall in the state. Other NCRC members likewise report success stories. New Jersey Citizens Action (NJCA), reports that in the past six years more than ten thousand New Jersey residents have received free mortgage and credit counseling, counseling that has been made directly available because of the CRA. NJCA enters into partnerships in which it provides homeownership counseling and banks make loans to graduates of its counseling programs. Since 1997 First Union has made 446 CRA mortgages to graduates of NJCA's loan counseling programs; only three of these mortgages have gone into foreclosure (NCRC 2000, 4).

Where Do We Go from Here?

Democratic dialogue and activism are necessary ingredients for community reinvestment. The CRA, HMDA, and the merger application process foster dialogue, partnership building, and increases in loans and investments for minority and working-class neighborhoods.

The CRA needs to be strengthened and brought up to date to keep pace with the revolutionary changes taking place in the financial marketplace, as banks merge with insurance and securities companies. Community reinvestment requirements must extend to all parts of financial conglomerates that are entrusted with safeguarding, lending, and investing the communities' wealth. CRA and fair lending factors must be considered in all merger applications, not just those involving banks merging with other banks. The public participation process and opportunities for public comment must be strengthened, not weakened.

The NCRC will be leading the fight to promote a CRA modernization bill. The CRA Modernization Act of 2001, introduced by Representatives Thomas Barrett and Luis Gutierrez and cosponsored by thirty-three other members of Congress, would extend the CRA to financial institutions not currently covered by the law, expand disclosure requirements, and provide enhanced data and public participation processes, all of which will enable activists to work with lending institutions and hold them accountable. More information and public participation, not less, is essential if further progress is to be made in community reinvestment (NCRC 2001b).

Congress also needs to step up its oversight of federal banking agencies. CRA grade inflation is a serious problem. Regulatory scrutiny too often reacts to community pressure, when there should be automatic penalties for banks that fail CRA exams or receive low scores. Likewise, federal regulators fail to monitor CRA pledges during the merger application process and rely too heavily on community groups when ruling on merger applications. Disparaging activists and cutting off debate does not only leave the country poorer on an intellectual level. It leaves the country, banks, and minority and working-class communities poorer on an economic level. While the CRA and CRA activists have gained many friends, powerful enemies remain. Our task is to demonstrate the democratic, win-win nature of the CRA for all parties in society. When we accomplish this, our abilities to reinvest together grow.

References

Avery, Robert B., Raphael W. Bostic, and Glenn B. Canner. 2001. Assessing the Impact of CRA on Banking Institutions. Paper presented at the Federal Reserve's Second Community Affairs Research Conference in Washington, D.C. April 5–6.

Bostic, Raphael W., and Breck Robinson. 2002. Do CRA Agreements Influence Lending Patterns? [Manuscript.] To be published in 2003 in *Real Estate Economics*. Available from the authors at <bostic@usc.edu> and <robinsob@be.udel.edu>.

Canner, Glenn, and Wayne Passmore. 1997. *The Community Reinvestment Act and the Profitability of Mortgage-Oriented Banks.* Washington, D.C.: Federal Reserve Board, Finance and Economic Discussion Series.

Federal Reserve System. 2000. *The Performance and Profitability of CRA-Related Lending.* Report by the Board of Governors of the Federal Reserve System, submitted to the Congress pursuant to section 713 of the Gramm-Leach-Bliley Act of 1999 (July 17).

Federal Trade Commission. 2001. FTC Charges One of Nation's Largest Subprime Lenders with Abusive Lending Practices. Press Release, <http://www.ftc.gov/opa/2001/03/associates.htm> (March 6).

Joint Center for Housing Studies, Harvard University. 2002. *The Twenty-fifth Anniversary of the Community Reinvestment Act: Access to Capital in an Evolving Financial Services System.* Prepared for the Ford Foundation.

Litan, Robert E. 2001. *A Prudent Approach to Preventing "Predatory" Lending.* Report prepared for the American Bankers Association.

——, et al. 2001. *The Community Reinvestment Act after Financial Modernization: A Final Report.* Washington, D.C.: U.S. Department of the Treasury.

——, and Charles W. Calomiris. Homeownership That's Too Important to Risk. 2001. *New York Times* (Aug. 20), available at <http://www.brook.edu/views/op%2Ded/litan/20010820.htm>.

John Stuart Mill. 1975. *Three Essays on Liberty, Representative Government, and the Subjection of Women.* New York: Oxford University Press.

National Community Reinvestment Coalition (NCRC). 2000. *Doing Well by Doing Good: CRA Lending is Profitable for Banks and Critical for Communities.* Available at <http://www.ncrc.org>.

———. 2001a. *CRA Commitments.* Available at <http://www.ncrc.org>.

———. 2001b. *Current Status of CRA and Fair Lending Bills.* Available at <http://www.ncrc.org>.

———. 2002. *Anti-Predatory-Lending Toolkit.* Available at <http://www.ncrc.org>.

Oppel, Richard A. 1998. Associates under a Microscope: Home Equity Firm Replies to Heightened Scrutiny. *Dallas Morning News* (Aug. 16).

Rohde, David. 1997. Banks Discover the South Bronx; Forced to Open, Branches Profit and Refute Stereotype. *New York Times* (April 16).

Peter Dreier

---

12   Protest, Progress, and the
      Politics of Reinvestment

In the late 1980s, a Canadian newspaper journalist who specialized in urban affairs took me on a tour of Toronto's neighborhoods. We drove through wealthy areas and more run-down sections. I asked him to show me the "worst" neighborhood in Toronto. There was nothing in the entire city comparable to an American slum or ghetto. I asked my tour guide if banks in Canada practiced "redlining." A sophisticated man with decades of experience analyzing urban policy and politics, this journalist had never heard the word. I explained that redlining was a well-known, although controversial, practice in the United States. He looked at me incredulously. "How can your government allow this to happen? Banks here simply couldn't get away with that. It wouldn't just be illegal. It would be unthinkable."

No other major industrial nation has allowed its cities to face the type of fiscal and social troubles confronting America's cities. Other industrial nations do not permit the level of sheer destitution and decay found in America's cities. We accept as normal levels of poverty, crime, and homelessness that would cause national alarm in Canada, Western Europe, or Australia. Compare, for example, cities in Canada—which has a similar economy and distribution of wealth—with our own. On every important indicator—crime, homelessness, poverty, infant mortality—Canadian cities seem to be on a different planet.

Persistent poverty, racial segregation, and fiscal crisis are the most fundamental problems facing our cities. More than three-quarters of America's 31 million poor people live in our metropolitan areas, and they are increasingly concentrated in ghettos and barrios (Dalaker 2001; Jargowsky 1997; Dreier, Mollenkopf, and Swanstrom 2001). While their poverty stems from both unemployment and low-wage work, their ghettoization results from racial discrimination. Black and Hispanic poor are much more likely than poor whites to live in mostly poor neighborhoods. Overall, levels of racial segregation have not significantly changed in the past thirty years, particularly in the older industrial cities in the northeast and Midwest (Glaeser and Vigdor 2001). In most metropolitan areas, three-quarters of blacks and Latinos would have to move to reach a random level of racial integration. At least two out of every three white Americans live in essentially all-white neighborhoods. Meanwhile, the level of *economic* segregation has increased, with the poor and well-off increasingly isolated from each other, and with a growing "spatial mismatch" between where the poor live and where job growth is occurring (Dreier, Mollenkopf, and Swanstrom 2001).

The community reinvestment movement emerged in the 1970s to address the reality of declining urban neighborhoods and persistent racial discrimination in housing and lending. Following in the wake of the Fair Housing Act of 1968—a key victory of the 1960s civil rights movement—the community reinvestment movement sought to focus attention on the role lenders played in exacerbating urban neighborhood decline and racial segregation. Its first major victory, the Home Mortgage Disclosure Act (HMDA), was passed by Congress in 1975. Two years later, it helped enact the Community Reinvestment Act (CRA). Community reinvestment advocates hoped that these laws would help reverse the private disinvestment in older cities and revitalize declining neighborhoods.

As other authors in this volume have pointed out, Lawrence Lindsey, former Federal Reserve Bank governor before becoming economic advisor to President George W. Bush, claimed that the world of community reinvestment is divided into those who engage in "noisy protest" and those who "grow up" and participate in "quiet accomplishment" (Lindsay 2000). But the reality is more complex. The movement has had to steer a difficult course. It has relied on community organizing as well as community development. It has engaged in confrontation and protest as well as collaboration and partnership. It is part of a grassroots activist crusade for social justice, but it is also part of the real estate and banking industry that cares primarily about the bottom line. Much of its success is due to its ability to walk a fine line between opposing worlds.

Without doubt the movement has made significant headway, but the political and economic forces shaping America's metropolitan economies today are much more powerful than the practices of the banking industry alone. On its own terms, the community reinvestment movement has been quite effective, but it will need to broaden its horizons—and forge wider political coalitions—if it is to build on its recent achievements and have a significant impact on revitalizing declining urban neighborhoods in the future.

Today, many are heralding the "comeback" of American cities (Grogan and Proscio 2000). The truth is that most of the trends that began in the late 1950s—private disinvestment from central cities, suburbanization, persistent racial segregation, wide income gaps between cities and suburbs—continued through the 1990s and into the next century. Although there have been some encouraging signs as we enter the twenty-first century, it is important not to overstate the gains or be lulled into complacency about the urban condition.

Disinvestment and Decline:
The Transformation of Urban Areas

The community reinvestment movement emerged at a time when America's older cities were in the midst of a dramatic transformation and, for the most part, decline. One haunting phrase seemed to capture these trends: "disinvestment."

The rush to the suburbs accelerated in the 1960s and 1970s. The older "rust-belt" cities were hemorrhaging jobs and people. Between 1960 and 1980, for example, Buffalo's population fell from 533,000 to 358,00; Chicago's from 3.55 million to 3 million; Cleveland's from 876,000 to 574,000; Detroit's from 1.67 million to 1.2 million; Milwaukee's from 741,000 to 636,000; Pittsburgh's from 604,000 to 424,000; and St. Louis's from 750,000 to 453,000 (Downs 1997). In most metropolitan areas where central cities lost population, suburbs gained population. In metropolitan areas where central cities gained population—primarily in the South, Southwest, and West—suburbs gained population even faster.

Bluestone and Harrison popularized the phrase "deindustrialization" to reflect the wave of factory closings occurring throughout the country, particularly in the northeast and Midwest (Bluestone and Harrison 1982). Within these older cities, once-stable middle-class and working-class neighborhoods were losing their commercial districts. Long-term residents witnessed the shutdown of large employers and the exodus of supermarkets, pharmacies, clothing stores, five-and-ten-cent stores, and other retail services. Their neighborhoods were also losing a growing part of their housing stock to abandonment and arson, as homeowners and landlords moved out. Passersby saw weed-filled vacant lots where homes once stood.

The proportion of poor people living in cities grew and became increasingly concentrated in ghetto neighborhoods. In 1970 the poverty rate for all central cities was 12.6 percent; by 1980, it was 17.3 percent; by 1990, 19 percent. (By 2000 it had declined to 16.1 percent [U.S. Bureau of the Census 2000; Dalaker 2001].) In the one hundred largest cities, the proportion of census tracts with at least 20 percent poverty population increased from 27.3 percent in 1970 to 39.4 percent in 1990; the proportion of census tracts with at least 40 percent poverty population increased from 6 percent to 13.7 percent during that period (Kasarda 1993).

Middle-class families left for suburban neighborhoods, and the income gap between residents of cities and suburbs widened. The gap between per-capita income in the cities and suburbs in the eighty-five largest metropolitan areas grew continuously wider between 1960 and 1990. Between 1970 and 1990 the suburban poverty rate rose from 7.1 percent to 8.7 percent, a slower increase than the central city rate. (By 2000, it had declined slightly to 7.8 percent). These gaps between central cities and suburbs were created both by the downward mobility of existing city residents and by the out-migration of the better off (U.S. Bureau of the Census 2000; Dalaker 2001; Lucy and Phillips 2000). The racial composition of metropolitan areas changed as well, increasingly resembling what sociologists termed "chocolate cities" surrounded by "vanilla suburbs" (Farley et al. 1978).

The growing concentration of poor people in cities, the exodus of the middle class to the suburbs, and the disappearance of decent jobs in urban areas made it almost impossible for city governments to raise the revenue necessary to provide basic services. To avert fiscal collapse, many cities closed schools, hospitals, health centers, police stations, and fire stations. They laid off essential employees and reduced basic services, such as maintaining parks, repairing roads, and enforcing housing and health codes. This fiscal straitjacket and decline of urban public services further exacerbated the exodus of middle-class residents and businesses.

These trends, underway since the late 1940s, accelerated in the late 1960s, particularly after the wave of urban riots. Within a relatively short period of time, America's metropolitan areas had undergone a dramatic demographic and economic transformation.

Bank redlining clearly played a significant role in the urban decline of the 1960s and 1970s, but it was only one of several culprits. In the postwar era, federal government policies pushed middle-income people out of cities and pulled them into suburbs (O'Connor 1999; Mohl 1993; Dreier, Mollenkopf, and Swanstrom 2001; Fishman 2000). These included highway-building policies that opened up the hinterlands to speculation and development; housing and tax policies that offered government-insured mortgages and tax breaks to whites in suburbia (but *not* in cities); bulldozer urban renewal policies that destroyed working-class neighborhoods, scattering their residents to blue-collar suburbs, to make way for downtown business development; low-income housing policies that concentrated public housing and Section 8 developments in already poor neighborhoods; and Department of Defense decisions about where to locate military bases and where to grant defense contracts. Urban disinvestment was not simply a result of market forces but of federal government actions.

It would be misleading to suggest that all federal programs encouraged urban disinvestment, economic segregation, and suburban sprawl. Most federal policies exacerbated central-city decline and racial segregation, but the federal government also adopted another (smaller and less powerful) set of policies to improve the economic and social conditions of central cities. In truth, these federal aid programs to cities—whether to revitalize downtowns, attract private jobs to inner-city neighborhoods, stabilize poor and working-class neighborhoods, or provide fiscal assistance to local governments—served, in effect, to "clean up the mess" created by the federal government's much larger subsidies for suburbanization and urban disinvestment. In Alice O'Connor's phrase, federal urban policy has been "swimming against the tide" of most federal domestic policies (O'Connor 1999).

Many Americans think that the federal government coddled cities and that they are worse off despite the expenditure of billions of federal dollars. Steven Hayward of the conservative Heritage Foundation has observed that the federal government spent $600 billion on cities between 1965 and 1990, yet older central cities continued to decline. Such federal policies are doomed to fail, according to Hayward, because they ignore the "logic of metropolitan development" (Hayward 1998). Conservatives are essentially correct that federal urban policies have failed, but they are wrong about the reasons. These policies did not fail because they violated the logic of the market but because other government policies, exacerbating market forces, had already set powerful anti-urban forces in motion.

The Origins of the Community Reinvestment Movement

As with most social and economic trends, these trends were not immediately obvious but crept up on residents of urban neighborhoods. In the 1970s, a family turned down for a mortgage loan was more likely to assume that it simply did not meet the bank's underwriting standards than to think that it was a victim of discrimination. But a number of astute activists began to see a pattern. They started to recognize that many long-term homeowners and small-business owners—even those who were obviously creditworthy—were finding it increasingly difficult to obtain loans to fix up their homes or expand their businesses. Even neighborhood-based savings and loans institutions—created to promote homeownership—were rejecting mortgage applications from stable families that wished to purchase homes in areas that policy experts and journalists started calling "transitional" neighborhoods.

It soon became clear that these were not the random actions of misguided loan officers. Banks seemed to have made some policy decisions. They would accept deposits from local neighborhood residents but lend money primarily to people who bought homes in suburbs.

As Joe Mariano explains in Chapter 2, in the mid-1970s small groups of community activists in cities across the country recognized that banks were engaged in redlining. In Baltimore, Boston, Chicago, Cleveland, New York, and other cities, neighborhood residents and small-business owners began to recognize a pattern in bank lending decisions. Banks were making choices and refusing to make loans to homes and businesses in certain neighborhoods, creating a self-fulfilling prophecy of neglect, deterioration, and abandonment. The invisible hand of the market, they learned, had a red pen in it.

Local activists and organizers—like Gail Cincotta and Shel Trapp in Chicago—concluded that their neighborhoods were experiencing systematic disinvestment and began efforts to persuade banks to revise their lending practices. Some were simply educational campaigns to change the way bankers—often suburban residents with stereotyped images of city neighbor-hoods—viewed the areas. Other efforts involved consumer boycotts—"green-lining" campaigns—of neighborhood banks that refused to reinvest local depositors' money in their own backyards.

Most of the efforts ended in frustration, with little impact on the banks' practices. But some neighborhood groups achieved small victories, including agreements between banks and community organizations to provide loans or maintain branches in their neighborhoods. Eventually, activists across the country who were working on similar issues discovered one another and rec-ognized their common agendas. From such localized efforts grew a national "community reinvestment" movement to address the problem of bank redlin-ing (Fishbein 1992; Schwartz 1998; Squires 1992).

In response to grassroots pressure from the emerging neighborhood move-ment, Congress sponsored a number of initiatives to promote community self-help efforts against redlining and discrimination. These included three key pieces of legislation—the federal Fair Housing Act (FHA) of 1968, the Home Mortgage Disclosure Act (HMDA) of 1975, and the Community Reinvest-ment Act (CRA) of 1977. The FHA was the outcome of a heated legislative debate and might not have been enacted for several more years, if at all, except for the assassination of Martin Luther King in April 1968. As other chapters in this volume have made clear, the HMDA and CRA have been particularly critical in supporting organizing activities against redlining. Given the stakes, the legislative battles over these two bills were surprisingly low-profile affairs, and the bills were enacted with little fanfare or public controversy.

The adoption of the HMDA created the momentum for the CRA. It pro-vided systematic data demonstrating the reality of redlining, which made it difficult for the banking industry to argue persuasively that it did not engage in widespread discrimination. Thanks to these laws and grassroots organiz-ing, the entire community reinvestment climate has changed dramatically in the past few decades. Banks are now much more proactive in working with community organizations to identify credit needs and create partnerships to meet them (Schwartz 1998; Taub 1988). Government regulators are more active in evaluating lenders' CRA performance and using regulatory incentives to ensure compliance.

As the chapters in this book demonstrate, the CRA had minimal impact at first but gained momentum in the 1980s, despite resistance from the Reagan and Bush administrations and their appointed federal bank regulators. From 1977 through the late 1980s, federal regulators mainly failed to monitor and enforce the CRA. As a result, community reinvestment activities primarily involved bottom-up enforcement: local campaigns by community organiza-tions or coalitions against local banks.

By the mid-1980s, these local activities had coalesced into a significant national presence. Thanks to the work of several national community orga-nizing networks—ACORN, the Center for Community Change (CCC), the

National Peoples Action/National Training and Information Center (NPA/ NTIC), and Citizen Action, aided later by the National Community Reinvestment Coalition (NCRC)—these local efforts became building blocks for a truly national effort that has produced dramatic results. Community groups learned how to use HMDA data to identify lending discrimination and used a variety of community organizing strategies to bring banks to the bargaining table, crafting community reinvestment "agreements." Even during the Bush years, the grassroots movement, with some Democratic Party allies in Congress, was able to use the savings and loan crisis as an opportunity to strengthen the CRA and HMDA laws.

In the 1990s, with a more sympathetic president in the White House and thus stronger enforcement by bank regulators, HUD, and the Department of Justice, the movement was able to build on its earlier work and increase the number and magnitude of its partnerships with lenders. Indeed, a growing number of lenders began to view its CRA-oriented lending as a profit center. The community reinvestment movement had pushed many banks reluctantly to increase their lending in minority and poor neighborhoods that had once been written off. Lo and behold, these loans performed well. Racial stereotypes had blinded the banking industry to the untapped market of the inner city. Ironically, it took a push from government regulation and grassroots organizing for bankers to pursue a neglected market opportunity!

The Community Reinvestment Movement: Ingredients for Success

The community reinvestment movement is probably the most successful example of grassroots community organizing since the mid-1970s. Of course, this is a little like being the tallest building in Topeka; there's not much competition. There are thousands of community organizations in cities across the country, but the hard truth is that most of them are not very effective. Many groups are able to "mobilize" protest action around immediate issues, but few groups are able to build strong organizations with genuine indigenous leadership that can sustain themselves over the long haul, overcome defeats, and build on victories (Dreier 1996; Warren 2001).

Community organizations have won many neighborhood-level victories. But despite the tens of thousands of grassroots community organizations that have emerged in America's urban neighborhoods since the 1970s, the whole of the community organizing movement is smaller than the sum of its parts. For every group that succeeds, there are many that do not. With some important exceptions, community groups that do win important local victories are not always capable of building on their success and moving on to other issues and larger problems. For the most part, despite local success and growth, community organizing has been unable to affect the national agenda—or, in most cases, even state-level policy. As a result, community groups often improve only marginally the conditions of life in many urban neighborhoods.

Any careful, honest examination of community mobilization must recognize that there are many false starts and dead ends. In fact, because we rarely hear about the efforts that went nowhere, we fail to note that many grassroots initiatives never get far beyond the first living-room complaint session, the first church basement meeting, the first leaflet that appeared in neighborhood mailboxes and went unacknowledged.

There are two major obstacles to successful community organizing. The first is that most neighborhood problems can't be solved at the neighborhood level; thus, to be effective, community organizations have to be able to influence corporate and government decision-makers outside the boundaries of their neighborhoods. The second is that most community organizations lack the capacity to mobilize sufficient resources—core constituents, external allies, media attention—to challenge existing power arrangements.

The sources of urban decay are found primarily outside neighborhood boundaries. Symptoms of urban decay—poverty, unemployment, homelessness, violent crime, racial segregation, and high infant mortality rates—have their roots in large-scale economic forces and federal government policy. These forces and policies include economic restructuring toward a low-wage service economy; corporate disinvestment (encouraged by federal tax laws); bidding wars among cities and states to attract businesses that undermine local fiscal health; redlining by banks and insurance companies; federal housing, transportation, tax, and defense spending policies that have subsidized the migration of people and businesses to the suburbs (exacerbating urban fiscal traumas); and federal cutbacks of various financial assistance, housing, social service, economic development, and other programs.

But success is not simply about winning victories on specific issues. It is also about changing attitudes. It is about overcoming hopelessness and the sense of futility that infect America's inner cities—which some have called the "quiet riots" of drug and alcohol abuse, domestic and street violence, and suicide. It is about giving people more confidence in themselves and in their neighbors. It is also about helping people recognize that there are few easy victories. While it is important to win short-term victories in order to maintain hope, no significant improvement in urban conditions will occur overnight; lasting change requires that people stay involved over the long haul. It is these changes in attitude that give people and neighborhoods the inner strength to organize around issues and to develop a vision that things can be different. Religious institutions often play a key role in community organizing, in part because they provide the moral solidarity that adds an important dimension to self-help efforts that transcend narrow concepts of self-interest.

Success depends on the ability of community groups to mobilize resources and generate external support for their activities from various members of the public (the "conscience constituency"), government officials, the media, and funding groups, including religious institutions, philanthropic organizations, businesses, and government. This means "reaching out" beyond neighborhoods, forging partnerships with allies, and learning when confrontation is called for and when negotiation and compromise are necessary.

Neighborhood organizations face enormous obstacles to repairing the social and economic fabric of their communities. What influence can neighborhood self-help organizations—neighborhood crime watches, tenant unions, community reinvestment organizations, and similar groups—have on policies made in state capitals or in Washington, D.C., and on decisions made in corporate boardrooms?

Although community-based organizations cannot, on their own, solve the major problems in their neighborhoods, they can provide the essential building blocks for doing so—*if* they are part of a broader social movement. That the community reinvestment movement did, eventually, expand from a disparate group of local efforts to a truly national movement helps explain its success. In light of the obstacles it faced, it is worth looking closely at this movement in order to understand the key ingredients that contributed to its success.

First, community reinvestment was an issue that affected many people and was clearly linked to economic and social conditions in urban neighborhoods. The movement identified a clear problem (redlining), a clear target (banks), and a clear solution (reinvestment).

The movement identified the "victims" of banks' redlining practices as entire neighborhoods, not individual residents. This stands in significant contrast to the "fair housing" movement, which seeks to identify individual victims of housing discrimination by realtors and landlords and to gain redress through legal settlements.[1] The victims of redlining were all the residents of a neighborhood experiencing decline. Organizing, therefore, did not depend on finding specific individuals who were denied loans by banks, which would have cut all others in the same neighborhood out of the potential constituency base.

By framing the problem this way, community organizers could use the social capital of these neighborhoods—the networks of formal affiliations through churches and other groups and informal affiliations through friendships—to forge a sense of solidarity and common purpose (Saegert, Thompson, and Warren 2001). Moreover, the community reinvestment movement was framed primarily in terms of place, not race. HMDA data clearly show that black and Latino applicants, and black and Latino neighborhoods, are much more likely to be denied loans than are white applicants and white neighborhoods. But while redlining was clearly motivated by racial stereotypes about urban neighborhoods and their residents, community organizers were able to mobilize both blacks and whites to challenge banks' disinvestment. The goal of the movement was not primarily to change patterns of racial segregation (to help blacks move into white neighborhoods or whites into black neighborhoods, for example), but to expand private credit into neighborhoods, to help existing residents fix up their homes, and to help people purchase homes in the neighborhood. The work of one coalition in Pittsburgh, recounted by Stanley Lowe and John Metzger in Chapter 6, is a good example of this organizing approach, which used social networks across racial and neighborhood lines to wage an effective campaign against major regional banks.

Second, the movement devised a clear "solution" to the problem it had identified. Activists pressured banks to invest more money in specific neighborhoods. This money (or, more accurately, credit) would go to individual homeowners and homebuyers, but it was not based on identifying specific victims who had been denied loans. Thus the benefits were spread quite widely. Even more important, one did not have to be a direct recipient of a CRA-inspired mortgage in order to benefit. By channeling mortgage credit into urban neighborhoods, banks were improving the entire neighborhood—raising property values, improving the physical condition of the neighborhood—so that even people who did not directly receive CRA-inspired loans could feel they were beneficiaries.

Moreover, the beneficiaries were not only individual homebuyers and their neighbors but specific organizations engaged in community development. The number of nonprofit Community Development Corporations (CDCs) working in urban neighborhoods expanded dramatically in the late 1970s and 1980s, due in large part to the community reinvestment movement and the CRA. By the late 1980s there were at least two thousand CDCs in the United States, mostly in older urban neighborhoods (Walker and Weinheimer 1998; Ferguson and Dickens 1999). Under pressure to channel credit into redlined neighborhoods, banks began to look for community-based "partners." To co-opt protest from community organizing groups and to win favor with regulators and politicians, banks forged partnerships with CDCs, providing them not only with credit to undertake a variety of housing and economic development projects, but also with philanthropic grants to underwrite their organizational operating expenses.

Community organizing and community development involve different approaches to urban reform. Community organizing involves mobilizing people to combat common problems and to increase their voice in institutions and decisions that affect their lives and communities. Community development involves neighborhood-based efforts to improve an area's physical and economic condition, such as the construction or rehabilitation of housing and the creation of jobs and business enterprises. There are clearly some tensions between some CDCs and some community reinvestment activists. Many CDCs are reluctant to bite the hand that feeds them—government officials and lenders—while some community organizing groups prefer confrontation.

In some cities, CDCs were part of the political coalitions engaged in community reinvestment protest. In most cities, however, CDCs were more cautious, unwilling to challenge banks directly but willing to take advantage of the outcomes of community protest. For the most part, protest groups shook the money tree and CDCs collected the rewards (Weir 1999; Dreier 1991).

Community organizations that engage in successful mobilization efforts sometimes branch out into community development. Efforts to balance these components are not without tension, however. Community groups that focus primarily on service delivery or community development often lose the energy and momentum required to do effective community organizing. Likewise, groups that do community organizing believe that getting involved in service delivery and community development can sap their strength and lead them to get "co-opted" by government and business elites. Despite this tension, some groups are able to combine the two successfully. For example, in a number of cities, ACORN (a national network of community organizations) has drawn on its success in challenging bank redlining to become involved in housing counseling for potential homeowners and in housing development. East Brooklyn Churches, a coalition of New York City religious congregations that is part of the Industrial Areas Foundation (IAF) network, spent a decade working on neighborhood issues before establishing its own housing development program (Nehemiah Homes), which has become one of the largest nonprofit development projects in the country.

Third, community reinvestment advocates made the "democratization of data" a key part of their overall strategy. In many disputes that engage community organizations, these groups are at an informational disadvantage. Their adversaries claim to have superior or "expert" information. The HMDA enabled community groups to identify the problem and gave them access to key information. In today's society, access to technology and financial expertise is critical to a community group's ability to deal with government and the private sector on complex issues. The HMDA helped level the playing field. It provided the data needed to analyze banks' lending patterns systematically (for housing loans but not commercial loans). It gave many community groups and university-based scholars—and some newspapers, local governments, and other agencies—the data with which to investigate geographic and racial bias in lending.

But, as Malcolm Bush and Daniel Immergluck note in Chapter 10, to make federal laws like the HMDA work, community groups must learn how to use them, and this usually involves having money to hire experts or to train staff in the computer skills needed to analyze complex data. The community reinvestment movement quickly learned how to take advantage of the HMDA data and translate them into reports understandable to the general public and the media. After Bill Clinton was elected president, community groups persuaded HUD to make HDMA data even more accessible. Foundations funded efforts—such as the Right-to-Know Network (<http://www.rtk.net>)—to help community groups learn how to use HMDA data. The dramatic expansion of the Internet helped this process along, since much of HMDA data is now available on line.

Fourth, the community reinvestment movement developed the capacity to develop allies among public officials, lawyers (as John Relman recounts in

Chapter 4), the news media, foundations, and even the banking industry. It was able to marshal external resources and engage "third parties." No movement can be successful without such allies. Learning how to recruit these allies and use these external resources is an important aspect of effective organizing (McCarthy and Zald 1977).

Initially, Senator William Proxmire, a liberal Democrat from Wisconsin, was the key advocate for anti-redlining legislation in Congress. Activists like Gail Cincotta worked closely with Proxmire and his staff to draft and then lobby for the CRA. In later years, Congressmen like Henry Gonzalez of Texas, Barney Frank and Joseph Kennedy of Massachusetts, and others, worked closely with community reinvestment advocates. A number of local officials, including Boston mayor Ray Flynn, also joined forces with community organizations on this issue.

Community groups formed alliances with university-based experts (primarily sociologists, economists, and planners) and consultants, who either wrote reports on behalf of these groups or taught community organization staffers how to use them. In the late 1970s, for example, ACORN's St. Louis chapter worked closely with a Washington University sociologist to produce HMDA-based reports. Groups like ACORN, the California Community Reinvestment Coalition, and others developed an internal capacity to use HMDA data in sophisticated ways.

The movement also cultivated reporters for major newspapers to report on redlining. The HMDA provided community groups with a dramatic story to tell. They could use HMDA data to produce multicolored maps and charts that demonstrated the reality of redlining. Newspaper reporters loved the HMDA. The data could reveal which neighborhoods in their circulation area were being starved for credit. It could reveal which banks were the culprits—and which banks were the "good guys." By the late 1980s—particularly as journalists became more sophisticated in using computers and quantitative data, a number of major newspapers began to report the redlining issue with some regularity. In fact, the *Atlanta Journal and Constitution* won a Pulitzer Prize for its 1988 series on this subject, "The Color of Money." Other newspapers followed suit. It is significant that an organization of investigative reporters even published a handbook on using HMDA and census data entitled *Home Mortgage Lending: How to Detect Disparities* (McGinty 2000).

Beginning in the 1980s, national and local foundations began providing grants to local community organizations and national networks engaged in community reinvestment organizing and advocacy. At the national level, the Ford Foundation, Surdna Foundation, and others invested in the community reinvestment movement. Even some bank foundations have provided grants to organizations involved in the community reinvestment movement.

Community activists also learned how to develop strategic alliances with some bankers. HMDA reports, for example, allowed them to make distinctions between "good" and "bad" banks in terms of lending performance. In some cities activists persuaded local governments to issue regular "report cards" on lenders using HMDA data; in other cities, community groups sponsored these reports on their own.

Sophisticated activists were able to take advantage of this. Rather than paint the entire banking industry with the same brush, they argued that community reinvestment laws were needed to push reluctant regulators and "bad" banks to live up to their legal and moral commitments. They also were able to get some of the "good" banks to support their legislative goals. Since no bank wants to be identified as one of the "bad" lenders, banks were sometimes willing to work with community reinvestment groups to avoid being subjected to public protests.

Within a decade after the CRA was enacted, many banks created separate "community reinvestment" divisions. These divisions were often staffed by "liberal" individuals who sympathized with the aims of the community reinvestment movement. Indeed, some of these people had themselves been community activists who were recruited by banks to serve as liaisons with community groups. These bank officials often became the internal allies of the community movement, providing it with useful information and advice.

Fifth, the community reinvestment movement's organizing strategy gave residents a clear set of remedies at the national, state, and local levels. It did not rely simply on neighborhood organizing. These remedies included local linked-deposit laws, state linked-deposit and anti-redlining laws, and, of course, the enactment, and then the strengthening and improved enforcement of, the federal HMDA and CRA. Consequently, groups could organize and achieve victories on several fronts, which allowed them to keep constituents "in motion" and to juggle a number of organizing campaigns simultaneously. It also permitted groups working at the local level to hook up with groups in different cities, and to join forces at the state and federal levels.

In Boston, for example—after the Federal Reserve Bank and the Boston Redevelopment Authority in 1987 produced separate reports revealing widespread lending disparities, both of which were reported in the local newspapers—community groups forged a coalition to push for changes. At the local level they worked to get the city government to adopt a linked-deposit law, which requires the city to do an annual "report card" of banking practices in Boston (using HMDA and other data) and to deposit city funds on the basis of banks' performance.[2] They also pushed the state government to adopt a community reinvestment law (for state-chartered banks) and to create a "soft-second" loan program for low-income homebuyers.[3] They pressured the Massachusetts Bankers Association and individual banks to create a consortium and to forge a community reinvestment agreement with specific targets for loans, new bank branches, and other services. And finally, through the National Community Reinvestment Coalition, they worked with other groups to pressure Congress to strengthen the CRA and HMDA laws (Dreier 1991; Campen 1992; Callahan, Chapter 5 of this volume).

In 2000 and 2001 a variety of organizations around the country—including ACORN, the AARP, and others—spearheaded a campaign to address the problem of predatory lending. This effort, too, involved working on multiple fronts.

Sixth, local groups working on the same issue were able to learn from one another through several national organizing networks and training centers, particularly National Peoples Action (NPA), ACORN, the Center for Community Change (CCC) and the National Community Reinvestment Coalition (NCRC), as well as the Woodstock Institute and Inner City Press.

These networks helped expand the capacity of local community groups to use the CRA and HMDA. They provided groups with training and linked them together to make the federal government—legislators and regulators alike—more responsive to neighborhood credit needs. Through these networks, acting on their own or in concert, grassroots groups pressured Congress to strengthen both the CRA and HMDA several times in the late 1980s. These were dramatic legislative victories against overwhelming political odds. In 1990 sixteen national organizations formed the National Community Reinvestment Coalition to strengthen the community reinvestment agenda. As John Taylor and Josh Silver noted in Chapter 11, within a decade the NCRC had grown to include more than eight hundred local community groups and local public agencies from across the country.

With funding from several foundations and technical advice from these national networks, community groups have been able to hire experts to help interpret HMDA data, publish reports, and expose systematic bank discrimination. Whereas in the past most HMDA studies focused only on one bank or one city, national groups such as ACORN have been able to demonstrate that the problem is widespread. In 1989 the Federal Reserve began to respond with several studies of its own.

Seventh, the CRA provided community groups and national networks with "organizing handles" and a place at the negotiating table. By requiring banks to meet community needs as a prerequisite for obtaining various approvals from federal bank regulators, and by giving consumer and community groups the right to challenge these approvals, the CRA provided the groups with leverage to bring banks to the negotiating table. Confronted with HMDA studies and community protest, banks invited community groups to negotiate in order to avoid further negative publicity and the possible loss of regulatory approval. Regulators—often under pressure from Democratic congresspersons from urban districts—often felt that it was necessary to respond to community groups' CRA challenges, especially when they were backed up by empirical studies and press attention. Some of these members of Congress held their own public hearings, or pressured the regulators to do so, which provided community groups with public forums at which to air their grievances.

The CRA did not mandate community participation. Community groups had to *earn* their place at the negotiating table by staging protests and actively challenging bank applications to regulators. Nor did the CRA provide funding for community organizations for operations or research. These groups had to rely on foundations and other funding sources to provide resources for staff, office space, and research. (In contrast, HUD provides funding to fair housing groups to do testing that identifies lawbreaking landlords and realtors.) Nevertheless, groups that were able to marshal these resources were able to gain a seat at the negotiating table with banks and regulators.

New Challenges, Obstacles, and Opportunities

CRA agreements alone have catalyzed more than $1 trillion in bank lending and services. Banks have channeled significantly more credit into low-income and minority neighborhoods than they ever did before passage of the CRA and HMDA. Even more important, many banks are now much more proactive in forming partnerships with community-based organizations and in making credit available in previously neglected neighborhoods (Joint Center for Housing Studies 2002; Hagg 2000).

But as the movement enters the twenty-first century, it confronts new challenges, obstacles, and opportunities. Urban America today is different from what it was in the mid-1970s when the movement began. Over the years, the movement has learned to adapt to changing circumstances. Dramatic changes in the metropolitan landscape, the political environment, and the banking industry will require the movement to make further adjustments. The discussion that follows briefly outlines some of those new realities.

During the 1980s and 1990s, CRA-related lending focused mostly on low- and moderate-income urban neighborhoods, primarily those populated by racial minorities. Community reinvestment activists, along with a growing chorus of bankers, take credit for the improvement in urban conditions that occurred during the 1990s. But some caution is called for. Just as bank redlining was only one of the causes of urban decline in the 1960s and 1970s, we cannot expect bank-driven community reinvestment initiatives to rebuild struggling cities and neighborhoods on their own.

To the extent that the CRA helped revitalize urban neighborhoods, it challenges the belief that cities can do fine on their own and do not need government to steer public and private investment into urban areas. The wave of CRA-inspired investment over the past two decades no doubt contributed to physical and economic improvements in urban neighborhoods. It is not clear, however, exactly who benefited. Did CRA loans promote "gentrification" or did they help lift the urban poor out of poverty by making it easier to gain access to wealth-generating assets?

It is true that many urban social indicators improved during the second half of the 1990s. Some urban analysts have even heralded a new era of "comeback cities." The 2000 census revealed that during the 1990s major cities such as New York and Chicago reversed their long decline in population. In most cities, unemployment, poverty, and crime rates declined, while the homeownership rate, particularly among blacks and Hispanics, increased. Banks made more loans in urban neighborhoods, and private investors built office buildings, retail stores, sports complexes, and other facilities. By the end of the decade, the long decline in wages among unskilled workers finally seemed to have stopped. Even air quality improved in many urban areas. These trends have led the media to herald an incipient urban revival.

This message is certainly preferable to the widespread stereotype that America's cities are cauldrons of social pathology past the "point of no return." But these trends are neither inevitable nor very robust. They stem largely from an unprecedented national economic expansion, reinforced by national policies that reduced unemployment, spurred productivity, lifted up the working poor, and targeted private investment to low-income urban areas (Freeman 2001).

None of these factors substantially changed the most fundamental urban problem—namely, the growing concentration of poverty in central cities (and now inner suburbs) and the growing separation between the poor and the well-to-do.[4] Nor does it appear that these positive trends have continued into the first decade of the new century. As the nation's economy drifted downward from 2000 through 2002, the indicators of urban revival—reductions in poverty, crime, and the proportion of families without health insurance among them—came to a halt.

In reality, the economic dynamism of cities persists alongside substantial poverty, social exclusion, and growing inequality. Indeed, the persistent vitality of many central cities has generated the vast disparities of wealth and poverty that are sometimes located only a few zip codes from each other.

Harvard Business School professor Michael Porter has argued that inner cities have a "competitive advantage" and will prosper if governments simply step out of the way and promote a favorable business climate (Porter 1995, 1997). But it is not simply a matter, as Porter implies, of government helping private-sector investors make the best of their opportunities. The playing field between and within American metropolitan areas is very uneven, putting central cities in particular at a disadvantage. Because of the fragmentation of local governments within metropolitan areas, municipalities engage in "bidding wars" to attract private investment, thereby undermining the fiscal health of their own jurisdictions (Harrison and Glasmeier 1997; Nowak 1997).

This fragmentation, along with federal and state tax laws, makes it difficult for cities to capture much of the wealth generated within their borders for use in reducing concentrated poverty and providing municipal services. As productive investments have become more mobile, even large, prosperous cities have cut back on spending for the poor. Between 1970 and 1990 New York City, with a long tradition of helping the poor, cut its per capita expenditures on the poor from $537 to $285 (in constant 1987 dollars).

Central cities and older suburbs have both the most severe social needs and the worst fiscal conditions, exacerbating their inability to provide adequate municipal services, such as public safety, education, housing, and infrastructure maintenance. All of this undermines their "business climate" and the eagerness of private firms to invest in inner-city neighborhoods. These conditions pose some serious challenges to those concerned about the future of the community reinvestment movement.

1. The United States is now a suburban nation, and many "urban" problems now confront older suburbs. The community reinvestment movement is basically an urban phenomenon. Its organizing work was based on the paradigm of urban decline amid suburban growth. Its initial campaigns focused on the concept that banks welcomed deposits of urban residents but then lent them to homebuyers in suburban areas. The problem of bank redlining and private sector disinvestment is no longer confined to inner-city neighborhoods. The community reinvestment movement needs to address the problems of these declining suburbs, which are also starved for credit, to revitalize declining neighborhoods and deteriorating housing.

The urban neighborhood conditions that triggered the community reinvestment movement in the 1970s have now spread to many suburban areas. The first wave of inner, working-class suburbs has long since been built out, their populations have aged, and their residents' incomes have stagnated since the early 1970s. These suburbs have developed increasingly "urban" problems that they cannot solve on their own. Decline has accelerated in many older suburbs, a troublesome trend, because they typically have even fewer institutional resources than do central cities to respond to the problems that have crept up on them.

Ironically, many families who flee central cities to escape urban deterioration end up in suburbs that are worse off than the cities they fled. A nationwide study of 554 suburbs found the popular image of suburban prosperity to be a myth. Using a suburb's median family income compared with the regional median as a measure of prosperity, William Lucy and David Phillips found that 20 percent of the suburbs declined faster than their central cities between 1960 and 1990 (Lucy and Phillips 2000). The process of suburban decline sped up after 1980, when almost one-third of the suburbs fared worse than their central cities. Between 1980 and 1990, more than half (57 percent) of the suburbs lost population. Based on these trends, the authors call the period after 1980 the "post-suburban era," or the era of suburban decline.

This trend continued in the 1990s. The number of poor people living within metropolitan areas but outside the central cities held steady during this decade, even as the number of central-city poor declined by 14.3 percent. (The poverty population also dropped in nonmetropolitan areas.) In a relative sense, poverty became more suburban.

Basically, rich suburbs have prospered while middle-income and poor suburbs have declined. As a result, the degree of income polarization in suburbs has increased rapidly. Census data for 554 suburbs show that the number of suburbs below 80 percent of the metropolitan median family income increased from 22 to 90 between 1960 and 1990, and the number above 120 percent of the metropolitan median fell only slightly (from 148 in 1960 to 142 in 1990). Just as the gap between rich and poor widened at the individual level, it widened tremendously between suburban locations. The number of solid middle-income suburbs fell 40 percent, and the average ratio between the highest- and lowest-income suburbs increased from 2.1 to 1 in 1960 to 3.4 to 1 in 1990 (Lucy and Phillips 2000, 170–77).

Decline most affected not the oldest suburbs but those built between 1945 and 1970. When these suburbs go downhill, they usually do so rapidly. Normally, all the housing within their borders was built at about the same time. After twenty-five years, major systems such as roofs and furnaces need to be replaced. Residents with money usually find that it makes more sense to purchase a new home on the suburban fringe, in exurbia, than to rehabilitate and expand older tract homes. Land prices are cheap there, and the latest construction technology gives buyers more bang for their buck. As Lucy and Phillips note, exurbanization is to the postwar suburbs what suburbanization was to central cities: it sucks the life out of older suburbs by siphoning off the most prosperous households.

Bank redlining is partly responsible for suburban sprawl. By denying loans to middle-income households who may have wished to remain in central cities, banks accelerated the exodus to the suburbs. But bank redlining is not primarily responsible for the shortage of affordable housing in better-off suburbs—a major cause of racial and economic segregation. Municipal exclusionary ("snob") zoning laws—and the unwillingness of state and federal governments to challenge local zoning autonomy—play an important part in limiting housing opportunities in many suburban jurisdictions.

2. *The racial and ethnic composition of the United States and its metropolitan areas is more complex and diverse than ever.* The community reinvestment movement was founded on the paradigm of urban areas populated by blacks and whites. But as Frey and Geverdt (1998), Frey (2001), Harris (1999), and a number of other social scientists have noted, the demographic trajectories of our major metropolitan areas are no longer dominated by the dynamic of whites fleeing to the suburbs as central cities become increasingly populated by blacks. In many respects, we are moving beyond the paradigm of "politics in black and white." Although most large central cities, such as New York and Los Angeles, are becoming less white, they are also becoming less black, as African Americans suburbanize and immigrants and their children take the place of the native born. Most suburbs are also becoming more heterogeneous in racial and ethnic terms. There is a growing number of "melting-pot suburbs." In contrast to the 1960s and 1970s, these transitions are not pitting whites against blacks but are creating more complex patterns.

The first two decades of the community reinvestment movement focused almost exclusively on gaps in mortgage lending and homeownership rates between blacks and whites. While blacks continue to lag behind whites in these two indicators, the growing Hispanic population in metropolitan areas requires a new approach. Levels of residential segregation, suburbanization rates, gaps in the homeownership rate, and mortgage lending gaps (as revealed in HMDA data) between whites and Hispanics are also significant. In the future, the community reinvestment movement will need to incorporate Hispanic organizations into a broader coalition.

The political implications of the changing racial and ethnic mix of America's urban areas have yet to play out fully, but the black-white racial cleavage that drove urban politics in the postwar period is no longer the major political dynamic. The emerging politics of interethnic relations is not going to be easy, but it may be less likely to be locked in racial polarization. More complex forms of interracial coalition are likely to arise.

3. Racial discrimination in housing and lending is generally less overt than it was a few decades ago. Public opinion polls consistently show that white Americans are considerably more supportive of racial integration in neighborhoods and schools than they were twenty-five or forty years ago. But it is difficult to know for certain whether racial discrimination has been reduced. Certainly discrimination is more subtle and less overt than it was in the past. Nevertheless, there is considerable documentation that landlords, real estate agents, appraisers, and lenders today treat whites differently from how they treat blacks and Latinos, even when income is factored in (Yinger 2001; Turner and Skidmore 1999).

The fair housing and community reinvestment movements have been able to demonstrate significant levels of racial discrimination by using "testing" and HMDA-based reports. The real estate and banking industries have responded in a variety of ways by educating their member institutions to avoid the most blatant forms of discrimination, which are obvious to consumers.

In other words, the success of the community reinvestment movement in reducing the most blatant forms of racial discrimination has made it more difficult to uncover and challenge more subtle forms of discrimination that generate less outrage. Public opinion and public officials are certainly more receptive now to contesting overt racism. Just as most Americans opposed Sheriff Bull Connor's use of fire hoses and billy clubs to attack civil rights activists, or overt racial profiling by police, so too do most Americans oppose racially restrictive covenants in property deeds and violent opposition to racial integration. Many Americans were understandably upset when early HMDA studies, using color-coded maps, demonstrated racist lending practices. But it is more difficult to mobilize around more subtle forms of racial discrimination or around institutional practices that result in racially disparate outcomes but that appear on the surface to be racially "neutral" in intent or procedure.

It may be possible that *intentional* discrimination has been reduced over the past few decades. But, as Squires notes in his introduction, what may remain are more covert, *institutional* forms of racial discrimination. These are more difficult to detect and more difficult to mobilize against, because they are much more subject to interpretation.

A good example is the recent debate over issues of "creditworthiness." Lenders now argue that underwriting standards that consider an applicant's credit history are a necessary part of any review process. It is well known that whites are more likely to have wealth assets and less likely to have poor credit records than are blacks and Hispanics with comparable incomes (Oliver and Shapiro 1995; Conley 1999). These realities are primarily a consequence of past racial discrimination. Thus blacks and Hispanics have inherited a disadvantage, which means that the playing field for obtaining a mortgage (or insurance) is uneven, even if lenders and insurers treat applicants in a "colorblind" fashion.

Banks claim that even if their loan-processing reviews result in racial disparities in *outcomes*, they are not evidence of racial discrimination. Lenders can use this argument to deflect accusations of racial discrimination. Studies based on HMDA data alone cannot account for creditworthiness. Studies that "control for" creditworthiness—such as the Boston Federal Reserve report—rely on private data to which only lenders have access.

Similarly, the accelerating decline of bank branches and the increase of ATMs and on-line banking appear racially neutral, but they have significant racial implications. Because poor and minority households are less likely to have computers, they are even more likely now than before to be served by pawnbrokers, check-cashing stores, predatory lenders, and other forms of "fringe banking" (Caskey 1994).

4. The emphasis on homeownership poses dilemmas for community reinvestment advocates. The community reinvestment movement has been premised on the expansion of homeownership. The HMDA, for example, focuses on home-purchase and improvement loans, though it also covers multifamily loans. Much of the evidence used to justify the CRA is the wide gulf in homeownership rates between racial groups and between neighborhoods, which are viewed as indicators of a "credit gap" and of racial discrimination.

Since the community reinvestment movement began, the nation's homeownership rate has inched upward and the homeownership gap between whites and racial minorities has narrowed. At the peak of the business cycle in 1999, the homeownership rate reached an all-time high of 66.8 percent.[5] Without doubt, much of this achievement is a consequence of the pressure on lenders and regulators by the community reinvestment movement, including pressure on Fannie Mae and Freddie Mac, as Allen Fishbein describes in Chapter 7.

Although the homeownership gap between white households and minority (black and Latino) households remains wide, even when household income is considered, it has narrowed, due in part to stronger enforcement of federal anti-redlining laws and increased efforts by lenders, as well as Fannie Mae and Freddie Mac, to reach minority and immigrant consumers (Williams, McConnell, and Nesiba 2001). Moderate interest rates, relatively stable home prices, and employment growth have also contributed to this trend.

But aggregate figures can be misleading. Compared with the early 1980s, the homeownership rate in the late 1990s had actually *declined* among all age cohorts under 55. For example, the homeownership rate for the 30–34 age group was 62.4 percent in 1978 and 53.6 percent twenty years later. Moreover, many families who have managed to become homeowners are on shaky ground. In late 1999, according to the Federal Reserve's Survey of Consumer Finance, American households, particularly those with incomes below $50,000, had an unprecedented level of debt, including mortgage debt (Earnest 2000; Evanoff and Segal 1996; Savage 1999; Segal and Sullivan 1998; Uchitelle 1999; Wolff 2000; U.S. Bureau of the Census 1999).

Some observers have worried that an economic downturn would see a significant increase in mortgage delinquencies and foreclosure (although this might be partly offset by lower interest rates). This is exactly what occurred in New York following the economic upheaval in the wake of the attack on the World Trade Center in September 2001. Many homeowners there have been late with mortgage payments since the attack, and are now on the brink of foreclosure (Kershaw 2002).

As many of the chapters in this volume report, pressure from community activists can push banks (as well as secondary mortgage market institutions and home insurers) to revise underwriting standards in order to make previously marginal households creditworthy. But surely there are limits to the financial ability of many low-income households to afford homeownership— or the willingness of low-income families to sink all their resources into a house in a neighborhood that may not appreciate in value at the same rate as homes in other neighborhoods (Rosenthal 2001).

If the community reinvestment movement continues to operate as an advocate for homeownership, it will need to address these concerns. One obvious goal must be to level the playing field in terms of the federal government's housing subsidies. The vast majority of federal housing assistance comes in the form of tax breaks for homeownership, and the overwhelming proportion of those subsidies go to better-off families living in relatively expensive homes (Dreier 1997, 2003). Revising the nation's tax laws to provide subsidies to low- and moderate-income families who want to become homeowners—perhaps in the form of a tax credit similar to the earned income tax credit—would be one step in this direction (Retsinas 1999; Green and Reshovsky 2001). Pushing the lending industry and the secondary mortgage market institutions to encourage diverse forms of homeownership—including limited equity cooperatives—would be another vehicle for increasing homeownership and housing security for those whom the current system does not serve well. Resident-owned cooperatives are widespread in Canada and Europe, but less well known in the United States, in part because of the reluctance of lending institutions to provide financing for this form of homeownership.

5. *The financial services industry is much more consolidated and concentrated than ever before.* When the community reinvestment movement began in the 1970s, its primary targets were neighborhood savings and loan institutions. Their depositors were primarily individuals who lived and businesses that operated in the surrounding area. These institutions were created to make loans for homeownership. Although some S&Ls were quite large, most of them were sufficiently small so that people who lived in these neighborhoods considered them part of the community. When local residents began to understand that these institutions were engaged in redlining, they viewed it as a breach of faith. But, more important, because the depositors in these S&Ls came disproportionately from the surrounding area, the activists had convenient organizing handles for bringing these institutions to the negotiating table.

As Matthew Lee indicates in Chapter 9, "the CRA provides that banks have a duty to the communities from which they draw their deposits." But what happens now that the reality has shifted from neighborhood S&Ls to national and transnational "financial services" companies? How are community-based groups supposed to challenge the practices of firms that are headquartered thousands of miles away, that operate in many metro areas and even many countries, and that engage in a variety of financial services, some of them beyond the reach of the traditional framework of federal regulations? How do you hold financial institutions accountable to communities when they are distant, complex conglomerates whose key officeholders have no ongoing connections to many of the places where they do business?

Much has changed in the past two decades. The S&L industry lobbied Congress successfully in the 1980s to remove many of the constraints imposed on it by New Deal legislation, especially the restriction on lending only for home mortgages. As a result, the S&L industry was dramatically transformed in the 1980s. Savings institutions were now able to make commercial loans. Small S&Ls were purchased by larger S&Ls and by commercial banks. The industry engaged in an orgy of speculation and mismanagement, leading to the "S&L scandal" of 1989. Many S&Ls went bankrupt, forcing the federal government to spend hundreds of billions of dollars to bail out the depositors. By the early 1990s the neighborhood S&L was virtually a thing of the past.

At the same time, the entire banking industry underwent a similar transformation. Large local banks bought out smaller banks. Regional banks gobbled up local lending institutions. Between 1975 and 1997, the number of banking institutions declined by 40 percent as a result of failures, consolidations, and relaxation of laws limiting interstate banking (Joint Center for Housing Studies 2002, 14). Then, after heavy lobbying from banking and insurance industries, the Financial Modernization Act of 1999 tore down the seventy-year old legal firewalls between commercial banks and other financial services companies—insurance, investment banks, and others.

The restructuring of the mortgage industry has also had a significant impact. Private mortgage companies, which are currently *not* covered by the CRA, are making an increasing proportion of mortgage loans. In 1980 mortgage companies and other nonregulated lenders (in contrast to banks and thrifts) accounted for 29 percent of all one-to-four-family mortgage loans; by 1997, they accounted for 56 percent of them (Joint Center for Housing Studies 2002, 13). In Boston in 1990, banks had roughly 80 percent of the market share of mortgage loans; by 2000 mortgage companies had 70 percent of the market share (Callahan 2002; Campen 2001). As a result, "CRA's impact may be waning" (Joint Center for Housing Studies 2002, v).

The twenty-first century will certainly see a growing concentration of power in a smaller and smaller number of financial services conglomerates, which will present daunting new challenges. How, for example, can a community group in San Francisco bring pressure to bear on a bank headquartered in Charlotte, North Carolina, that purchased the San Francisco-based Bank of America?

Chapters 5, 8, and 9 of this volume address different aspects of this new problem. In the future, a major challenge to all community organizers will be the capacity of groups to organize "up to scale." Only groups that have a national base (such as ACORN) or are part of the national network (such as the NCRC, CCC, and NTIC) will have any reasonable chance to challenge the financial services giants.

This concern is not unique to the community reinvestment movement. Labor unions, environmental groups, and others have increasingly confronted the reality of unregulated "free" trade and economic globalization. Not only do many financial services firms operate globally, they provide the capital for other companies to expand investments around the world, often to take advantage of cheap labor, lax environmental regulations, and a union-free workforce held in check by authoritarian governments, many of them supported by the U.S government with military and economic aid. Indeed, U.S. banks are financing the flight of American jobs and the expansion of sweatshop conditions overseas or in low-wage areas of the United States. In many cases they use the deposits of American working families, including their pension funds, to do so. But none of these activities is currently within the scope of the Community Reinvestment Act.

Unless the community reinvestment movement is able to address these economic and political realities—in part by joining forces with labor unions and environmental groups—the new world of lending will increasingly be beyond their reach. The past decade has witnessed a growing willingness on the part of organized labor to forge coalitions with community groups, such as the living-wage crusades in dozens of cities around the country. Labor unions have been noticeably absent from all but a handful of community reinvestment campaigns, though they are beginning to work with affordable housing groups to address the housing concerns of the nation's working families (Dreier 2000a, 2000b; Dreier and Candaele 2002). It makes sense for community reinvestment advocates to forge alliances with unions, whose members live in low-income and working-class neighborhoods, in central cities and inner-ring suburbs that are subject to the redlining practices of lending institutions.

6. The political environment is likely to shift away from support for community reinvestment unless a broad coalition can forge a counterweight to the financial services industry lobby and to suburban domination of Congress. The community reinvestment movement gained momentum in the mid-1970s, a time when American politics was in backlash against urban rebellion, civil rights activism, and urban renewal programs. It was certainly swimming against the tide. If anything, the political climate is likely to be even less hospitable in the future unless a number of conditions change.

In the 1970s cities still had a significant voice in Congress and were able to stem or mitigate the backlash. This is no longer true. Congress is now dominated by members from suburban districts, a reflection of both demographic changes and congressional gerrymandering, which has increasingly isolated urban voters into a smaller and smaller number of "safe" seats dominated by liberal (increasingly minority) Democrats (Teixeria and Rogers 2000; Schneider 1992; Gainsborough 2001; Sauerzopf and Swanstrom 1999; Nardulli, Dalager, and Greco 1996; Wolman and Marckini 1998; Dreier, Mollenkopf, and Swanstrom 2001). If Democrats regain a majority in the House of Representatives, many of these liberal Democrats from urban districts will become chairs of key committees and subcommittees, but they will be operating in an environment requiring cooperation and compromise with suburban Democrats, many of them from "swing" districts where their electoral margins of victory are relatively narrow. The same dynamic is increasingly true in state governments as well (Weir 1996).

Any effort to address urban problems will require forging a political coalition with some elements of the suburban electorate, most likely the inner-ring suburbs that are facing increasingly "urban" problems. As noted above, many of these older suburbs confront problems of disinvestment and decline. The community reinvestment movement needs to build bridges across city lines, particularly in those "swing" inner-suburban districts.

The Financial Services Modernization Act of 1999, which rolled back some CRA provisions, was a clear indication that while the banking industry has learned to live with the CRA, it would still prefer to operate with fewer regulations. As Squires and other contributors to this volume make clear, banks have often touted their CRA agreements to improve their public relations and to win approvals from regulators, but CRA commitments are often vague, difficult to monitor, and difficult to enforce. With a few exceptions, grassroots community groups lack the capacity to monitor these agreements. In 1999, as Squires notes, "Congress could have established CRA or CRA-like requirements for all providers of financial services," but chose not to do so.

The political influence of the increasingly concentrated financial services industry is likely to grow, as major lenders, insurance companies, and others join forces to reduce federal government regulation of their industry. Banks and insurance companies have long been among the more generous contributors to political campaigns, spreading their largesse to both political parties. Despite the passage of the McCain-Feingold campaign finance reform law in 2002, business and industry groups will continue to have an overwhelming advantage in influencing elected officials.

The community reinvestment movement cannot hope to match the political influence of the financial services industry—through the legislative process (lobbying for amendments to strengthen the CRA), through the regulatory process (pressuring regulators to enforce existing laws), or through the political process (working to elect sympathetic politicians to Congress and state government)—on its own. Community reinvestment coalitions are quite fragile. Many lack the staying power to maintain their constituency base and to sustain mobilizing after initial victories. This is particularly true as the financial services industry becomes increasingly concentrated and distant from community accountability. The movement will need allies who share some of its specific agenda and who share a broader agenda to promote activist government to protect and expand the rights of working-class and low-income Americans.

The most effective vehicle for addressing these concerns is organized labor. Union strength reached a peak of 35 percent in the mid-1950s, enabling blue-collar Americans to share in postwar prosperity and join the middle class. Union pay scales even boosted the wages of nonunion workers. The erosion of America's labor movement since the 1970s has contributed to declining wages and living standards and the nation's widening economic disparities. In 2000 only 13.5 percent of the workforce belonged to unions, with less than 10 percent of the private workforce unionized.

Despite this decline, organized labor remains the strongest progressive political force in the country—one with the capacity to mobilize voters and influence the outcome of elections, especially in swing districts, and influence legislation. In recent years, the labor movement, under the new leadership of AFL-CIO president John Sweeney, has pledged to expand union organizing, and union membership has increased modestly in recent years. Recognizing their own political limitations, unions have also increasingly reached out to religious, community, and environmental organizations—in campaigns for local living wages and in efforts to put limits on unregulated global trade. The labor movement's future—among nonunionized service-sector and light manufacturing sector employees—is concentrated in cities and inner-ring suburbs.

As noted earlier, labor unions are dealing with an increasingly global and concentrated economy, and are seeking new tools to organize and new approaches to get governments to regulate conglomerate business operations.

Unions face their own version of economic redlining—the runaway company, financed by large-scale lenders. There is an obvious natural affinity between community organizations seeking to improve urban neighborhoods and labor unions that represent and seek to expand their membership among low- and moderate-income workers.

Conclusion

Gregory Squires calls the community reinvestment movement part of the "struggle to democratize access to capital." The next phase of this struggle, he observes, will be the battle over some version of the Community Reinvestment Modernization Act of 2001, sponsored by Congressmen Tom Barrett of Milwaukee and Luis Gutierrez of Chicago. As Squires notes, this bill would "extend CRA or CRA-like provisions to all mortgage lenders, insurers, and security firms. It would establish HMDA-like disclosure requirements for the property insurance industry. And it would revise those sections of the Financial Services Modernization Act [of 1999] that weakened the CRA." Squires acknowledges that "the prospects for this legislation are uncertain" and claims that it "depends on community-based organizing efforts."

In reality, no legislation as bold as the Barrett-Gutierrez bill is likely to make much headway without being part of a much broader progressive agenda. The struggle to democratize access to capital has many fronts. These include efforts to give employers a greater voice in their workplaces and over the investment of their pension funds; efforts to promote full employment at decent wages; efforts to shift our nation's public and private investment, and scientific talent, away from military spending and toward civilian needs, especially in our urban areas; efforts to limit to influence of big money on our elections and political system; efforts to increase the nation's investment in our *human* capital, including our schools, health care, and child care.

Today there are thousands of community organizations based in urban neighborhoods around the country. Most engage in relatively modest efforts, such as pressuring the police to close down a local crack house or getting city hall to fix potholes. Some are more ambitious. Their community organizing has included forming tenant unions, building community development corporations, combating redlining, challenging police abuses, fighting against environmental and health problems, mobilizing against plant closings and lay-offs, and reforming public education and (as ACORN has done in New York City) even setting up charter schools sponsored by grassroots organizations. National networks like ACORN, the Industrial Areas Foundation, US Action, and others have helped improve the capacity of these local groups to develop leaders, mobilize campaigns, and win local victories.

Urban activists also sank their roots in the labor movement, focusing their organizing efforts among workers in low-wage industries such as hospitals, hotels, janitors, garment workers, home health care workers, and others. This work has primarily been among women, immigrants, and people of color. Unions that have made the most headway in recent years have drawn on the tactics and themes of civil rights crusades and grassroots organizing campaigns that emphasize dignity and justice, and that forge alliances with community and church groups. In a number of cities, unions have formed ties with community activist groups like ACORN and the Industrial Areas Foundation. Recently, unions and community groups in several cities have conducted exciting "living-wage" campaigns to require private firms with municipal contracts or subsidies (such as tax breaks) to pay their employees decent wages and benefits. A growing number of these urban activists have built electoral coalitions—forging ties between community, union, environmental, women's rights, civil rights, and other organizations—to win a stronger voice in government decision-making.

Indeed, for the past twenty-five years, progressive grassroots movements have gained a stronger foothold in running local governments. In a few cases, progressive coalitions have actually taken power in City Hall. Their leaders and allies have been catapulted to elective office, including mayor and city council. Most of these progressive regimes took root in smaller cities with prominent universities, such as Cambridge, Madison, Berkeley, Santa Cruz, Santa Monica, and Burlington (Vermont), where Independent Congressman Bernie Sanders served as mayor and helped forge a progressive coalition that is still in power. But there have also been successful progressive electoral governing coalitions in Cleveland, San Francisco, Chicago, Boston, St. Paul, Pittsburgh, and other cities.

But the lessons of the past three decades of local activism are ambiguous. When progressive community and union activists forge alliances with progressives in local government, they can clearly make a difference. They can put pressure on banks to stop redlining and force landlords to fix up slum buildings and stop rent gouging. They can provide support to union organizing campaigns and improve the wages and working conditions of public employees as well as of employees of firms with municipal contracts. They can help restore confidence in government by doing an efficient job of "civic housekeeping"—picking up snow and garbage, recycling waste, fixing potholes. They can shift spending priorities to discourage gentrification and promote rebuilding of poor neighborhoods by community-based groups. They can add more women and minorities in public employment and push private employers to do likewise. They can restrict police abuses and even get local police departments to work more closely with neighborhood groups.

These community organizations, local union struggles, progressive mayors and city councilors have won many local victories. But the hard truth is that despite the existence of thousands of grassroots community organizations, despite the many progressive union locals, and despite the hard work of many progressive municipal officeholders, the whole of "progressive urban activism" is smaller than the sum of its parts. Progressive urban activists can gain a foothold in government and create models of successful public policies. But ultimately cities cannot, on their own, solve the urban crisis. Even the most radical mayors and city councilors simply lack the economic resources, tax base, or legal authority to address the many problems they confront. As a result, all this local activism has not yet added up to a progressive national political movement that can significantly influence federal policy. In large part this is because all these local efforts are fragmented, isolated from each other, unable to build on each other. With some exceptions, local community groups and even national networks that are essentially engaged in the same thing basically ignore each other's work rather than find ways to work together strategically.

A new political majority must be built around identifying and building on concerns that unite those who live in central cities with residents of the inner suburbs and community organizers with labor unions, environmental smart-growth advocates, and inner-city church activists. Finding common ground between these groups requires elected officials and organized citizens alike to show political leadership.

We need to understand three fundamental realities: outer metropolitan areas cannot prosper as much as they might without healthy central cities; the interests of inner suburbs are now closer in many respects to those of central cities than to those of better-off outer suburbs; and many problems that vex suburbanites as well as central-city residents have their roots in, and are exacerbated by, the competition for resources, including private investment, that now characterize our metropolitan areas.

This may seem to be a long way from the community reinvestment movement's initial organizing efforts in the 1970s, but it is part of the longer arc of social justice organizing that has inspired union, civil rights, environmental, and other progressive crusades to limit the power of big business and expand American democracy. The specifics may change, but the basic principles are the same. As Frederick Douglass wrote almost 150 years ago: "If there is no struggle, there is no progress."

Notes

1. In 1968 the Kerner Commission, appointed by President Johnson in the wake of ghetto riots, recommended enacting a national "open occupancy" law and changing federal housing policy to build more low- and moderate-income housing outside ghetto areas. By passing the Fair Housing Act, Congress addressed the first recommendation but not the second. Of course, much of the fair housing advocacy work over the past three decades—in the form of individual complaints or lawsuits—has helped more people than just the named plaintiffs. (See Kushner 1992, Keating 1994, and Saltzman 1971.) Some local organizations created to address fair housing have also organized around community reinvestment issues, however. This was the situation in Milwaukee, as described in Chapter 3 of this volume.

2. A number of cities and some states now have linked-deposit programs. An example of Boston's annual linked-deposit "report card" is available at: <http://www.cityofboston.com/treasury/1999banking.pdf>. For an analysis of the impact of community reinvestment advocacy in Boston, see Campen 2001.

3. A "soft-second" mortgage reduces a borrower's monthly costs by dividing the loan into two components: a conventional thirty-year fixed-rate loan (usually for 75 percent of the purchase price); and a subsidized second mortgage for 20 percent of the purchase price (interest only for a shorter period of time—for example, ten years). The program lowers monthly costs by eliminating the requirement to pay mortgage insurance premiums. The program typically requires a low down payment and has more flexible underwriting than many conventional mortgage products, and lower closing costs as well.

4. Data from the 2000 Census on the concentration of poverty and affluence are not yet available. For the most recent analyses, see St. John 2002; Abramson et al. 1995. For recent trends in income and wealth inequality, see Mishel, Bernstein, and Schmitt 2000.

5. This was the rate at the end of 1999. It has increased slightly since then to over 67 percent.

Bibliography

Abramson, Alan J., Mitchell S. Tobin, and Matthew R. VanderGoot. 1995. The Changing Geography of Metropolitan Opportunity: The Segregation of the Poor in U.S. Metropolitan Areas, 1970 to 1990. *Housing Policy Debate* 6 (1): 45–72.

Bluestone, Barry, and Bennett Harrison. 1982. *The Deindustrialization of America.* New York: Basic Books.

Callahan, Thomas. 2002. Private communication to Peter Dreier. April 19.

Campen, Jim. 1992. The Struggle for Community Investment in Boston, 1989–91. In *From Redlining to Reinvestment.* Ed. Gregory D. Squires. Philadelphia: Temple University Press: 38–72.

———. 2001. *Changing Patterns VIII: Mortgage Lending to Traditionally Underserved Borrowers and Neighborhoods in Greater Boston 1990–2000.* Boston: Massachusetts Community and Banking Council (Dec.).

Caskey, John P. 1994. *Fringe Banking Check-Cashing Outlets, Pawnshops, and the Poor.* New York: Russell Sage Foundation.

City of Boston. 1999. *Linked Deposit Banking Report to the Mayor.* Accessed at: <http://www.cityofboston.com/treasury/1999banking.pdf>.

Conley, Dalton. 1999. *Being Black, Living in the Red: Race, Wealth and Social Policy in America.* Berkeley: University of California Press.

Dalaker, Joseph. 2001. *Poverty in the United States: 2000.* Current Population Reports. Washington, D.C.: U.S. Census Bureau (Sept.): 60–214.

Downs, Anthony. 1997. The Challenge of Our Declining Big Cities. *Housing Policy Debate* 8 (2): 359–408.

Dreier, Peter. 1991. Redlining Cities: How Banks Color Community Development. *Challenge* 34 (Nov./Dec.): 15–23.

———. 1996. Community Empowerment Strategies: The Limits and Potential of Community Organizing in Urban Neighborhoods. *Cityscape: A Journal of Policy Development and Research* (May): 121–59.

———. 1997. The New Politics of Housing: How to Rebuild the Constituency for a Progressive Federal Housing Policy. *Journal of the American Planning Association* 63 (winter): 5–27.

———. 2000a. Labor's Love Lost: Rebuilding Unions' Involvement in Federal Housing Policy. *Housing Policy Debate* 11 (2): 327–92.

———. 2000b. Why America's Workers Can't Pay the Rent. *Dissent* (summer): 105–11.

———. 2003. The Truth about Federal Housing Subsidies. In *Housing: Foundation of a New Social Agenda.* Ed. Rachel Bratt et al. Philadelphia: Temple University Press.

Dreier, Peter, and Kelly Candaele. 2002. Housing: An LA Story. *Nation* (April 15).

Dreier, Peter, John Mollenkopf, and Todd Swanstrom. 2001. *Place Matters: Metropolitics for the Twenty-First Century.* Lawrence: University Press of Kansas.

Earnest, Leslie. 2000. Household Debt Grows Precarious as Rates Increase. *Los Angeles Times* (May 13), 1, 17.

Evanoff, Douglas D., and Lewis M. Segal. 1996. CRA and Fair Lending Regulations: Resulting Trends in Mortgage Lending. *Economic Perspectives* 20 (6): 19–46.

Farley, Reynolds, et al. 1978. "Chocolate City, Vanilla Suburbs": Will the Trend toward Racially Separate Communities Continue? *Social Science Research* 7: 319–44.

Ferguson, Ronald F., and William T. Dickens, eds. 1999. *Urban Problems and Community Development.* Washington, D.C.: Brookings Institution.

Fishbein, Allen J. 1992. The Ongoing Experiment with "Regulation from Below": Expanding Reporting Requirements for HMDA and CRA. *Housing Policy Debate* 3 (2): 601–36.

Fishman, Robert. 2000. American Metropolis at Century's End: Past and Future Influences. *Housing Policy Debate* 11 (1): 199–213.

Freeman, Richard B. 2001. The Rising Tide Lifts . . . ? In *Understanding Poverty.* Ed. Sheldon Danziger and Robert Haveman. Cambridge: Harvard University Press: 99–126.

Frey, William. 2001. Melting Pot Suburbs: A Census 2000 Study of Suburban Diversity. Washington, D.C.: Center on Urban and Metropolitan Policy, Brookings Institution (June).

Frey, William, and Douglas Geverdt. 1998. Changing Suburban Demographics: Beyond the "Black-White, City-Suburbs" Typology. Research Report, Population Studies Center, Institute of Social Research, University of Michigan (June): 98–422.

From, Al. 1999. The Next Battleground: Suburbs Are the Key to Democratic Victories in 2000. *New Democrat* (March/April): 35–36.

Gainsborough, Juliet F. 2001. *Fenced Off: The Suburbanization of American Politics.* Washington, D.C.: Georgetown University Press.

Glaeser, Edward L., and Jacob L. Vigdor. 2001. *Racial Segregation in the 2000 Census.* Washington, D.C.: Brookings Institution, Center on Urban and Metropolitan Policy (April).

Green, Richard K., and Andrew Reschovsky, eds. 2001. *Using Tax Policy to Increase Homeownership among Low- and Moderate-Income Households.* Madison: Institute for Research on Poverty.

Grogan, Paul, and Tony Proscio. 2000. *Comeback Cities: A Blueprint for Urban Neighborhood Revival.* Boulder: Westview Press.

Hagg, Susan White. 2000. *Community Reinvestment and Cities.* Washington, D.C.: Center on Urban and Metropolitan Policy, Brookings Institution.

Harris, David. 1999. All Suburbs Are Not Created Equal: A New Look at Racial Differences in Suburban Location. Research Report, Population Studies Center, Institute for Social Research, University of Michigan (Sept.): 99–440.

Harrison, Bennett, and Amy K. Glasmeier. 1997. Why Business Alone Won't Redevelop
the Inner City: A Friendly Critique of Michael Porter's Approach to Urban Revitalization. *Economic Development Quarterly* 11 (1): 28–38.

Hayward, Steven. 1998. Broken Cities: Liberalism's Urban Legacy. *Policy Review*
(March/April).

Jargowsky, Paul. 1997. *Poverty and Place: Ghettos, Barrios, and the American City.*
New York: Russell Sage Foundation.

Joint Center for Housing Studies, Harvard University. 2002. *The 25th Anniversary of
the Community Reinvestment Act: Access to Capital in an Evolving Financial Services System.* Cambridge: Harvard University Joint Center for Housing Studies
(March).

Kasarda, John. 1993. Inner City Concentrated Poverty and Neighborhood Distress:
1970–1990. *Housing Policy Debate* 4 (3): 253–302.

Keating, Dennis. 1994. *The Suburban Racial Dilemma.* Philadelphia: Temple University Press.

Kershaw, Sarah. 2002. Failed Mortgages Soar in New York: Big Increase in Defaults
Seen among Poorer Families. *New York Times* (March 27).

Kushner, James. 1992. Federal Enforcement and Judicial Review of the Fair Housing
Amendments Act of 1988. *Housing Policy Debate* 3 (2): 537–99.

Lindsay, Lawrence B. 2000. Community Development at the Crossroads. *Neighborworks Journal* (winter): 54–55.

Lucy, William H., and David L. Phillips. 2000. *Confronting Suburban Decline.* Washington, D.C.: Island Press.

McCarthy, John, and Mayer Zald. 1977. Resource Mobilization and Social Movements.
American Journal of Sociology 82 (6): 1212–41.

McGinty, Jo Craven. 2000. *Home Mortgage Lending: How to Detect Disparities.*
Columbia, Mo.: Investigative Reporters and Editors, Inc.

Mishel, Lawrence, Jared Bernstein, and Mohn Schmitt. 2000. *The State of Working
America 2000–2001.* Ithaca: Cornell University Press.

Mohl, Raymond. 1993. Shifting Patterns of American Urban Policy since 1900. In
Urban Policy in Twentieth Century America. Ed. Arnold Hirsch and Raymond
Mohl. New Brunswick, N.J.: Rutgers University Press.

Nardulli, Peter, Jon Dalager, and Donald Greco. 1996. Voter Turnout in U.S. President
Elections: An Historical View and Some Speculation, *PS* 29 (3): 480–90.

Nowak, Jeremy. 1997. Neighborhood Initiative and the Regional Economy. *Economic
Development Quarterly* 11 (1): 3–10.

O'Connor, Alice. 1999. Swimming against the Tide: A Brief History of Federal Policy
in Poor Communities. In *Urban Problems and Community Development.* Ed.
Ronald Ferguson and William Dickets. Washington, D.C.: Brookings Institution
Press.

Oliver, Melvin, and Thomas Shapiro. 1995. *Black Wealth/White Wealth: A New Perspective on Racial Inequality.* New York: Routledge.

Porter, Michael. 1995. The Competitive Advantage of the Inner City. *Harvard Business Review* 73: 55–71.

———. 1997. New Strategies for Inner City Development. *Economic Development Quarterly* 11 (1): 11–27.

Retsinas, Nicholas. 1999. *Toward a Targetted Homeownership Tax Credit.* Washington, D.C.: Brookings Institution, Center on Urban and Metropolitan Policy and Harvard University, Joint Center for Housing Studies.

Rosenthal, Stuart S. 2001. *Eliminating Credit Barriers to Increase Homeownership: How Far Can We Go?* Washington, D.C.: Research Institute for Housing America, Working Paper No. 01-01, March.

Saltzman, Julia. 1971. *Open Housing as a Social Movement,* Lexington, Mass.: Heath.

Saegert, Susan, J., Phillip Thompson, and Mark R. Warren, eds. 2001. *Social Capital and Poor Communities.* New York: Russell Sage Foundation.

Sauerzopf, Richard, and Todd Swanstrom. 1999. The Urban Electorate in Presidential Elections, 1920–1996. *Urban Affairs Review* 35 (1): 72–91.

Savage, Howard. 1999. Who Could Afford to Buy a House in 1995? Current Housing Reports. Washington, D.C.: U.S. Bureau of the Census.

Schneider, William. 1992. The Suburban Century Begins. *Atlantic* (July): 33–43.

Schwartz, Alex. 1998. From Confrontation to Collaboration? Banks, Community Groups, and the Implementation of Community Reinvestment Agreements. *Housing Policy Debate* 9 (3): 631–62.

Segal, Lewis M., and Daniel G. Sullivan. 1998. Trends in Homeownership: Race, Demographics, and Income. *Economic Perspectives* 12 (2): 53–72.

Squires, Gregory, ed. 1992. *From Redlining to Reinvestment.* Philadelphia: Temple University Press.

St. John, Craig. 2002. The Concentration of Affluence in the United States: 1990. *Urban Affairs Review* 37 (4): 500–520.

Taub, Richard P. *Community Capitalism: Banking Strategies and Economic Development.* Boston: Harvard Business School Press.

Teixeira, Ruy, and Joel Rogers. 2000. *America's Forgotten Majority: Why the White Working Class Still Matters.* New York: Basic Books.

Turner, Margery Austin, and Felicity Skidmore. 1999. *Mortgage Lending Discrimination: A Review of Existing Evidence.* Washington, D.C.: Urban Institute.

U.S. Bureau of the Census. 1999. Housing Vacancies and Homeownership Historical Tables. Available at: <http://www.census.gov/hhes/www/housing/hva/historic/histt15.html> (accessed 1999).

U.S. Bureau of the Census. 2000. Poverty of People, by Residence: 1959–1999. Available at: <http://www.census.gov/income/histpov/histpov8.txt> (accessed 2001).

Uchitelle, Louis. 1999. In Home Ownership Data, a Hidden Generation Gap. *New York Times,* Sept. 26, Sec. 3: 4.

Walker, Christopher, and Mark Weinheimer. 1998. *Community Development in the 1990s.* Washington, D.C.: Urban Institute.

Warren, Mark R. 2001. *Dry Bones Rattling: Community Building to Revitalize American Democracy.* Princeton: Princeton University Press.

Weir, Margaret. 1996. Central Cities' Loss of Power in State Politics. *Cityscape* 2 (12): 23–40.

———. 1999. Power, Money, and Politics in Community Development. In *Urban Problems and Community Development.* Ed. Ronald F. Ferguson and William T. Dickens. Washington, D.C.: Brookings Institution.

Williams, Richard A., Eileen McConnell, and Reynold Nesiba. 2001. The Effects of the GSEs, CRA, and Institutional Characteristics on Home Mortgage Lending to Underserved Markets. *Cityscape* 5 (3): 9–106.

Wolff, Edward. 2000. Recent Trends in Wealth Ownership 1983–98. Working Paper No. 300, Annandale-on-Hudson, N.Y.: Jerome Levy Economics Institute of Bard College (April).

Wolman, Harold, and Lisa Marckini. 1998. Changes in Central City Representation and Influence in Congress since the 1960s. *Urban Affairs Review* 34 (2).

Yinger, John. Housing Discrimination and Residential Segregation as Causes of Poverty. In *Understanding Poverty*. Ed. Sheldon Danziger and Robert Haveman, 359–90. Cambridge: Harvard University Press.

Gregory D. Squires

13   Epilogue:
Where Do We Go from Here?

Organizing and advocacy, of course, are primarily means to various ends. If the basic objective is to increase access to capital on equitable terms to all segments of metropolitan areas, the question remains, what new policies and practices will achieve these ends? The Community Reinvestment Modernization Act of 2001 (H.R. 865), introduced in the first session of the 107th Congress by Representatives Tom Barrett of Milwaukee and Luis Gutierrez of Chicago, provides a fairly detailed outline of policies that would result in appropriate practices.

This bill was motivated by two basic trends. First are continuing disparities in wealth, home ownership, and access to financial services between economically distressed, predominantly nonwhite central cities and more prosperous, disproportionately white, outlying urban and suburban communities. Second is the continuing consolidation within and among financial services industries that was reinforced by the Financial Services Modernization Act, which allowed banks, insurers, and securities firms to enter into each other's business in ways that had previously been prohibited by federal law. The three primary objectives of this bill were to 1) enhance access to financial services for citizens of all economic circumstances and in all geographic areas, 2) enhance the ability of financial institutions to meet the credit needs of all communities, and 3) ensure that community reinvestment keeps pace with affiliations in the financial services marketplace. This bill would broaden application of the CRA beyond federally chartered depository institutions, increase data disclosure requirements, and strengthen oversight responsibilities of appropriate authorities, in part by restricting certain activities of financial service providers that do not have a satisfactory record under the Act.

Major Provisions of the Community
Reinvestment Modernization Act of 2001

Broadening the Reach of CRA

Under the proposal, all nonbank affiliates of bank holding companies that engage in lending would be subject to the CRA. It would also place CRA-like obligations on securities firms, mortgage banks, and insurers. Firms in each of these industries would have a continuing and affirmative obligation to provide services to all segments of the communities where they do business, including low- and moderate-income neighborhoods. For mortgage banks and insurers the CRA exam would consider service to minority communities and economically distressed areas. And in those cases where mortgage banks and insurers persist in failing to meet their obligations, Fannie Mae and Freddie Mac would be prohibited from purchasing mortgage loans made by these institutions. In those cases where a bank or an affiliate is engaged in predatory lending, its CRA rating would be reduced. Each securities, mortgage banking, and insurance affiliate of a financial holding company would be required to have at least a satisfactory rating before it could merge with another holding company. The reach of the CRA, and the consequences for noncompliance, would be enhanced by these provisions.

Increasing Disclosure

The bill would establish new data disclosure requirements for the insurance industry. Property insurers would be required to submit HMDA-like data on the location of the policies they write (along with those they cancel and nonrenew), type of policies (e.g., full replacement, actual cash value), premiums, losses, location of agents and agents that are terminated, along with the race, income, and gender of applicants and disposition of their applications. Insurers would also be required to submit data on their investments, including the number of loans for commercial real estate transactions, small businesses, and homes, along with other community development investments.

The bill also calls for improvements in current reporting requirements. Small business and farm disclosure requirements would be expanded to include the race and gender of applicants, revenue of applicants' businesses and farms, census tract of applicants' residence, and disposition of applications.

The additional disclosure provisions would provide substantial new information that would facilitate the formation of partnerships among community organizations and lenders, assist regulatory agencies in the targeting of scarce enforcement resources, and enable financial service providers to identify missed opportunities in various markets.

Strengthening Oversight Responsibilities

The Community Reinvestment Modernization Act would require public notice and opportunity for public comment prior to approving most mergers or acquisitions involving a financial holding company. And the Federal Reserve Board would be obligated to take into consideration the community reinvestment record of the involved entities. Where bank holding companies expand into new nonbank activities, affiliates would be required to maintain at least a satisfactory CRA rating.

This bill would also require CRA examinations of small banks (those with less than $250 million in assets) every four years for those with an outstanding rating, and every three years for those with satisfactory ratings. Under the Financial Services Modernization Act of 1999 these institutions are to be examined every five years.

The "sunshine" requirements of the 1999 bill would also be modified. While the initial CRA agreements would be disclosed, the new bill eliminates the annual reporting requirements, deletes the requirement that ties disclosure to prior testimony or discussion of CRA with banks, and removes the penalties for nongovernmental parties resulting from noncompliance with the disclosure requirements.

Finally, this act would remove most exemptions from the HMDA (for smaller banks and banks where mortgage lending is a small share of their total loans) and expand the HMDA to include pricing information and the number of loans that were subprime loans.

The Community Reinvestment Modernization Act of 2001 would represent a logical extension of the legal protections secured by the Fair Housing Act, the HMDA, and the CRA.

Feasibility?

The political prospects for this bill are another story. Its sponsors did not expect it to become law in the near future and, indeed, it did not receive serious consideration in Congress. Most of its provisions are not considered politically feasible today. But the political center does change, and it does so in response to organizing and advocacy efforts.

Three or four years prior to their passage, most of the civil rights legislation of the 1960s would have been considered unrealistic. The same could be said about the sweeping welfare reform legislation passed by the Clinton administration. It took the martyrdom of Martin Luther King Jr. to secure passage of the Fair Housing Act in 1968. It took a Democratic president advocating what had long been a conservative Republican policy to get welfare reform. But in both instances there had been years of scholarly research, intellectual debate, conflict, and struggle. And there had also been years of organizing and advocacy (on all sides), from the neighborhood level to state legislatures to the Congress and White House.

The community reinvestment and fair lending victories that have been achieved—in part through the use of tools like the FHA, HMDA, and CRA—reflect a similar history. Local neighborhood organizations, working with supportive members of the media, the academic community, and sympathetic elected officials and representatives of financial institutions themselves (sometimes brought kicking and screaming to the bargaining table) have used a variety of tools to change the way lenders do business in the nation's cities. And the Community Reinvestment Modernization Act would probably not have been produced were it not for the advocacy efforts of the National Community Reinvestment Coalition. But there are few if any permanent victories. Future goals for community reinvestment and fair lending do seem reasonably clear, as do the tactics and strategies for achieving them. Sustaining the type of effort responsible for past victories and required for future ones remains the challenge of the day.

About the Contributors

GREGORY D. SQUIRES is the chair of the Department of Sociology at George Washington University. His recent books include *Capital and Communities in Black and White* (1994), *Insurance Redlining* (1997), *Color and Money*, with Sally O'Connor (2001), and *Urban Sprawl: Causes, Consequences, and Policy Responses* (2002).

JOE MARIANO, executive director of the National Training and Information Center, has a thirty-plus-year career in organizing. He has worked for the United Farmworkers, helped organize the Buckeye-Woodland Community Congress, was executive director of the Logan Square Neighborhood Association in Chicago, served as training director of the Gamaliel Foundation, and has been with NTIC since 1994.

WILLIAM R. TISDALE is president and CEO of the Metropolitan Milwaukee Fair Housing Council (MMFHC) and was the founding president of the National Fair Housing Alliance. He has served on numerous state and national advisory boards and has taught classes in sociology at the University of Wisconsin, Milwaukee.

CARLA J. WERTHEIM is executive vice president of MMFHC and is on the faculty of NFHA's Fair Housing School. She has been a consultant to HUD on numerous occasions and has co-taught courses at the University of Wisconsin, Milwaukee, with Mr. Tisdale.

JOHN P. RELMAN is the founder and director of Relman & Associates and teaches discrimination law at the Georgetown University Law Center and American University's Washington College of Law. He formerly served as the director of the Fair Housing Project at the Washington Lawyers' Committee for Civil Rights and Urban Affairs and as a staff attorney at the National Office of the Lawyers' Committee. He is the author of *Housing Discrimination Practice Manual*.

THOMAS CALLAHAN is the executive director of the Massachusetts Affordable Housing Alliance (MAHA). He previously served as coalition coordinator at Tenants United for Public Housing Progress in Boston and as a community organizer at Massachusetts Fair Share.

STANLEY A. LOWE is vice president for Community Revitalization of the National Trust for Historic Preservation in Washington, D.C., and vice president of Preservation Programs for the Pittsburgh History and Landmarks Foundation. He served previously as executive director of the Pittsburgh Housing Authority, director of Neighborhoods and Planning Policy for Pittsburgh mayor Tom Murphy, CEO of the Manchester Citizens Corporation, and founder and representative of the Pittsburgh Community Reinvestment Group.

JOHN T. METZGER is assistant professor of Urban and Regional Planning at Michigan State University and was on the visiting faculty of the Graduate School of Public and International Affairs of the University of Pittsburgh. He was the first coordinator of the Pittsburgh Community Reinvestment Group and has published widely on a range of community reinvestment issues.

ALLEN J. FISHBEIN recently rejoined the Center for Community Change, where he serves as its general counsel and codirector of the Neighborhood Revitalization Project. He served previously as senior advisor for Government Sponsored Enterprises Oversight at HUD, and as a board member of or advisor to the National Neighborhood Coalition, Fannie Mae, Freddie Mac, the National Community Reinvestment Coalition, the American Bar Association, and the Federal Reserve Board.

MAUDE HURD is the president of ACORN. She is a longtime resident of Dorchester, Massachusetts, and has served as chairperson of her neighborhood ACORN chapter, board member for Boston ACORN, national ACORN board member, and, since 1992, national president of the organization. In her day job she develops and conducts anti-drug, tobacco, and alcohol training in low-income communities of color.

STEVEN KEST has served as ACORN's executive director since 1990 and has been an ACORN community organizer since 1975, working in Arkansas, Connecticut, and New Jersey. In 2001 he served on the HUD/Treasury Task Force on Predatory Lending.

MATTHEW LEE, executive director of Inner City Press/Community on the Move (ICP), is a community activist and public interest lawyer. He cofounded Inner City Press/Community on the Move in the South Bronx of New York City in 1987. He is currently working on a new project, the Fair Finance Watch.

MALCOLM BUSH has been president of the Woodstock Institute, a community economic development think tank, since 1992. He has held regular faculty appointments at Northwestern and the University of Chicago and is the author of *Families in Distress: Public, Private, and Civic Responses.*

DANIEL IMMERGLUCK is assistant professor of Public and Nonprofit Administration at Grand Valley State University in Grand Rapids, Michigan. He has written on CRA and related issues and served as senior vice president of the Woodstock Institute.

JOHN TAYLOR is president and CEO of the National Community Reinvestment Coalition. He has received the Martin Luther King Jr. Peace Award and two U.S. Congressional Citations, among other awards, and has appeared on ABC's Nightline, CBS, Fox News, CNN, CSPAN, in the *New York Times, Washington Post, Chicago Tribune,* and hundreds of other print, television, and radio media. He was also appointed by President Clinton to the Community Development Fund Advisory Board.

JOSH SILVER is vice president of Research and Policy of the National Community Reinvestment Coalition. He was a policy analyst at the Urban Institute for five years before coming to NCRC.

PETER DREIER is the E. P. Clapp Distinguished Professor of Politics and director of the Urban and Environmental Policy Program at Occidental College in Los Angeles. From 1984 to 1992 he served as director of housing and senior policy advisor to Boston Mayor Raymond Flynn. He is the coauthor of *Regions That Work: How Cities and Suburbs Can Grow Together* (2000) and *Place Matters: Metropolicies for the Twenty-first Century* (2001).

Index

AARP. *See* American Association of Retired Persons

Abacha, Sani, 149

abandoned properties: HUD mismanagement and, 36; reclaiming of, 136; subprime lenders and, 40

academic research, *vs.* activism, 154–55

accountability of financial institutions, 148

ACORN. *See* Association of Community Organizations for Reform Now

ACORN Housing Corporation (AHC), 119, 120–21, 124–25

activism: *vs.* academics, 154–55; efficacy of, 2–3; history of, 29–35; against HUD, 37–38; legislation and, 8, 131–32, 223; national networks, 193–94, 201, 213, 215; need for, 28–29, 100, 154–55, 166–67, 169–70; tactics, 10, 12, 28–32, 40, 91, 120, 124–25, 127–29, 131. *See also* community reinvestment movement

Advisory Commission on Regulatory Barriers to Affordable Housing, 112

Aetna Insurance Co., 48

affirmative action, CRA and, 11–12

Affordable Housing Goals, 105, 112–16

Affordable Housing Program (AHP), 111

affordable mortgages. *See* CRA loans

AFL-CIO, 128–29

African Americans: and creditworthiness, 207; economic status of, 86; ghettoization of, 188–89; homeownership rates, 2, 87, 162, 203, 207–8; mortgage approval rates, 5, 8, 59, 92, 126; property values and, 3; share of mortgage loans, 1, 18, 21, 80–81; subprime loans and, 123; suburbanization of, 205

Against Investment Discrimination, 34

AHC. *See* ACORN Housing Corporation

"Ain't I a Woman" homeownership initiative, 92

Aldinger, William, 128

Alinsky, Saul, 8, 21, 157

Allegheny Conference on Community Development, 88

Allegheny Valley Bank, 98

Alleyne, Sonia, 82

Allstate Insurance Co., 47

American Association of Retired Persons (AARP), 130, 132, 201

American Banker, 128, 137, 138

American Bankers Association, 16

American Civil Liberties Union (ACLU), 46

American Family Mutual Insurance Company, 4, 20, 46, 47

American Institute of Real Estate Appraisers, 4

Ameriquest, 125–26

Ameritrust Bank, 34, 35

Anchor Savings Bank, 137

Anderson, Adrianne (of Boston), 78

Anderson, Adrianne (of MAHA), 75, 79

Apgar, Bill, 38

appraisals, discrimination in, 20, 121

arbitration, mandatory, 122, 127

Associates First Capital Corporation, 40, 126, 146, 150

Association of Community Organizations for Reform Now (ACORN): ACORN Housing Corporation (AHC), 119, 120–21, 124–25; activities of, 120; affordable loan activism, 129–30; core philosophy of, 124; Financial Democracy Campaign, 108–9; GSEs reform and, 107, 109, 110, 113–15; HMDA data use, 199; national networking and, 193–94, 201, 213; predatory lending activism, 119–33; role of, 198; structure of, 120; unions and, 214

Atlanta Journal-Constitution, 8, 199

Babcock, Frederick, 4

Banamex, 150

Banc One, 157, 158

bank(s). *See* financial institutions